AMERICAN LIBERAL DISILLUSIONMENT

IN THE WAKE OF WORLD WAR I

AMERICAN LIBERAL DISILLUSIONMENT

IN THE WAKE OF WORLD WAR I

STUART I. ROCHESTER

The Pennsylvania State University Press
University Park and London

Library of Congress Cataloging in Publication Data

Rochester, Stuart I   1945–
   American liberal disillusionment.

   Includes bibliographical references and index.
   1. European War, 1914–1918—United States.
2. Liberalism—United States.   3. United States—
Politics and government—1913–1921.   I. Title.
D619.R53   940.3   76-47613.
ISBN 0-271-01233-1

Designed by Larry Krezo

Printed in the United States of America

To my parents

CONTENTS

ACKNOWLEDGMENTS

My obligations are manifold. I am especially indebted to Edward Younger of the University of Virginia for his wise counsel and unfailing encouragement throughout the several stages of this project; as mentor and good friend he commands my lasting esteem and affection. William H. Harbaugh, despite the pressures of a taxing schedule, graciously read an earlier version of the manuscript; his matchless biography of Theodore Roosevelt was itself an inspiration to grace and erudition. For their generous advice, I am grateful, also, to Norman A. Graebner, a master diplomatic historian, and Don Higginbotham, chairman of the Frederick Jackson Turner Prize Committee. I thank Phi Alpha Theta for the award of its 1974 manuscript prize and Lynn W. Turner and his committee for their cogent suggestions on readying the manuscript for publication.

Grants from the Ford Foundation and the National Endowment for the Humanities and a summer research stipend from Loyola College enabled me substantially to broaden my research and refine my insights. Librarians at Columbia, Cornell, Yale, the University of Virginia, and the Library of Congress contributed time and courtesies which mere acknowledgment cannot adequately repay. John M. Pickering, Carole Schwager, and their talented staff at The Pennsylvania State University Press saved me from more faults than I would care to admit. Among many colleagues who lent cheer and assistance, I would be remiss if I did not mention the collaboration of a beautiful friend who typed a dozen pages and inspired countless words.

Lastly, for years of both good humor and spirited criticism, I dedicate this book with special gratitude to my parents.

S.I.R.

"What did you think
    We should find," said a shade,
"When the last shot echoed
    And peace was made?"
"Christ," laughed the fleshless
    Jaws of his friend;
"I thought they'd be praying
    For worlds to mend;

"Making earth better,
    Or something silly,
Like whitewashing hell
    Or Picca-dam-dilly."

—Alfred Noyes
"A Victory Dance"
June, 1920

Into this world of mechanical progress and human amelioration,
the World War came like a baleful meteor from outer space.

—Lewis Mumford
"The Aftermath of Utopianism," 1941

1 INTRODUCTION

The years between roughly 1914 and 1940 witnessed a remarkable intellectual metamorphosis that found passionate liberals converted to doddering conservatives, Pollyannas transformed into despairing cynics, and men of faith and conviction reduced to ideological vagabonds. In 1914, Walter Lippmann busily blueprinted a new society that would have total mastery over its affairs; Reinhold Niebuhr, graduated from Eden Theological Seminary, eagerly prepared sermons on the Social Gospel; John Dos Passos serialized anticapitalist pieces for the *Harvard Monthly*; and Max Lerner, a precocious twelve-year-old, was already drinking at the fountains of progressive education and Young Democratic politics. By 1940, Lippmann was behind a desk at the New York *Herald Tribune* pontificating on the hopelessness of democracy; Niebuhr was formulating a fundamentalist neo-orthodoxy that bared the Social Gospel as a pious fraud; Dos Passos was well along on a course that would take him to the *National Review* and a kinship with Barry Goldwater; and Lerner, though still nominally a liberal, was writing a flattering introduction to Machiavelli's *The Prince*.

No doubt a large measure of this dramatic reversal can be explained by the phenomenon of the older, wiser, "tired radical" who, Walter Weyl observed, would marry a pleasant wife, beget interesting children, and be content to live out his life peacefully in the country.[1] But the process of change for the generation that drew its early nourishment from Rooseveltian or Wilsonian progressivism was more profound and convulsive than a simple aging process. Most of them did not simply melt into suburbia or the business culture. They were victims not of the creeping conservatism of age but of a dislocating, unhinging disillusionment.

Lewis Mumford, writing in 1940, described the failure of these liberal minds in their formative years to understand the limitations of man and society. Those who were children before 1914, Mumford said, "were brought up in a relatively innocent world. . . . We certainly did not believe, as Fourier had suggested, that the very ocean would some day turn into lemonade, in proof of human harmony and amity. But we were quite as well prepared to see it turn into lemonade as we were prepared for the actual developments that . . .

followed." Mumford and his young associates—progressives, socialists, radicals, whatever their liberal persuasion—glibly assumed that
"certain kinds of cruelty and violence could never occur on a large
scale again." Progress seemed unilinear, assured by either the application of human intelligence or the historical process itself. They
thought, in characteristic progressive terms, that the good society
could be engineered, that institutions could be managed, that evils
could be eliminated; and they were convinced, like the socialist
Charles Edward Russell, that ideals and common interests tran-
scended the parochial concerns of race, language, and nationality.
Even the intrusion of war in 1914 presented itself initially as an opportunity for them. They talked about democracy in Russia, a new spirit
of internationalism and public responsibility, the possibility for permanent peace, and the likelihood of a world government supported
by all the peoples and rulers of the earth. The prospect of a new
international order and social reconstruction at home on a grand scale
made warriors of pacifists, enthusiasts of cynics, well-wishers of radicals.[2]

It was the war, however, that eventually punctured their innocence. The years 1914–1920 were whirlwind, torturous ones that
placed hopes, convictions, even reputations on the line. They were a
time of infinite possibilities that would see either the consummation
or eclipse of progressive dreams. For liberals they turned out hellishly
bad. With shattering effect, the war demonstrated the frailty of both
the human condition and their own utopian philosophy. In the oppressive outcome—in the wartime hysteria, the duplicity at Versailles,
and the ensuing descent from the lofty heights of Wilsonian idealism
to the "bungalow minds" of normalcy—even the most strong-willed
were compelled to question their cherished assumptions about the
rationality of man and the inevitability of progress. Thus were
launched the journeys of disillusionment of the twenties and thirties
that brought some liberals full circle to conservatism, some through
the way station of communism, some on a never-ending trail of soul-
searching.

This book is an effort to explain the dynamics of disillusionment in
the American liberal community. Its underlying assumption is that
the great twentieth-century "liberal disillusionment" evolved largely
out of the experience of the First World War, that the war episode
was in fact a kind of pivot or mainspring that sent a galaxy of
liberal-minded men on what I have called their journeys to and from

conviction. It is an assumption that is made advisedly, with due regard for the arguments of Henry May, Christopher Lasch, and other historians who in recent years have played down the theme of "war as watershed."[3] For decades, popularizing historians and indulgent memoirists exaggerated the watershed impact of the struggle. Armageddon became a convenient hinge on which chroniclers could turn a new chapter and the disillusioned could hang their conversion. The sophisticated works of May and Lasch were salutary in refining a worn stereotype and reminding us of the longer vicissitudes of illusion and disillusion. But in putting the war in longer perspective they inadvertently obscured the salient role that the war *did* play. Lincoln Steffens's progressive faith may have been flickering, perhaps even spent, before Sarajevo, but it was the war experience that soured him for good and sealed his estrangement; likewise in the case of alienated young writers who were temporarily rejuvenated, then irrevocably demoralized by the encounter. I deal with this important matter at length in chapter 8.

The bulk of the book is concerned with the seminal years 1914–1920—with the seeds, the roots, the early manifestations of disillusionment. Chapters 2–7 comprise a narrative reconstruction of the process of disillusionment, leavened with an analysis of liberals' aspirations and failures as they moved through their stances from peace to war to peacemaking. Specifically, chapter 2 surveys the illusory prewar atmosphere. Chapters 3, 4, and 5 discuss the liberal reaction to the outbreak of the war, to American intervention, and to the foundering of the Wilsonian crusade. Chapters 6 and 7 trace the liberals' predicament at the peace conference, from their determined arrival in Paris to their bitter repudiation of the settlement at Versailles. Chapter 8 offers a postmortem examination by the liberals themselves and by subsequent historians.

In a chapter-length epilogue, I explore the nature of the disillusionment itself—its various currents, or "journeys," charted roughly from 1920 to 1940—and take up a number of outstanding questions: How pervasive actually was the "great disillusionment"? Were *all* the liberals "disillusioned"? For those who were disillusioned, what did "disillusionment" consist of precisely? Did it involve a questioning of basic assumptions and complete loss of faith, or did it involve a rejection of personalities (Wilson) and methods (war, progressivism) and *re*-illusionment in the direction of communism and farmer-labor politics? In other words, to what extent were illusions *destroyed*, and to what extent were they merely *displaced*? Historians who have tracked the intellectual orbit of the twenties have generally chosen either to minimize the disillusionment (accenting instead the resumption of reform and business as usual) or, at the other extreme, to dwell on its cosmic proportions. I attempt to establish that the disillusionment was widespread but diffuse, that it had many nuances, and that there were at least three separate routes traveled by the prewar liberals.

Obviously, there is enough material in these residual years for a companion volume. For now, I hope to illumine the convulsive experience of 1914–1920 that spawned the disillusionment and to suggest the broad outlines of a continuing investigation. The postwar odyssey of Lippmann, Niebuhr, Dos Passos, Lerner, and their fellow liberal travelers remains one of the most fascinating, important, and neglected phenomena in American intellectual history.

A word about definition should be stated here at the outset. The writer on some "liberal" philosophy or movement is at once placed in a vulnerable position by using a term that defies adequate definition. Some readers of this introduction no doubt have already bristled at what they consider too casual or ambiguous employment of the term. The most scrupulous attention, however, cannot solve the semantic problem. The men who are the subject of this study were themselves vexed by the meaning of "liberalism." In 1938 Max Lerner called it the most disputed term of his generation. Newton Baker, the Wilsonian progressive, defined "liberalism" hazily as "a state of mind . . . a sure feeling that things get better in this world rather than worse and have their best chance of improvement when they rest for approval upon the informed conscience of the common man." In 1932 Carl Becker was both amused and befuddled at how radicals were suspecting liberalism of being "an *agent provocateur* [sic] of Capitalism," while conservatives treated it "as a Bolshevik masquerading in a rented dress coat."[4]

If the term had fallen into disfavor by the time Becker was speaking in the 1930s, in the years of the First World War it was embraced freely by nearly everyone at one interval or another. A scholar studying the League of Nations debate of 1918-1920 has cited the difficulties in identifying "liberal" opinion—the defections to and from the liberal camp during the war, the discrepancy between "liberalism" in domestic matters and "liberalism" in international affairs, "the almost constant, frequently confusing, and sometimes breathtaking shifts or reversals of position with regard to America's role in the war and in the world after the war."[5]

Faced with the semantic dilemma, the historian has two choices. He can either try as best he can to distinguish among different "liberal" factions, which inevitably becomes clumsy and artificial;* or he can take Baker's expansive definition and deal with liberalism as a transcendent "state of mind" or "intellectual attitude." In this broadest sense, Arno Mayer has grouped individuals as seemingly incompatible as Max Eastman, Robert La Follette, Randolph Bourne, and Herbert Croly under the banner of "forces of movement" and allowed that even Wilson and Lenin were "merely men with different methods."[6] With a bit less license, I have chosen to do the same. I examine a wide range of "liberals" from members of the insurgent Socialist and Communist parties to the editors of respectable reformist journals like the *Nation* and the *New Republic*, from avuncular old-stock progressives to orphaned, irascible writers of the so-called lost generation. Thus Charles Edward Russell, Upton Sinclair, Herbert Croly, Oswald Garrison Villard, William Allen White, Randolph Bourne, John Dos Passos, and their assorted colleagues all emerge as "liberals." It is a wide spectrum, but necessarily so, as the intellectual life of these years is remarkably protean and diversified. My purpose is to recreate a climate of opinion, a sense, an atmosphere of what these essentially liberal-minded men were experiencing, even as they bickered among themselves and mercurially shifted positions. Distinctions and qualifications are made where warranted, but the work as a whole remains a study less of individuals or groups than of a phenomenon. I am concerned less with the arrangement of the intellectual spectrum than with the dynamics of disillusionment.

Russell, Sinclair, Croly, Villard, White, Bourne, Dos Passos, Eastman, Niebuhr, Lippmann, Becker, Mumford, Weyl, Steffens, Charles Beard, William Bullitt, Brand Whitlock, Malcolm Cowley, Ray Stannard Baker, John Dewey, Frederic Howe, Stephen Wise—all of those who are part of this story, though perhaps differing in their specific prescriptions or temperaments, qualify as "liberal" in the generous intent, the progressive intellectual outlook, and the expansive vision of a better society which they shared in common. The ethos of the Progressive Era—the common commitment to progress and peace—was such that men who subscribed to widely divergent politics and ideology could still participate in it together. This affinity, however vague and imprecise, joined them like soul brothers. They participated in the illusions of the prewar years and they participated in the disillusionment that followed and crystallized as the events of war and peace unfolded.

*See, for example, Christopher Lasch's distinction between "war liberals" and "anti-imperialists" in *The American Liberals and the Russian Revolution* (New York, 1962), a distinction that is essential to his study but clumsy (by his own admission) and unsatisfactory because of the myriad inconsistencies in liberal opinion even within his chosen groups.

2 THE PREWAR ILLUSION

For all the advances in industrialization and urbanization, the increases in crime and pollution, the improvements in communication and transportation that made the world unprecedently small and intruding, Americans in 1914 were still for the most part provincials. The "end of American innocence" may, as Henry May suggests retrospectively, have had its roots before 1914, but it was a phenomenon of which the average American was scarcely aware at the time. Matthew Josephson recalled growing up in Brooklyn between 1900 and 1914 in a world still illuminated mostly by gas and "appearing very much as it did in the time of President Grant." The tempo of life was at the pace of the family's old carriage horse, "about six miles an hour." Born in Chicago in 1896, John Dos Passos remembered a boyhood when "a man could circle the globe without a passport and the police were harmless fellows in funny hats and barbed wire was used to keep cattle in their pasture." Elmer Davis looked backward from 1931 in a salute to "good old 1913 . . . when you could get a dinner with wine for what the hors-d'oeuvres cost now, when traffic and livers were less congested." Memories, especially postwar memories, often prove faulty or sentimental, and can be as unreliable as the historian's hindsight, but in these cases memory seems to serve correct. The prewar years, by nearly all contemporary accounts, were good ones. One does not have to rely on reminiscences to gather that these were extraordinarily sanguine times—not as idyllic as memoirists have drawn them but still years of innocence, of romps and frolics, of small regrets and great expectations. In Lewis Mumford's phrase, they were years of "sweetness and light." Above all, for American liberals, they were years of illusion.[1]

There was, first of all, the illusion of peace. Jane Addams, in 1907, detected a "cosmic patriotism" that would utilize the war virtues—loyalty, dedication, sacrifice—for the task of planetary reconstruction. As people became committed to the peaceful improvement of their lives, war would become an anachronism—relegated to the history books and to remote aboriginal lands. Scott Nearing counted war "among such defunct social practices as cannibalism and chattel slavery." "All three," Nearing believed, "had their places in social history. All three cropped up occasionally. But they belonged in the past, were being outlived in the present, and would play little or no part in the human future." To most progressives, the sporadic fighting in the Balkans signified the last gasps of the old nationalism. Newton Baker, in a speech in October 1917, estimated that if a poll had been taken in the United States prior to 1914 as to the possibility of world war, the result would have been "substantially unanimous" that such an event was inconceivable. In *The Great Illusion* (1911) Norman Angell had demonstrated that war was no longer profitable even to the victors. The pacifist spirit was unmistakable. There was the Olympianlike eminence of The Hague Court, the swelling corpus of international law and treaties, and a profusion of energetic organizations like the Carnegie Endowment for International Peace (founded in 1910), the World Peace Foundation (1910), the Church Peace Union (1914), and the American School Peace League (1908). Even the dormant American Peace Society, founded in 1828, enjoyed a revival.[2]

Peace was merely one of the illusions consuming American liberals in the prewar years. As early as 1907 Upton Sinclair prophesied that socialism would triumph in the United States within a decade; William English Walling allowed in 1914 that it would take a while longer—perhaps fifteen years. Brand Whitlock, the reform mayor of Toledo, wrote a rhapsodic autobiography in 1913 touting the American promise and heralding a new sense of commitment "pressing with the irresistible urge of moral sentiment" that "will renovate the cities and recreate the lives in them." Whitlock was convinced that Jeffersonian ideals were being realized in an industrial society through the construction of new schools and civic centers, the elimination of pretense and privilege, and the zealous efforts of progressives like John Peter Altgeld and Samuel "Golden Rule" Jones. Men were working together to fulfill this promise. Lawyer Donald Richberg recalled that the progressive leaders were different in methods and that Roosevelt, Bryan, La Follette, and Wilson each had his adherents, but "their common goal was to lift up the level of the average well-being." Carl Becker wrote in 1912 that the notion of "Perfectibility" had perhaps been watered down since its eighteenth-century conception, but was far from extinguished. "Transformed into the idea of Progress—the belief that society can by its own efforts indefinitely increase the happiness and welfare of all men," said Becker, "it is perhaps the one really vital faith of our day."[3]

At the bottom of the prewar illusion was this conviction that individuals could actively and creatively shape their own society. Progress was certainly not a new conviction in America, but its foundation had always rested largely on providential or impersonal forces—the frontier, the immigrant heritage, manifest destiny—never on the conscious, daily application of human intelligence and ingenuity. The new pragmatism of William James and John Dewey changed all this. *Creative Intelligence* was a collection of essays by eight exponents of James's philosophy. Dewey, as one of the contributors, elaborated on the significance of the title with his statement that the salvation of progressive society lay in "the power of intelligence" to project a desirable future and to invent "the instrumentalities of its realization." Progress now came to be construed as something programmatic rather than automatic—based solidly on the calculations of the human will and intelligence rather than on the vagaries of geography or Providence. There was the belief, as Oliver Wendell Holmes, Jr., remarked contemptuously of the *New Republic* men, that you could "legislate bliss." Such presumption accounted for much of the liberals' indefatigable optimism even through the war period, as epitomized by the brash manifesto of educator Horace Kallen: "Regard a free league of free peoples—if you *will* it, it is no dream."[4]

Indispensable to the new pragmatism was a trust in education and environmental change as correctives to social ills. Kallen, Dewey, and Jane Addams wrote at length on the subject of education as preparation for life and on the vital relationship between school and society. William Allen White included a chapter entitled "Schools the Mainspring of Democracy" in *The Old Order Changeth* (1910), and Randolph Bourne contributed two noteworthy studies on *The Gary Schools* and *Education and Living*, a follow-up to his mentor Dewey's *Democracy and Education*. If school failed to cure the delinquent boy or civilize the promiscuous girl, then a change in environment was a ready resort. The progressives believed that if you provided tough kids with playgrounds or channeled their energies into team sports, if you took precocious girls off the streets and into supervised dance halls, if you ran reformatories like "junior republics" so that bad kids would emulate their virtuous political environment, then prospective delinquents would turn into model children and society, through simple tact and ingenuity, would spare itself a generation of vice. Jane Addams believed that even the "ancient evil" of prostitution could be eradicated with a new conscience and the application of the new pragmatic techniques. Addams insisted also that the "juvenile delinquent" was a simple case of maladjustment—the country boy thrown into the city without the opportunity for play or open spaces and with unaccustomed freedom to roam because of looser family ties; when he stole from pushcarts he was merely practicing the habit of picking up surplus food in the open country, and when he carried a knife or shotgun he betrayed his rural instinct to hunt rabbits and coons.[5]

It was presumed that men and women were essentially rational. The job for progressive society was to redirect those occasionally wayward or misguided impulses. Newton Baker in a wartime speech spoke of the dance halls, YMCA's, and Boy Scouts as "healthy and stimulating substitutes" for the old temptations. "The discovery was made," Baker said, "that the way to overcome the temptations and vices of a great city was to offer adequate opportunity for wholesome recreation and enjoyment; that if you wanted to get a firebrand out of the hand of a child the way to do it was neither to club the child nor to grab the firebrand, but to offer in exchange for it a stick of candy!"[6]

Even more sober progressives subscribed to this meliorist philosophy. Walter Lippmann, in two prominent prewar books that surveyed the new challenges and complexities of American life, warned against wishful thinking and easy solutions, and urged, like Dewey, the pragmatic application of creative intelligence on an ongoing basis—constant, creative, dynamic statesmanship. For all his caution, however, he shared with Dewey, Addams, Baker, and other liberals like his *New Republic* coeditors Herbert Croly and Walter Weyl the conviction that society could be cleansed of most of its imperfections and "mastery" accomplished. That labor and management could come to terms, that corruption could be eliminated, that intelligent, creative statesmanship could be achieved in a democracy—all goals that he would declare hopeless after the war—were for Lippmann in 1914 "not idle dreams [but] concrete possibilities."[7]

Mumford later remarked that among progressives and liberals, "there was scarcely one who did not assume that mankind either was permanently good or might sooner or later reach such a state of universal beatitude." "They thought," he quipped, "that, with good economic and political arrangements, life might become a long picnic on a sunny summer afternoon, a picnic in a world from which even the mosquitoes might, with a vigilant Public Health Service, be kept away."[8]

It is striking how pervasive the prewar spirit actually was. Much has been made of the "cult of disillusion" that existed before the war among the younger liberal intelligentsia—pouting collegians like Randolph Bourne, Max Eastman, William Bullitt, and F. Scott Fitzgerald. No doubt young writers were frustrated by the genteel standards of a *Scribner's* or *Harper's* which frowned upon their experimentation and scoffed at their profanities. No doubt there was a rebelliousness among the young against what Henry May has called "the custodians of the old culture." Malcolm Cowley wrote that they were disillusioned at seventeen. "We felt . . . that our lives were directed by Puritan standards that were not our own, that society in general was terribly secure, unexciting, middle class."[9] Matthew Josephson remembered the young writers waiting restively in the musty offices of the Century Company while the aged editors took their noon siesta. Fresh out of Yale, Bill Bullitt was a cub reporter chafing at his inactivity in the city rooms and hankering for assignment overseas. Certainly, progressivism's *enfants terribles* were an impatient, petulant lot. But their restlessness was borne more of *illusionment* than despair. They were dissatisfied, to be sure, but they had great hopes for an American renaissance that would crack the barnacles of the old order. The avant-garde New York Armory art show in 1913, the cornucopia of new magazines and little theaters, the new feminism and New Freedom, the spirit of change everywhere, hinted, in Josephson's own words, "a New Day, the universe changing before our eyes." Cantankerous Ezra Pound talked of an American Risorgimento that would "make the Italian Renaissance look like a tempest in a teapot." Van Wyck Brooks discerned expanding cultural contacts with Europe signaling an end to the old provincialism and wrote a book celebrating America's "coming of age." As May himself notes, even in its most iconoclastic and pessimistic moments, the prewar rebellion was always exuberant.[10]

It was a curious mood that prevailed among these young people— fledgling liberals and cultural radicals like Cowley and Bourne, Fitzgerald and Bullitt, all of them serving their literary or political apprenticeships. Henry Piper has called it an "intellectual schizophrenia"—a simultaneous disillusion and hope. Bourne wondered to a friend in September 1913 "what perverse fate has imposed on me a philosophy so cross-grained, so desperately unpractical as mine of scorn for institutions, combined with a belief in their reform." The question was one they would confront more squarely after 1914, as the prewar years moved precipitously into a new phase. For the time being, they joined their progressive elders in the crowded ranks of the illusioned.[11]

The charged atmosphere of the prewar years sparked a "golden age of American radicalism," Heinz Eulau has observed. "Liberals and radicals, socialists and anarchists settled their differences by rational argument rather than personal calumny." Mabel Dodge's Fifth Avenue salon became a microcosm of the ferment, visited by packs of single-taxers, poets, birth-controlists, and socialists. The *New Republic*, *Seven Arts*, *Masses*, and other magazines newly established or in the process of being created—which were to become the rallying points around which rival liberal camps would cluster after 1914—were now partners in the common effort of prodding society. The more frivolous basked in the aimless euphoria of Washington Square, while the serious ones served on the board of the American Peace Society or gathered material to expose municipal corruption. One group found progress in reform legislation, another in cultural emancipation, another in the unprecedented prestige that the country enjoyed. All were heady with "a sense of secret comradeship and immense potentialities for change."[12]

This is not to say that skeptics crouched in the closet in 1914. Maintaining a high profile were the misanthropic Veblen, the sulking Adams brothers Henry and Brooks, and the septuagenarian Holmes who freely and publicly admonished giddier colleagues. Holmes wrote his young friend Harold Laski, just graduated from Oxford and teaching at Harvard, that he, for one, did not believe "that universal bliss would ensue if the world [would] only get a move on and obey when the *New Republic* says Hocus-Pocus-Presto-Chango." Laski replied affirmatively. Croly and Lippmann seemed to him "really theologians—for they believe either in goodness or in sin as original and they have what I take to be a pathetic trust in environmental change. . . . Here, I think there is too great confidence in the power of men to do anything to which they turn their attention." A rather remarkable friendship developed between Laski, in his early twenties, and the crusty Holmes. Their correspondence provides a valuable record of the thought of two men who abstained from progressivism's intoxication.[13]

Lincoln Steffens had turned increasingly cynical since his muckraking days and by 1914 was more debunker than reformer. In *The Shame of the Cities* (1904) and *The Struggle for Self-Government* (1906) he found the entire American system, from top to bottom, from congressmen to big businessmen to small farmers, honeycombed with corruption. He blamed the purblind masses who so easily succumbed to the bosses, and perceived that graft was not so much a crime as a social process of which all the elements in the society were cogs. By the eve of the war Steffens was convinced that all the muckraking and exhorting in the world could not change society. He wrote to a fellow reformer that the people would not listen to them. "They cannot read, not anything that is longer than a meal." In his autobiography he mentioned that "muckraking looked useless. Society moved like a glacier, slowly; if it progressed, it grew like an oak tree—slowly." Poet-philosopher George Santayana was weaving his five-volume *The Life of Reason* in 1905–1906, during the embryonic period of the new pragmatism and new nationalism, and, like Steffens, paused to reflect on the possibilities for social democracy. "For such excellence to grow," he sighed, "general mankind must be notably transformed."[14]

In 1914, at least one liberal, Walter Rauschenbusch, the Social Gospel minister, realized the urgency of the moment and the fragility of the prewar spirit. Rauschenbusch spoke at a dinner at the St. Denis

Hotel in New York City in April, two months before Sarajevo. "We are told," he said, "that we must be patient, must bide our time: Rome wasn't built in a day!" "Don't believe it," he cried. "We have not a moment to lose. *Now* is the hour—perhaps the last hour for us of this generation. For any moment—tomorrow, the day after—a war may break out, and then our chance will be gone. The world will revert on [*sic*] an instant to reaction, autocracy, perhaps to barbarism and savagery. We shall then have to fight, if we can fight at all, not for progress, but for elemental things which we think achieved when war comes. . . . So it's now or never! Once America gets into war with Mexico, Japan [he did not mention Germany]—our enemies will be in the saddle, to ride roughshod for years."[15]

The skeptics formed a significant minority, and they pointed to very real reasons for alarm and misgiving, but they were voices in the wilderness in the balmy prewar years. America was not yet paradise, but, as Walter Lord has noted about the period between the turn of the century and the outbreak of the war, "these years were good because, whatever the trouble, people were sure they could fix it." More typical than Justice Holmes's debunking or Rauschenbusch's foreboding was the quiet injunction of William Allen White to a Phi Beta Kappa class at Columbia that progress to some upward ideal was "the surest fact of history." Or Whitlock's rhapsody in 1913, on the eve of war: "Notwithstanding all the ignorance and all the woe in the world tonight, never before has there been such widespread opportunity for enlightenment, never such widespread comfort, never so much kindness." John Chamberlain, writing from the disillusioned perspective of the twenties, recaptured the enchanting sound of "the fiddles . . . tuning all over America." "The fiddles," Chamberlain wrote nostalgically, "could be heard lightly, sweetly, as early as 1912 and 1913, the years of Great Expectations when the Millennium, Woodrovian-fostered, seemed just around the corner. . . . Could any note of hope, any time, any place, have been so universal?"[16]

3 THE WAR, 1914-1916

"A DUMB SHOW"

"The war" for Americans in the summer of 1914 was the Mexican War. The *Literary Digest* of June 20 headlined its "Topics of the Day" section with a spread on "Mexican Gun-Running," the *Atlantic Monthly* featured in its June issue a sketch of the Mexican president Victoriano Huerta, and *Munsey's* chose Mexico for its June "popular geography" lesson. Albert Shaw's *American Review of Reviews* in its "Progress of the World" column listed sixteen entries relating to the Mexican imbroglio, five on the Canal tolls question and other problems in the Caribbean, and one on the ominous tremors emanating from Europe. *Scribner's* offered some European commentary, though its coverage was restricted to "Chamois-Hunting in Switzerland." The annual summer of violence in the Balkans had arrived on schedule, and elicited the usual mixed response among Americans of mild concern over the commotion of clashing troops and considerable amusement at the vagaries of European politics. It appeared as if the Europeans were resuming their joust over a few sacred mounds and cow pastures. As the great powers began mobilization, few Americans bothered to ascertain the cause or magnitude of the hostilities. The advent of a steamy June had enervated even their anxiety over the volatile Mexican situation, and the assassination of Archduke Francis Ferdinand on 28 June hardly interrupted the casualness with which they retired for the season. [1]

The major cares of midsummer 1914 were the next predicaments of the heroes in the melodramas that were being serialized in magazines and movie theaters. *Collier's*, a long-time indicator of the pulse of American opinion, studded its covers with sports figures who were captivating the country with sensational feats and record performances. Yachting, rowing, and polo were suddenly in vogue, but baseball and tennis were still predominant, and Americans were relieved to hear that German Davis Cup ace Otto Froitzheim would be permitted to play in America despite the threatened restrictions on travel. Other excitement was generated by the National Balloon Race eliminations, the Sells-Floto circus and its magnificent calliope, and the fortieth edition of the Chautauqua with its motley company of pedagogues, minstrels, and mountebanks.

The rush of events in the Balkans scarcely penetrated even the more sensitive liberal community. As the war approached, liberals were relaxing from the year's round of reform, savoring recent successes and dreaming new pipe dreams. In their memoirs, it became a literary convention for these liberals to sketch the change of seasons of 1914 in gossamer tones. Novelist Edith Wharton wrote in Paris that "an exceptionally gay season was drawing to its close." The dust of ideas "sparkled like motes in the sun." Brand Whitlock, who had just succeeded Theodore Marburg as minister to Belgium, remembered a leisurely spring at his new post punctuated only by garden strolls, state dinners, and trips to the museum. Harold Stearns, a crony of Bourne's who was graduated from Harvard in 1913, found it difficult to recall "the intellectual stage-setting of those days, for everything was shortly to undergo such a violent disorientation." Stearns thought of a large-scale European war "only as I might think of a comic opera war in the Balkans, perhaps accompanied by such gay music as we were then hearing, with Mitzi Hajos singing in 'Sari.' "[2]

Even when the Balkan situation exploded in July and August, the liberals were oblivious to the proportions of the conflict. Lippmann sailed for England a few days after the assassination and spent a "delightful" month in London and at Beatrice and Sidney Webb's school in the country. "I do not remember hearing any discussion of the Serbian crisis," he later wrote, "and so little concern did I have with it that in the last week of July I crossed over to Belgium, loitered at Ostend and Bruges and Ghent, went on to Brussels and then bought a ticket for a journey through Germany to Switzerland, where I meant to spend my vacation walking over mountain passes." In western New York, the erudite faculty of the Chautauqua summer school routinely delivered their lectures and traded daily gossip at lunch, rejecting out of hand a report on 31 July of a general European war. Scott Nearing recalled them sitting at the big round table in the main dining room, momentarily aghast at the news, and then reassuring one another it was all a fabrication. Charles Edward Russell wrote, "We saw the whole eloquent drama of the Balkans played out before us and there we sat like spectators at an inexplicable dumb show and wondered what the row was all about."[3]

Why such detachment and indifference while Europe was in convulsion? William Allen White years later drew a self-portrait of pure innocence. White pictured himself as the proverbial "babe in the woods" in European affairs. His "introduction to European politics" did not come until a conversation with Norman Angell while crossing the Atlantic to Paris and the peace conference. "I was just Republican precinct committeeman in the Fourth Ward of Emporia, Kansas,"

White explained. "The vast complexity of European politics, built on centuries of tradition, usage, prejudice and conflicting desires, was not even remotely in any corner of my consciousness." White and some others could be excused their provincialism, however flimsy a rationalization, but for most American liberals it was not a case of pure innocence that blinded them to the convulsions in Europe. Wharton, Whitlock, Stearns, Lippmann, and a host of others touring or temporarily living on the Continent were immediately on the scene. Among liberal intellectuals and writers at home, almost all had a cosmopolitan sophistication acquired from Ivy League educations and travels abroad.* Even the average American, according to Elmer Davis, "had daily first-hand knowledge of the growing internationalism of business, travel, sport [and] amusement that promised to make frontiers in Europe no more than lines on the map."[4]

The international awareness *was* present. As early as 1909 Herbert Croly, in his bible of progressivism *The Promise of American Life*, matter-of-factly suggested the possibility of a general European war and the active role the United States would necessarily play in it. American liberals were not as uninitiated as some of them later pretended to be. In the disappointments they would suffer during the war and at Paris, they were victimized not by their *inexperience* but by their *illusions*. Even White's self-portrait of the "babe in the woods" belies the fact that he and his compeers overestimated their own backyard neighbors' rationality and goodness and their own country's promise of progress. Locally, nationally, and internationally, they thought in terms that were too optimistic. And so in the spring and summer of 1914, although many of them were equipped by knowledge and experience to recognize the significance of events, by inclination they overlooked or misread them. As one confessed:

> To lift up our eyes and see the world as it really was seemed in some of us a physical impossibility. Because the German that lived next door to us in Janesville was an ingenuous and peaceable man the government of imperial Germany must be ingenuous and peaceable. Because when the Kaiser of Germany met the

---

*Of the *New Republic* men, Lippmann, Croly, and Philip Littell were Harvard graduates, as were the Hapgood brothers Norman and Hutchins, *Nation* editor Oswald Garrison Villard, and "lost generation" types like Dos Passos, Cowley, Granville Hicks, and John Reed. Max Eastman went to Williams, Walter Weyl to Pennsylvania's Wharton School. Among the cultural radicals who gathered around the *Seven Arts* magazine, Bourne was graduated from Columbia, Stearns and Van Wyck Brooks from Harvard, and Paul Rosenfeld and Waldo Frank from Yale. Lippmann, Croly, Dos Passos, Bourne, Brooks, and the Hapgoods were among those who had studied and traveled extensively in Europe before the war.

Kaiser of Austria they kissed and said they loved peace it was apparent neither could ever draw the sword; the kiss proved that. Because it cost $1470 to fire a great gun there could never be a war; where was the money to come from? And because Germany had some kind of an elected parliamentary body Germany after all must be more or less democratic and hence could not be very unlike us.

It was a myopia that left them blind to the harsh realities of a world now glowing with peril.[5]

Germany declared war on Russia on 1 August and on France 3 August. The next day, with the German invasion of Belgium, England, too, was locked in combat. The "dumb show" had become a full-scale conflagration engulfing the entire continent. Initial reaction among liberals verged on absolute shock. "It was a protected little historic moment of peace and progress we grew up in," Eastman said. "We were children reared in a kindergarten, and now the real thing was coming. History was resuming its bloody course." Edith Wharton wrote, "There were moments when I felt as if I had died, and woken up in an unknown world." David Starr Jordan, recently retired president of Stanford University, was at work putting the finishing touches on a study entitled, ironically, *War's Aftermath*, which examined the disastrous and lasting effect of the Civil War on the American South. He inserted a gratuitous comment on the European situation, written melancholically in London in August 1914: "Thorns and thistles grow in the harassed mind as in the devastated field. The higher life withers in the atmosphere of poverty and pestilence. The muses flee from the wolf at the door."[6]

Santayana, having retired from the Harvard faculty and moved to Europe in 1912, also found himself in England at the outbreak of the war. Writing from Oxford on 16 August, he said he was restless, hardly knew which way to turn. The war upset his plans and lacerated his sympathies. He had come to Oxford "in the fond hope of finding peace." But the war was "too atmospheric. It pervades every retreat." Minister John Haynes Holmes was astonished at how suddenly—"in the wink of an eye"—"three hundred years of progress is cast into the melting-pot." Charles William Eliot, the distinguished president emeritus of Harvard, addressing a women's club in October, broke into tears while discussing how profoundly the war had affected the progressive philosophy.[7]

Despite the initial wave of shock and disillusion, most American liberals rebounded quickly in these early months of the war, resumed reform activities at home, and took comfort in their own country's remoteness from the turmoil. As Henry May has noted, "The outbreak of the war in Europe shocked American intellectuals but did not immediately become their main preoccupation. Until about the winter of 1916, radical and progressive politics, together with the new literary and philosophical tendencies, get more space than the war in the liberal and literary periodicals." "The sound of marching feet," recalled Dos Passos, "came dimly through the walls of the sanctum upstairs in the Harvard Union where we edited the *Monthly*." Harold Stearns, in London, was closer to the reverberations of booming artillery and tramping infantry and dramatically aware of the momentous events unfolding before him, but his response was one of relief, even celebration. He and his compatriots congratulated one another on their good fortune to be Americans. "Whatever else happened in a world which had fallen to pieces," he rejoiced, "*we* were out of it. We were safe behind the broad stretches of the Atlantic; we had a sanity and a sense of humor that contrasted only too sharply with the strain and nervousness of our foreign friends." Randolph Bourne was another American in Europe when the war broke. Initially stunned by the turn of events, he left for the United States in August and, like so many others, was prepared to let the war run its course. "I do not even want to think about Europe," he wrote on the boat home, "until the war is over and life is running again."[8]

The war, however, did not go away, and into 1915 it became luminously clear even to blinkered liberals like Stearns and Bourne that the conflict would be protracted. The weeklies replaced their gay bits of Americana with grisly pictures of the war theater and reports of German atrocities. Unrestricted submarine warfare raised doubts about the wisdom of isolationism and unpreparedness. Many books and films appeared early in 1915 dealing with the theme of invasion—climaxed by an article in the May issue of *McClure's* entitled "The Conquest of America!" Journalist Richard Harding Davis, novelist William Dean Howells, and academicians George Beer and Arthur Lovejoy were among those urging Americans to join the cause of England and France, while Harvard psychologist Hugo Münsterberg detailed the German case in two compelling volumes. In the unsettling climate created by these pressures, liberals inevitably, sooner or later, had to confront the fact of war and the formidable questions that the crisis posed.[9]

Social Gospel minister Holmes had been one of the first to confront the issue squarely. In September 1914 he asked, "Who in these United States is thinking at this moment of recreation centers, improved housing, or the minimum wage? If, as now seems probable, the nations fight to the point of exhaustion, the question facing the world at the conclusion of peace will not be that of social progress at all, but simply and solely that of social survival!" And now a year later, Croly and Lippmann in the *New Republic* confirmed the exigency and implored fellow liberals to "face a world very different from that with which our current imaginations have grown up." In a lengthy editorial entitled "Mental Unpreparedness" they placed the war in icy perspective:

> To a younger generation brought up with a humanitarian and evolutionist philosophy the war has been a shock that has dislodged all the old ideals. If the conflict had been over speedily, we might have dismissed it as a momentary aberration of our civilized world. . . . But the war has not been speedy. And now after a year what was a shock in which the very universe seemed to reel has become almost the normal background of European affairs. We no longer ask how it can all be got back to its original state, but what the outcome will do to our world. While a year ago we could not have believed that we lived in such a world, we have now been fairly dragooned into accepting the fact that it is exactly in the sort of world where such things happen that we live, and may live for years to come.

"We are at the parting of the intellectual ways," the editors declared. "We can put our ideals behind us and turn and worship them, or we can put them ahead of us and struggle towards them."[10]

Unfortunately, even as they assumed the burden of confronting the war head-on, the liberal response turned characteristically to nostrums. Where the *New Republic* editors had called for thoughtful analysis and probing study, most liberals set about organizing peace expeditions or developing disarmament plans. Few doubted that the war would be brought to a clean conclusion or that the peace would be an enduring one. Few challenged William Howard Taft's reassuring prognosis that after the horrible expenditure of blood and treasure "there will be every opportunity for common sense to resume its sway." "It is an awful remedy," said Taft, "but in the end it may be worth what it costs, if it makes this the last great war." Even the *New Republic* men, for all their solemnity, were confident of a happy ending. The war was "the first real test" of the pragmatic philosophy—of the ability of men to adapt and respond intelligently to a serious crisis. As in the campaigns against municipal corruption and prostitution, they were certain of success. Perhaps only a handful of liberals in 1915 cushioned themselves for the failures and disappointments that lay ahead.[11]

A symposium of "Peace Proposals and Programs, 1914-1916," compiled by Bourne and published in 1916 by the American Association for International Conciliation, reveals much about liberal expectations during the first two years of the war. The various proposals, collected from among such notables as Lippmann, Eliot, William English Walling, and Norman Angell, demonstrated a surprisingly sophisticated grasp of the complexities of international relations and of the fundamental political and economic issues underlying the war polemics. H.N. Brailsford, English political commentator and frequent contributor to the *New Republic*, recognized that "when two embassies compete in Peking for a railway concession, the issue may be determined by the balance of naval power in the North Sea." Eliot observed that small states could not exist except "united in an offensive and defensive alliance, or under guarantees given by a group of strong and trustworthy nations." Not one subscribed to the dreamy pacifist notions of Jane Addams or William Jennings Bryan that war could be abolished simply by disarmament. But more significant and more revealing than their relatively sophisticated analysis of the causes of war was the gross naïveté of their prescriptions for peace.

The very appearance and title of the collection (*Towards An Enduring Peace: A Symposium of Peace Proposals and Programs, 1914–1916*)—like the peace contests and peace banquets and other paraphernalia of the peace movement—indicated the cavalier conviction on the part of leading liberal editors, intellectuals, and statesmen in 1914-1916 that peace could indeed be contrived or engineered. They advanced plans like consulting architects submitting blueprints. Some presented altogether quixotic solutions, such as the proposal of A. A. Tenney, a professor of sociology at Columbia, that a "world-wide like-mindedness" be developed. More cerebral proposals, such as Eliot's, suggested an elaborate system of international courts and tribunals backed by an international police force. But nearly all worked from the assumption that peace, and no less than *absolute* and *permanent* peace, was a possibility in human affairs. Socialist Walling conceded that war could not be abolished by disarmament, but was hopeful of "abolishing the *causes* of war," a goal perhaps even more remote.

John Bates Clark, a director of the Carnegie Endowment for International Peace and professor of political economy at Columbia, believed here in 1915 that "something having the characteristics of a league of peace is rapidly evolving and in all probability will, at the close of the war, require only a small modification to enable it to prevent, so long as it lasts, the recurrence of a great war on the Continent of Europe." Nicholas Murray Butler, another director of the Carnegie Endowment and the president of Columbia, proclaimed himself an "unconquerable optimist" and proceeded to interpret the war as a "catharsis," as "history's way of teaching" the fallacy of the old ways. "Surely," Butler exulted, "that struggle for the balance of power . . . has proved its futility. Surely we can see the vanity of Ententes and Alliances and of a division of the world into heavily armed camps. . . . Surely the international politics of a Palmerston, or a Disraeli, or a Bismarck, striking and splendid as they were in their own way,— surely those policies are put behind us and are outgrown forever."[12]

Like firemen—instinctively, mechanically—peacemakers rushed in to put out the war. Some individuals undertook peace expeditions. The New York Peace Society called for a reconvention of The Hague Conference. The World Peace Foundation pressed for the nationalization of the manufacture of armaments. The American Socialist party urged the abolition of all private profit in munitions manufacturing, international ownership of all strategic waterways including the Bosporus, Dardanelles, Strait of Gibraltar, and the Suez, Kiel, and Panama canals, and the declaration of "offensive" warfare solely by the direct vote of the people. Additionally, there were proposals by the Church Peace Union, the International Peace Congress, the School Peace League, and the Women's Movement for Constructive Peace. Some of the more ludicrous solutions included "interchangeable citizenship" and "the incorporation of the golden rule into international law." All were hopelessly unrealistic. The liberals who contributed to the Bourne symposium represented the more informed and responsible elements in the pacifist community between 1914 and 1916, but even they failed to realize the enormity of the task or to perceive that the precious goal of peace—however and whenever obtained—might be slippery and evaporable.[13]

The travail and illusions of these early years can perhaps best be discerned on a personal level. Charles William Eliot is a good example of both the graces and the limitations of the liberal mind. Eliot, president of Harvard from 1869 to 1909 and a tough-minded Democrat who voted for Roosevelt and Taft rather than the flatulent Bryan, studied the war on assignment for the Carnegie Endowment. In numerous addresses and in a series of article-length letters to *The New York Times* he undertook to explain the issues of the war and its significance for Americans. In remarks to the Lake Mohonk Conference on International Arbitration in 1907 he had delivered one of the few sensible statements by an American on the subject of disarmament, asking how Germany could consent to an arbitration on the reduction of armaments when surrounded by alien armies and in the absence of adequate safeguards. Eight years later, in May 1915, in another speech to the Lake Mohonk Conference, Eliot reiterated the same theme, lamenting how little their thinking had matured and calling for "the creation of an international legislative and executive council, or other political body, backed by an international force." Eliot's objective throughout the prewar and wartime discussions on peace and disarmament was the establishment of this international council backed by an authorized peacekeeping force—a far sounder mechanism for peace than the "pledges" and "petitions" that others were bandying about. But was it reasonable to expect that such an organization could be established or function effectively? Eliot later gave his warm endorsement to the peace treaty and heralded Wilson's League of Nations as the fulfillment of his hopes and as a real solution to the international anarchy. But even if America had joined the League, how could any kind of genuine concert have been achieved or sanctions and force meaningfully employed amid the welter of hatreds and irredentism of 1919?

However astute his analysis, Eliot succumbed to a catalogue of progressive fallacies. He overestimated the good will and intelligence of the masses. He held an inflated faith in institutions as cure-alls for the world's evils. And, as evident in nearly all of his letters to the *Times*, he exaggerated the virtue of "public discussion" and the villainy of secret diplomacy and conspiring politicians. A forceful League of Nations, free institutions at home, the democratic forum, and public diplomacy—these were the instruments on which Eliot counted to reverse the tide of war and insure a lasting peace. It was a program that was certainly not folly, perhaps not even unreasonable, but, like other, more farfetched proposals, so presumptuous that it primed its author for disillusionment.[14]

Almost alone among the participants in the Bourne symposium to grasp the true dimension of the problem—the *impossibility* of permanent peace—was the budding prophet Arnold Toynbee. "Humanity," Toynbee offered, "has an instinctive craving for something eternal. . . . Whenever the European organism proves its instability by breaking down, we start in quest of a perfect mechanism, a 'permanent settlement.' We are invariably disappointed, but invariably we return to the quest again." Toynbee recalled the efforts of statesmen at Vienna a century earlier who labored to produce a definitive peace. "In 1915 the belligerent democracies are preparing to lead themselves the same dance. 'Europe is in a mess,' we are all saying: 'Let us tidy her up once and for all, and then we can live comfortably ever after.' " Toynbee admonished that the impending settlement would not be permanent, "and the better it fits the situation, the less permanent will it be. . . . Our real work will be to regulate this immediate settlement so that it varies in harmony with the subsequent growth of Europe."[15]

Walter Lippmann amplified Toynbee's sobering observations in a book entitled *The Stakes of Diplomacy*. Lippmann was distressed by the increasing tendency among his countrymen, his liberal colleagues in particular, to regard the war in abstract, simplistic terms. He bristled at their "thin solutions [to] intricate questions"—Bryan's arbitration treaties, the socialists' referendum on declarations of war, women refusing to buy lead soldiers for their children. Although he endorsed the proposal for a world senate and international organization, Lippmann recognized the difficulty of drafting a peace and the necessity of maintaining peace by ongoing negotiations and *Realpolitik*, however unsavory such methods might be to the liberal mentality. He knew that any plan for peace would be tenuous at best, and he presented his own ideas as a "compass" and not a "panacea." Like Toynbee, he urged a sense of humility, patience, and a tough-minded attention to proximate solutions. "We shall end war," he concluded, "by dealing effectively with our problems, not by reiterating that war is horrible."[16]

Voices of moderation chimed in from other quarters as well. In March 1915 David Starr Jordan, à dedicated pacifist, reviewed the goals that he and his associates faithfully supported, acknowledging how tortuous the road ahead might be. "Let us assume," said Jordan in an extremely perceptive passage,

> that there will be no victory for either side, but that all the nations concerned will find themselves defeated. The treaty of peace must be written at last. There are many things which we would like to put into this treaty, things essential to the future security and well-being of Europe. But we shall not get many of them. We may not get any. It may be that the drawn game will end in a truce, not of peace but of exhaustion.
>
> After the war is over then will begin the work of reconstruction. Then will come the test of our mettle. Can Europe build up a solid foundation of peace amid the havoc of greed and hate? Constructive work belongs to peace; it may take fifty years to put the Continent in order.

More caustically, Harold Laski wrote Justice Holmes how little he cared "for the upward and onward trend" and that "really I am sick and tired of benevolent amateurs and peace leagues and birth-control and all the other means by which the reformers are going to make the tough discipline of life sufficiently tender for a generation which likes even to read its classics in translations." For Laski, the war was the crowning proof of human infirmity. He told Holmes he "might have yielded to the perfectibilists before the war" but that the flames in Europe had "surely demonstrated our humanity." A similarly chastened Harvard senior, John Dos Passos, reflected glumly upon his graduation on the "ponderous suicidal machine" called civilization. [17]

One improbable expression of moderation appeared in *The Book of the Homeless*, a potpourri of poems, articles, and sketches put together in 1916 by Edith Wharton and sold for the benefit of the Franco-Belgian Relief Committee. Contributors included the likes of William Dean Howells, Paul Elmer More, Theodore Roosevelt, and Henry James. Most of the pieces were chauvinistic and emotionally charged. The chief exception was the contribution of William Butler Yeats, a poem entitled "A Reason for Keeping Silent":

> I think it better that at times like these
> We poets keep our mouths shut, for in truth
> We have no gift to set a statesman right;
> He's had enough of meddling who can please
> A young girl in the indolence of her youth
> Or an old man upon a winter's night. [18]

Yeats's message was plain enough, as was the advice of Toynbee and Lippmann. But few liberals found reason to keep silent—or sober. As on the eve of war when Walter Rauschenbusch's words of apprehension fell on deaf ears, in the commotion of 1916 skeptics were again overwhelmed by a chorus of sloganeering and bravado.

At precisely the same time that Dos Passos was penning his "humble protest" and Jordan was composing a scenario in which the war would run on indefinitely, an organization called the League to Enforce Peace convened in Washington to unveil yet another ambitious formula for peace. A conglomeration of liberal and conservative editors, ministers, intellectuals, and statesmen who were brought together by a cosmopolitan outlook and a common commitment to internationalism,* they proposed to limit future wars through an international police force to which each nation would contribute a specified quota. They also advocated a boycott and other economic sanctions "to provide the peace movement with a spinal column." Their feeling was that a league or alliance among the principal nations, utilizing their joint economic and military resources, could effectively enforce peace. "That was something everybody could understand," a leader explained. "Every city and town has its police force, every village its marshal, every rural precinct its constable. . . . To

---

*Members included William Howard Taft, Alton Parker, Lyman Abbott, Victor Berger, Charles Van Hise, William Allen White, Rabbi Stephen Wise, Hamilton Holt, A. Lawrence Lowell, Theodore Marburg, and John Bates Clark.

compel a whole people to obey the law of nations is but to carry a step farther a practice with which all the world is familiar in its daily life." To their credit, they realized that a league could not eliminate war, but their extravagant illusion here was the assumption that nations would cooperate in the cause of peace and self-preservation— that international law and relations were merely an extension of everyday community relations, and that nations, like people (yet another illusion), were rational.[19]

By the fall of 1916 most liberals had surrendered their expectations for an instant conclusion to the war or a perfect peace. But they remained optimistic about the outcome and enthusiastic over the prospect for democracy and freedom in the postwar world. Secretary of War Newton Baker explained that the peace of Vienna had failed because "it stood upon the pleasure of a half-dozen gentlemen, interested in the pretensions of princes and the destinies of dynasties, who sat around the table with a map of Europe and some lead pencils." Baker was convinced that it would be different this time, that the United States would exert its influence and its example of democracy to inspire Europe to a just and lasting peace.[20]

Former Social Gospeler George Herron, living in Italy during the war, wrote his friend Upton Sinclair that "the outcome will be social revolution in every country and the sweeping away of all the old institutions of government, with new conceptions of morality and social responsibility." The new and nobler world would come "only out of a great tribulation," he said; "half a generation" might pass before they settled down to an orderly course.[21] Herron's vision was fuzzy at best. His timetable was downright fanciful. This was the stuff of which disillusionments were made. In two years at war, liberals tragically failed to perform the severe reckoning and unsparing self-examination which the occasion required. They failed to scale down their expectations sufficiently or to cushion themselves for disappointment. And they persisted in the same flabby assumptions of peace and progress that had worked well enough in reform activities at home but were betraying them in the more formidable arena of the European combat.

No one was riper for disillusionment in 1916 than Brand Whitlock, a liberal acquaintance of Herron's beginning his third year as U.S. minister to Belgium. Whitlock looked ahead to the presidential race of 1916, the role that Woodrow Wilson was destined to play in the peacemaking, and the likely verdict of history. "It is too soon now to talk about the campaign," he wrote Colonel House from Brussels in May 1916, "but I think it is pretty safe to predict that the great issue will be between Democracy and Imperialism." Whitlock believed it was an issue that could decide the election. "All we have to do," he said, "is sincerely to make that issue clear, and that should be a simple and congenial task for those who see no hope for the world except in democracy and in the American ideals. How superbly the President has upheld these ideals! When the fumes of the passions of these times shall have been cleared away, he will take a place in history beside Lincoln." "I write this now," he added, "not because you don't know it already but because some day when we are old, sitting around the fire, having taken our place among the back numbers, I wish to be able to say: 'I told you so.' "[22]

4 THE WAR, 1916-1917

"THE GREAT CRUSADE"

Whitlock's characterization of the presidential campaign of 1916 signified a dangerous new upswing in the liberal illusionment—the tendency to imagine the war as something of a crusade and America's role in it as messianic. It was a temptation that had beguiled many liberals from the start[1] but was only in 1916 becoming altogether seductive. The "crusade" theme was foreshadowed as early as August 1914 in the letters and diary of John Jay Chapman.* Chapman had written his mother from London that the war would have no beneficial result if the victors were allowed to aggrandize at the end. He tried personally to convince the British that they should take the initiative in disavowing any claims to territory and proclaiming their intention to disarm. "Such a declaration," he said, "would arouse a wave of enthusiasm among neutrals, and make the war into a crusade." In a diary entry of 28 August he told of his suggestion to Lord Grey "that he should give utterance on Disarmament as the object of the war—as soon as possible—and that this should be the beginning of what the Americans would call a publicity end of the war—a thing as important as the battles, i.e. continuous explanation to the grand public of the aims of the Allies."[2]

Through 1915 and 1916, as the war dragged on to an uncertain conclusion, an ever-increasing number of liberals became intoxicated with Chapman's concept of a "crusade" that would articulate war aims, enlighten the public, and in general ennoble the entire war effort. What seemed a salutary boost to the liberal cause, however, amounted to a reckless escalation of emotional involvement and intellectual commitment at precisely the time when the liberal pulse should have slowed. How could the mere enunciation of war aims or

*Chapman was actually more free spirit or "religious mystic" (as his friend and biographer DeWolfe Howe described him) than liberal. A very complex individual, he was distressed by the exclusion of Negroes from freshman dormitories at Harvard but WASPish in regard to Jews and Catholics and insensitive to many social issues. Still, he has been depicted as a radical (see Melvin Bernstein's essay, "John Jay Chapman and the Insurgent Individual," in *American Radicals: Some Problems and Personalities*, ed. Harvey Goldberg [New York, 1957], 21-33), and in any case his example is instructive.

gesture of noble intention—so cheap, so insubstantial—affect the outcome? How could mere rhetoric and publicity get people to overlook historic grievances or fight for anything less than the traditional stakes of spoils and vengeance? How could any true sublimation of spirit or purpose be accomplished anywhere except in state drawing rooms and the liberal press? Chapman himself was moved to confess on board ship from London to New York that "my ideas of disarmament, etc., may be like reaching for the moon."[3]

Nonetheless, having initially ignored the war and then been shocked by its magnitude, liberals were fast becoming obsessed with it as an apocalyptic event. Chapman had Lord Grey leading the crusade, but by 1916, almost by default, Wilson and America were being cast as the messiahs. For the first time since the outbreak of the war in 1914, American liberals were seriously considering the question of United States intervention. For all their bluster, the overwhelming majority of them had been content before 1916 to do their shouting from the sidelines and to let America's role in the conflict be one of Olympian detachment: America's proper position was to stand on the mountain, guard the sanctity of neutral rights, and urge Britain and France on to a victory over the German militarist government and a generous democratic peace with the German people. But as both liberal and American interests became imperiled by the protraction of the war and neutrality seemed suddenly a stale and precarious course, a number of fidgeters were looking in new directions.

Eliot wrote to *The New York Times* in March, "It is time to feel and speak more strongly about something more than the rights of neutrals. It is time for the deepest rooted and strongest of Republics to consider how it can best bring direct help to harassed and bleeding France and Great Britain." Eliot called on Americans to "take sides openly with the European peoples who are now resisting military despotism and dangerous national ambitions, and to discharge their obligations to the liberty-loving generations of the past and the future." Ray Stannard Baker had gone the route of most prewar liberals: through 1914 and 1915 he attended and addressed peace rallies, signed pacifist petitions, espoused the cause of disarmament, and listed proudly among his credentials charter membership in the League to Enforce Peace. But by 1916 he was troubled by America's ostrichism and chafing for some action. At an autumn meeting of the American Academy of Arts and Letters, in which Theodore Roosevelt delivered a warmongering address, Baker quarreled less with the Colonel's militancy than with his small-mindedness. He believed that Americans were "as willing to fight as any people on earth: if they can be assured that they are fighting for their own spiritual ideals:

their own vision of their nation." Baker was ready to go to war—as long as it was in the service of idealism. For most of these men now contemplating intervention—whether out of a sense of danger to the national interest or opportunity to bring new purpose to a feckless struggle—it was natural that they should seize upon the crusade concept for their rationale. To undertake a selfless campaign for "spiritual ideals" was an honorable and compelling motive for intervention, one that would both meet the challenges of a widening war and accommodate their carefully guarded idealism.[4]

The change in the liberal position unfolded most dramatically in the editorial pages of the *New Republic*, a magazine conceived during the summer of 1914 that eventually became the chief organ for the liberal interventionist viewpoint. Of the three controlling editors, Herbert Croly was a curious blend of mugwump, Hamiltonian, and democrat who perhaps more than any other living American personified the magazine's keynotes of pragmatism and progressivism; Walter Lippmann had flirted with socialism in his college days at Harvard but was gradually coming around to a more stringent Hamiltonian philosophy with his 1913 *Preface to Politics* and 1914 *Drift and Mastery*; and Walter Weyl was an economist in the New Nationalist school but so concerned with individual virtue that he has customarily been portrayed as the Jeffersonian of the trio. Lippmann later said that the three often disagreed and that Croly as senior editor usually prevailed.[5] Together they groped their way through the thicket of international relations on a tortuous course that by the winter of 1916 had them deep into the crusade psychology and, like Baker, tacitly supporting an American intervention. Since they wielded considerable influence in liberal circles, and in official circles as well, it is worthwhile to trace their evolution in some detail.

Pacifists like Jane Addams and Randolph Bourne later depicted the *New Republic* men as plunging headlong into support of intervention, but in fact their decision was painstakingly deliberate and came only after three years of constant vacillation and agonizing. The crowded summer of 1914 was an explosive time to launch a magazine of commentary. The suddenness with which the war was upon them did not permit the editors to develop a well-defined policy. Lippmann remarked that they had to improvise on very short notice. Initially, on impulse, they called for the "end of American isolation" and the abandonment of "timid neutrality," and berated mollycoddles like Addams who were "more passivist than pacifist." But they recoiled quickly into a position of "watchful waiting," and by the outset of 1915 had shucked their combativeness altogether for a policy of strict and benevolent neutrality.[6]

Although more power- and preparedness-conscious, more in the "realist" mold than most of their fellow liberal journalists, the *New Republic* editors were as sensitive to the horrors of war and as troubled by the implications of intervention. Accordingly, they busied themselves with much the same peace schemes that occupied other liberals—a favorite of theirs was the "league of neutral nations"—and were content for the time to woo the belligerents to the conference table and impress upon the Allies in particular the need for a generous peace initiative. After the *Lusitania* disaster in May, they became alarmed over the possibility of premature action by the American government. They urged continued restraint and discretion. Even after German authorities delivered a grossly unsatisfactory note to Wilson explaining the *Lusitania* incident, the editors rationalized the reply as justifiable in view of the "German temper":

> It is easier to get into war than to get out of it, and the ultimate horror of a struggle should be avoided unless everything else fails: It cannot be avoided if American opinion hardens and demands the kind of answer which a government like Germany's cannot give and still retain the support of a people in the present temper of the Germans. . . . If German officials are seeking to find some compromise of safety, we who are free and powerful can well afford to give them the chance.

In an editorial entitled "Not Our War" they could find no reason for abandoning America's "traditional attitude of neutrality and isolation."[7]

But circumstances worsened rapidly during the next year—the Germans refused to seek "some compromise of safety," the Allies for their part talked more each day like plotting imperialists, and the strident nationalism of Roosevelt and James Harvey's *North American Review* gathered fresh converts—until a settlement congenial to liberal goals and American interest seemed impossible unless a more decisive action were taken. Through the remainder of 1915 and into 1916, *New Republic* editorials reveal mounting frustration. While continuing in the effort to elevate the Allies' terms of peace and enlighten public opinion and persisting in the hope that Germany could be coaxed to the conference table, the editors seemed to have sensed the inadequacy of their desultory course. Drifting uncertainly, they were discrediting their own severe pragmatic philosophy, which called for positive action. By the fall of 1916 they acknowledged the gravity of the German offensive and the hollowness of their lectures to the Allies on dealing magnanimously with the Germans. In an editorial of 2 December they wrote, "Clearly we cannot now urge the Allies to make overtures of peace to a Germany which is still ascendant." Still they procrastinated, effusively praising the program of the League to Enforce Peace and vainly proposing a "show-down" conference among neutrals and belligerents to resolve the outstanding questions. What stymied them was the dilemma that hounded all conscientious liberals who contemplated an American intervention: how to move the nation into a more forceful and constructive peacemaking role without in the process fueling the tide of war?[8]

The rapid acceleration of events finally compelled the *New Republic* editors to attempt a solution, which they developed in a relentless series of editorials during the winter of 1916. They were at last prepared to risk American intervention, provided certain conditions and guarantees were met. They applauded the President's decision to send a note to the belligerents pointedly asking their intentions and explaining the conditions under which America would intervene (all stock liberal goals—reduction of armaments, restoration of Belgium, recognition of the rights of small nations, etc.). It is "a move in the direction of a positive national policy," they wrote in an editorial of 30 December, "which . . . will create for the American democracy a living and serviceable relation to the ultimate issues of the European war." The editors believed the belligerents would take the President's earnestness seriously. "No one in Europe who is honestly fighting simply for security and a measure of justice," they declared, "can in the end regard this offer of ours as anything but friendly and hopeful. For what it says to Europe is this: we will guarantee with our resources and our lives the objects of the western democracies, but before we do that those objects must be distinguished from the objects of the imperialists." The *New Republic* was courting intervention on terms that would enhance a liberal settlement of the war: America would intervene only upon securing a suitable guarantee from the Allies—or for that matter from the Germans at this point in December 1916—that they would pursue a nonimperialist, nonvindictive conclusion to the war.[9]

It was the crusade gambit. America's purpose was selfless and unimpeachable. "It is aggressive only in the manifest interest of international order and security. It is national in the sense that it brings certain national ideals a little nearer to realization." America was ready to fight for the "popular objects" of the war—disarmament, no annexations, a league of nations—higher stakes than power, territory, or honor. Weapons were to be ideals; objectives, supranational. The editors were confident of a favorable response to Wilson's note. When the initial replies from the German government and the Northcliffe press in Britain ranged from lukewarm to hostile, they chalked it up to the reactionaries in those countries who were still in power but fading as liberal sentiment mounted:

> The first exclamations need not disturb us, nor cause us to
> swerve. They were exactly what was expected, and they will
> not dominate. The logic of the situation is so powerfully on the
> side of the President that the complexion of the talk will inevita-
> bly change. The movement which he has initiated cannot fail to
> grow, and everywhere it will assume sooner or later the form of a
> struggle between the progressives and the extremists.[10]

Thus, by the close of 1916, the *New Republic* men had elevated the
prosecution of the war to the level of a crusade. It was a precipitous
new step for men who were accustomed to dealing in practical concerns and hard realities, men who throughout their deliberations and
even during their wishful peace maneuvers had been absorbed with
matters of "power" and "national interest." Harold Stearns later
wrote of their awkward transition that "nothing was more pathet-
ically amusing during the war than to watch . . . very severe pragmatic minds [turn to] the task of formulating ideal terms of peace."[11]
But the lure of idealism was too great in 1916 for even "realists" to re-
sist (and progressivism's "realists" had always been prone to such
lapses). The crusade formula seemed the perfect answer to the liberal
dilemma. It would accomplish, by force if necessary, the most immediate task—the elimination of the German threat to neutral rights,
freedom of the seas (Lippmann's special concern), and the welfare of
the "Atlantic community" (as the editors were coming to call the common Allied interest); and it would do so in such a way, they thought, as
to check jingoist emotions and imperialist designs. Further, the leverage exerted by American intervention would assure liberalism a domi-
nant voice at the peace table and promise that the new world order
would be constructed according to democratic principles.

Lippmann, Croly, and Weyl thus joined an expanding body of restive liberals uncomfortable with America's spectator role and willing
to hazard intervention if the conditions were right. Significantly, they
were also converging upon the official position of the government, as
the crusade campaign found its biggest booster in the White House in
the person of Wilson.

Despite the conditional backing of the *New Republic* and the open ad-
vocacy of respected leaders like Eliot, American intervention remained something less than a popular cause in the liberal community
through 1916. Many liberals balked at the crusade injunction and refused to consider intervention on any grounds whatsoever. There

were doctrinaire pacifists like Jane Addams (who was sensitive to the charge and preferred to bill herself as an "aggressive pacifist"); ministers John Haynes Holmes, Norman Thomas, and A.J. Muste, who huddled around the newly formed Fellowship of Reconciliation; philosopher-economist Scott Nearing; Amos Pinchot, who became so exercised over the hint of American aggressiveness that he financed the leftist *Masses*; and Oswald Garrison Villard, whose *Nation* and New York *Evening Post* became virtual stewards of the peace movement. The pacifists could not countenance joining forces with the Lodges and Roosevelts, and rejected the *New Republic* argument that intervention would "liberalize" or shorten the war. Pinchot wrote just prior to Wilson's war declaration, "It will make Germany desperate, close the fist of the militarist government upon the people, and hold down the democratic impulses that stand for peace. . . . It will solidify the British Government's determination not to make peace until a decisive victory is won, and to offer no terms in the meantime that will not impel Germany to fight on to the bitter end."[12]

There were, too, the colony of liberal intellectuals who frequented Greenwich Village and other haunts of art and literature and feared that intervention would bring a crackdown on expression and creative activity. They could not reconcile themselves to the corrosion of aesthetic values that they believed would inevitably accompany American involvement: the suppression of free speech, the impositions of conformity, the intensified destruction of human life, and the desecration of a German culture in which they found much to admire. Matthew Josephson wrote, "We were skeptical when reading Allied propaganda about the alleged war atrocities committed by the countrymen of Goethe and Beethoven." They did not follow the war with the daily concern of those on the mainline and were not as vocal as the pacifists, but in the *Seven Arts*—the magazine around which they gathered in November 1916—they took potshots freely at the war enthusiasts. Among the prominent writers attracted to the magazine, many of them defectors from the *New Republic*, were Waldo Frank, Harold Stearns, Van Wyck Brooks, James Oppenheim, and the brilliant hunchback Randolph Bourne, whose *Untimely Papers* collection is perhaps the most trenchant expression of their position. As Bourne explained, they were not doctrinaire pacifists, but opposed intervention rather on the *New Republic*'s own pragmatic grounds that the application of additional military force could not truly resolve the conflict.[13]

The antiinterventionist ranks were augmented on the left wing by numerous socialists and Marxists who mocked the campaign for American intervention as a capitalist stratagem. The American Union

Against Militarism paraded a papier-mâché dinosaur named "Jingo" and spent $50,000 to discourage Wilson's preparedness program. Max Eastman, Floyd Dell, and John Reed overhauled the old *Masses* and proceeded to unmask the enemy as not Germany but "the 2% of the people of the United States who own 60% of the national weath," and who were now planning to make a soldier out of the workingman "to defend their loot." According to Eastman, their strong feelings against the war toned down their proletarian revolutionism and "mixed it in a rather opaque solution with 'bourgeois pacifism.' " Scott Nearing, chairman of the People's Council for Freedom and Democracy, a conglomerate of diverse peace organizations, claimed 800,000 members among individuals and trade unions.[14]

Nearly all liberals, the *New Republic* men included, had been instinctively opposed to intervention. But as the international situation deteriorated in late 1916 and into 1917 and the German threat became more menacing, American involvement seemed every day more inevitable, and liberals like Pinchot and Bourne who remained on the sidelines became increasingly relegated to the position of gadflies and shadow figures. A key development was the decision of Wilson himself to take the lead in announcing America's purpose and cultivating the moralistic rationale for intervention. The *New Republic* had called continually for "firm and courageous leadership" to sell the liberal program to the Allies and to make their own countrymen aware of the importance of a democratic triumph for both the United States and humanity at large. In the early stages of the conflict Wilson had staunchly maintained a neutral rights stance, but his "strict accountability" dictate was becoming maddeningly untenable and embarrassing. As he followed the *New Republic*'s beaconing editorials, the unfolding spectacle of a holy war with all its moral and religious trappings must have been tantalizing to his Puritan disposition. As Norman Graebner has written, "At the core of Wilson's thought was the conviction that the nation's political, social, and moral uniqueness had assigned to it a transcendent mission to serve humanity. . . . As the struggle on the Western front moved from trench to trench and the contestants became locked in a process of futile destruction, Wilson informed the American people that Europe beckoned, not for material aid, but for leadership in creating a better world." "Why is it that all nations turn to us with the instinctive feeling that if anything touches humanity it touches us?" he asked. "Because it knows that ever since we were born as a Nation we have undertaken to be the champions of humanity and the rights of men."[15]

Wilson's idealized conception of international relations and bumptious interpretation of America's role were perfect grist for the crusade mill. The *New Republic* did not have to press very hard. Indeed, because of the close correspondence between the pronouncements of the Administration and those of the *New Republic*, critics charged variously that the magazine was feeding Wilson his material or that Wilson was using the magazine as his personal forum. There is little evidence to support either allegation. Lippmann explained some years later:

> Our relations with Wilson were never personal. I don't think Croly ever saw Wilson when he was President; in the winter of 1916 I had two or three interviews such as any journalist has with the President. Croly and I did begin to see something of Colonel House, It was a curious relationship. Wilson was preparing to run for his second term; his main problem was the management of American neutrality. We discussed the problem perhaps once a fortnight with Colonel House. He never told us what the President was going to do. We never knew anything that hadn't appeared in the newspapers. In our own minds we followed the logic of the situation as we saw it. Partly by coincidence, partly by a certain parallelism of reasoning, certainly by no direct inspiration either from the President or Colonel House, The New Republic often advocated policies which Wilson pursued.

Whatever the mechanics of the fateful policy shift, by the close of 1916 Wilson had reached a palpably new plateau of "aggressive neutrality," and the *New Republic* editors were voicing satisfaction that "those who have cried for a leadership expressive of American idealism and interest have it now."[16]

In his famous address to the Senate on 22 January 1917, Wilson borrowed the *New Republic*'s "peace without victory" phrase (which Croly and Lippmann coined in a series of December editorials) to drive home the crusade theme. Wilson suggested the outlines of an enduring peace, one in which America could participate and lend her authority, and adumbrated a number of aims—freedom of the seas, reduced armaments, security for weak nations—that would receive their classic expression in the Fourteen Points a year later. Although some liberals were offended by the President's intrusion (George Perkins, the Bull Mooser, commented in *The New York Times* that "not content with butting into Mexico, with all its dire consequences," Wilson now proposed to butt into European affairs) and others, like Charles Beard, felt that he was "just preaching a sermon," in general the message elicited warm approval. Socialist Morris Hillquit believed that it was "a courageous act, and it will have an excellent effect upon the fortunes of the war." More lavishly, Ray Stannard Baker called it "the very quintessence of the American ideal applied to world affairs . . . expressing exactly the inner beliefs of thousands of Americans."

Wilson's vision, said Baker, was "strong and true." Among those who apparently agreed was Rabbi Stephen Wise, a staunch pacifist who had vigorously used his pulpit to criticize Wilson's preparedness program. Wise, outdistancing Wilson's own pace, became convinced that "the time had come for the American people to understand that it might be our destiny to have part in the struggle to avert the enthronement of the law of might."[17]

Entertaining a war and fighting one were two different matters, and liberals—Wilson most of all—still blanched at the prospect of actual involvement. In such an event, the road ahead would be strewn with unknown perils. Thousands of young Americans would undoubtedly be sacrificed. The agenda of reform, already proceeding haltingly, would likely be postponed or drastically curtailed (although, as we shall see, many liberals invited the war as a possible stimulant for a slumping progressivism). The impact on the public mind and the national psyche—for a country nursed on illusions of peaceful isolation—would be incalculable. And, most disturbingly, there was no guarantee that American intervention would accomplish any of the crusaders' exalted objectives; for the Allies seemed hellbent on ignoring Wilson's good auspices, and responded equivocally at best to Wilson's queries about their intentions. The *New Republic* could not update its cheerless report on 6 January that "the war of words like the war of armies is so far a stalemate." In a tormented editorial of 13 January the editors bared their uneasiness: "To sit by as a neutral and refuse to consider the awful complications of the struggle is to wash your hands of it. . . . Yet the effort to find a way through is difficult beyond precedent. Journalists . . . can hardly help feeling that they are stumbling and stuttering most of the time." Through January they sifted diplomatic correspondence and scanned troop movements in Europe searching desperately for some sign of a breakthrough—a more concrete Allied pledge, feelers for a negotiated settlement, a lull in the fighting—that would obviate or at least ease American intervention, make its consequences less traumatic and imponderable.[18]

But the die had been cast. Events were overtaking them all. Croly, Lippmann, and Weyl affirmed their commitment with a pronouncement on 27 January that "our vitality, our strength and our potentialities are too great for the mere pursuit of our own interests. All that is valuable in our tradition cries out that we must not sit still in grudging isolation." Four days later, with the German resumption of submarine warfare, their decision was abruptly sealed, the Allied response academic. The cover of their 3 February issue proclaimed in boldface type: "Without delay diplomatic relations must be broken. The navy should be mobilized. Steps should be taken to arm all merchant ships. The terms and conditions of our entrance into the war should be discussed and announced.'"* As Arthur Link has observed, the President and probably a majority of liberals hoped to the end for a *deus ex machina* that would make intervention unnecessary, but the Zimmermann dispatch and the overt attacks on American merchant vessels made any eleventh-hour conciliation impossible. Additionally, the March revolution in Russia, uniting the forces of democracy and "dumocracy" in an imposing moral coalition, cast the conflict suddenly in an irresistible light. Even the guarded editorials of Villard's *Nation* granted that the Petrograd revolution administered a "spiritual cleansing" to the cause of the Allies and "enormously enriched the issues for which the Allies are contending."[19]

Brinksmanship exhausted and the liberal hand strengthened by events in Russia, the President reluctantly but solemnly sealed his own decision. On 2 April, before a joint session of Congress, Wilson delivered his war message, eloquently certifying the idealistic foundation for American intervention:

> The right is more precious than peace, and we shall fight for the things which we have always carried nearest our hearts—for democracy, for the right of those who submit to authority to have a voice in their own Governments, for the rights and liberties of small nations, for a universal dominion of right by such a concert of free peoples as shall bring peace and safety to all nations and make the world itself at last free. To such a task we can dedicate our lives and our fortunes, everything that we are and everything that we have, with the pride of those who know that the day has come when America is privileged to spend her blood and her might for the principles that gave her birth and happiness and the peace which she has treasured. God helping her, she can do no other.

The great crusade was launched.

It is a familiar story how quickly and dramatically the American public broke with its isolationist tradition and rallied to Wilson's commission in 1917. Frederick Lewis Allen, reporting for the *Nation*, spotted a

---

*The editors even now stepped in gingerly, vowing only money and munitions. "If the Allies wish us to put an army in the field we can do so only when they have defined their terms so specifically that we are assured of a just settlement" ["America's Part in the War," *NR* (10 Feb. 1917), 34]. By 17 February, however, they urged the full commitment. Terms or no terms, they decided, "the time to strike is now" [untitled editorial (17 Feb. 1917), 57]. Through the remainder of February and March and right up until the official declaration of war, they ran ahead of Wilson's "armed neutrality" policy, noting impatiently on 24 March, "It is increasingly apparent that no policy short of war will rescue and reestablish the imperiled American interests and rights" [untitled editorial (24 Mar. 1917), 210].

"rebirth of American patriotism," the flag flapping in the wind "everywhere up and down the streets," every day looking like Washington's Birthday. From London, former American foreign minister to the Netherlands Henry van Dyke wrote a poem celebrating the occasion. On 11 April Rabbi Wise wired the President his congratulations, exulting that Wilson's message was "destined to become a Magna Charta for all the peoples and places of earth." Charles Edward Russell noticed that "minds that had been buried in cash drawers came forth to forget them and all things else except the triumph of the nation's ideals; eyes that had been fastened on stock tickers took in a novel survey of the world's horizon." Harold Stearns recalled conversation at a Long Island dinner party "where the devastation of French provinces was spoken of with more horror and understanding of what it meant than would have been the case if it had been Arizona or California which had been invaded." At Harvard Malcolm Cowley remembered with disaffection how his professors preached about duty and sacrifice and an "abstract patriotism that concerned the right to self-determination of small nations, but apparently had nothing to do with better schools, lower taxes, higher pay for factory hands or restocking Elk Run with trout." Eagerly Americans accepted the universality of the cause. Public opinion was mobilized faster than the troops.[20]

Confronted with Wilson's stirring mandate and the plain actuality of war, it is not surprising that Americans responded so enthusiastically. George Kennan has observed of democracies that they are slow to go to war but once embattled see it through with a righteous passion, and such was the reaction among impressionable democrats in 1917. What is more striking, however, is the number of formerly dissenting liberals—confirmed pacifists, balky radicals, sheepish fence-sitters—who now came to the support of the war. Kansas editor William Allen White became enthralled with the injunction to "make the world safe for democracy." White had in fact abandoned his neutral position as early as the German invasion of Belgium, but he had never been very demonstrative because, like so many other Americans, he was not certain of what exactly was at stake; with the goals of American intervention clearly spelled out now, he exalted the war as a "struggle of the world away from the gross materialism of Germany to a higher spiritual standard of life contained in the word Democracy." With similar expectations, moderate socialists like Russell, John Spargo, and William English Walling, hankering for something more palatable than a philosophy that focused on materialistic ends, welcomed the sloganeering as a refreshing tonic.[21] One of them, Upton Sinclair, felt such a kinship with Wilson's policy that he

published at his own expense ten issues of a monthly magazine entitled *Upton Sinclair's: For a Clean Peace and the Internation.* [22]

David Starr Jordan, who had crisscrossed the country between 1909
and 1914 delivering addresses on the theme of international pacifism
(for the World Peace Foundation, of which he was director), voluntarily muzzled himself, refused speaking engagements tendered by
fellow pacifists, and, at least tacitly, gave his approval to the American intervention. On 8 April he wrote the San Francisco *Bulletin* that
he would not change a word he had spoken against the war. "But
that is no longer the issue," he said. "We must now stand together in
the hope that our entrance into Europe may in some way advance the
cause of Democracy and hasten the coming of lasting peace." Even
the stubborn *Nation* loosed its anchors and sailed with the crusaders,
informing readers on 3 May, "The coming into the war of the greatest
democracy, with all thoughts of conquest put away from it, and every
form of material gain renounced in advance" would sooner or later
convince "even the most absolutist rulers" that "the extinguishment
of nationalities and the seizure of their land" would no longer be tolerated. With a quickening pulse, on 17 May, the *Nation* found
America moving in earnest. "Neither fear nor vainglory is the impel-
ling motive, but a gradually deepening sense of what is at stake—
what is, in Lincoln's phrase, to be either 'nobly won or meanly lost.'"
Scholars who have investigated Oswald Villard have concluded that
he never completely reconciled himself to American intervention.*
However, his editorials in the *Nation*, as well as in his New York *Evening Post*, amounted to an implicit approval provided the Allies
moved closer to Wilson's conditions for peace and America preserved
its own "free hand" through the negotiations. [23]

With the grudging conversion of Villard and the *Nation*, the struggle
engaged the most reluctant of warriors. What in the liberal community
had been tantamount to heresy in 1914—the espousal of American
intervention—had become fashion by the summer of 1917. The early
shock and cynicism had given way to a gradually more sanguine and
expansive view of the war, culminating in an apocalyptic vision of
America and the Allies fighting their way through to a new world order.
Liberals like White and Jordan had performed a shifty job of rationalization between 1914, when they instinctively opposed the war and American involvement, and 1917, when they, at least silently and in the
extreme fanatically, gave their support to the intervention. Why did
these men, many of them previously skittish or plodding, change their

---

*See, for instance, Robert Endicott Osgood, *Ideals and Self-Interest in America's Foreign
Relations* (Chicago, 1953), 265-66 and Michael Wreszin, *Oswald Garrison Villard*
(Bloomington, Ind., 1965), 91-93.

step so dramatically? There was, of course, the rush of events that propelled Eliot, the *New Republic* editors, and Rabbi Wise toward their commitment even before Wilson's official declaration. There was, too, after April, the plain fact of war and the prodigious display of sentiment and compassion that Wilson's message evoked. White, Jordan, Walling, and Sinclair certainly had their special reasons for going in, as did others. The improvisational nature of the intervention makes it difficult to unravel the intricate web of motivations that influenced their action and to separate surface rationalizations from genuine concerns. But there were at least three factors that seemed to operate generally throughout the liberal community and that placed tremendous pressure upon them all to join the war movement.

There was, first of all, the human impulse to be in on the action. Veteran reformers like Samuel Hopkins Adams and Ida Tarbell found that by working for the Creel Committee on Public Information they could garner more glamour and excitement than they enjoyed in their finest muckraking days. With retread reformers as its nucleus, the Creel Committee, in the phrase of Louis Filler, read like a "roll call of the muckrakers." Max Lerner later said that liberal intellectuals followed the Wilsonian lead so that they could be in a more effective position to influence government policy. "Better to swim with the current and thus retain some influence," wrote Lerner, "than to remain frustrate outside the current." Charles Forcey, focusing on the *New Republic* men, has traced their decision more to opportunism, depicting them not as gadflies but as moths who veered "toward the brighter centers of power." In any case, the pressure to enlist was great. Jane Addams wrote, "We were constantly told by our friends that to stand aside from the war mood of the country was to surrender all possibility of future influence, that we were committing intellectual suicide, and would never again be trusted as responsible people or judicious advisers." Stearns, who along with Bourne and most of the *Seven Arts* group elected to stay out, admitted that the inducements to become "mobilized" were very strong—the invitations to join prominent organizations and mingle in the stylish company of Washington officials, the pleasure of having one's name displayed in posters and advertisements, "the charm of being important and 'on the inside,' . . . the human desire to keep in touch with the main current of events."[24]

On a less personal level, a second factor was the liberals' estimation of the domestic scene, where progressivism seemed to be losing its vitality and in desperate need of invigoration from some new source. The progressive state of the prewar years had been unsurpassed as an agency of reform and embodiment of national purpose. But the recession of 1913-1914, the Administration's flagging commitment to domestic reform, and the intrusion of the war stalled the momentum and cast grave doubts on the future of the movement. For some time prior to American intervention, liberals had been distressed by the apparent stagnation of the reform effort and the breakdown of national purpose. Journals such as the *New Republic* and the *Nation* expressed great concern over indiscriminate labor strikes (particularly upsetting was the railroad crisis in the summer of 1916) and the sudden retrogression in the caliber of state government after years of vigorous attention and improvement. Of the latter, the *New Republic* was moved to remark in November 1916, "Perhaps the most ominous aspect of the contemporary American politics is the prevailing attitude of helplessness and discouragement in the presence of the recognized and flagrant failures of state government." With labor restless, reform languishing, and the domestic situation in general deteriorating, progressivism seemed to be caught in the rudderless drift and reaction which Rauschenbusch had warned against in 1914. Not surprisingly, then, many liberals seized upon the war as a vehicle that might reverse the decline and give American society new direction. With its unchallenged potential for national integration and social reorganization, the war presented a perfect opportunity to rejuvenate national purpose, encourage concerted effort, and perhaps, with the right kind of attitude and spirit, enhance progressive reform.[25]

Such hopes were not freshly conceived in 1917. From the start, liberals had shared a certain fascination with the war as an instrumentality for social change. Albert Beveridge speculated in 1915 that the collective effort and efficient organization required by the war would give impetus in peacetime to a movement he called "democratic collectivism." "It is not unthinkable," he wrote, "that when the war is over, the common man, thus taught in war time, will demand the application of the same methods to great industries which affect the public welfare in peace."[26] Pragmatists like Dewey and Lippmann envisaged the "routineers" (Lippmann's term in *Preface to Politics* to describe stale bureaucrats and standpatters) finally being replaced by the "inventors" and social engineers. Even radicals like Bourne and Dos Passos, despite their moral outrage, were impressed with the liberating capacity of the war, Bourne viewing it as a force promoting cultural liberation and Dos Passos as a catalyst for the dismantling of the entrenched capitalist system.

By 1917, with the domestic malaise deepening, the war acquired a growing significance as a solution to progressivism's problems. Lured by the prospect of large-scale human cooperation and social reorganization that the war promised, many otherwise disinclined liberals decided to throw in with the interventionists. Jane Addams described their transition:

> After the United States had entered the war there began to appear great divergence among the many types of pacifists, from the extreme left, composed of non-resistants, through the middle-of-the-road groups, to the extreme right, who could barely be distinguished from mild militarists. There were those people, also, who although they felt keenly both the horror and the futility of war, yet hoped for certain beneficent results from the opportunities afforded by the administration of war; they were much pleased when the government took over the management of the railroads, insisting that governmental ownership had thus been pushed forward by decades; they were also sure that the War Labor Policies Board, the Coal Commission and similar war institutions would make an enormous difference in the development of the country, in short, that militarism might be used as an instrument for advanced social ends. Such justifications had their lure and one found old pacifist friends on all the war boards and even in the war department itself. Certainly we were all eager to accept whatever progressive social changes came from the quick reorganization demanded by the war.

Thorstein Veblen, seldom disposed toward anything, became excited over the talk of organization and efficiency, lifted his veil of cynicism, and volunteered his services to the Food Administration. Even a freethinker like Clarence Darrow, an eminent pacifist, was persuaded to place his faith in the war as an engine for reform and reconstruction. "I am not naturally an optimist," Darrow reflected in December 1917. "I don't know whether this war will be the last or not. It may not be. . . . But I have some faith, and I believe that this world will not be the same world again after this war is done. It will change old ideas and old institutions." "It may be," said Darrow, "after the rich and the poor and the high and the low have helped each other in war, they may learn to help each other in peace."[27]

However compelling the pressure to swim with the current and the lure of reviving progressivism, the key in swinging reluctant liberals around to support of the war was Wilson's summons to make the world safe for democracy. Wilson's moralistic-idealistic rationale alone made intervention conscionable. No liberal could quarrel with the intention or question the urgency of the task outlined by the President. The crusade formula, as Eric Goldman has maintained, "became the ideological bridge by which most of the progressive group moved with their leader from neutrality to intervention." It was the route taken by the *New Republic* men, by converted pacifists like Wise and Jordan, and by unsure stragglers like White and Villard looking for a light in the forest. Brand Whitlock was essentially a pacifist, but he could go to war for the right cause, and Newton Baker remembered he was "thrilled by the exposition of an idealistic and Christian philosophy." Russell said, "We went in for the sake of an ideal. . . . This war, in its most important phase, was not a struggle against the German people; it was a struggle between two ideas, the idea of democracy and the idea of autocracy." No one welcomed the evangelical overtones more than Protestant Social Gospel ministers, who, as Donald Meyer has noted, "were presented with a supreme challenge to the policy of partnership in the culture." Wilson's inspiration enabled them to participate with a cloak of respectability. Although a few prominent clerical figures (most notably Muste, Thomas, Rauschenbusch, and Holmes) never could reconcile themselves to the campaign, the great majority of them easily managed to translate the Social Gospel from a peace to a war creed. Meyer wrote that they transferred "the same high tone justifying peace to the justification of war, preaching the war not simply as national but also as religious necessity."[28]

The predicament of the clergymen suggests the tangle of motivations and pressures, the concocted sophistries and conscientious concerns that nudged them all into war. The international mission was foremost—it was the most convenient and purposeful rationale, the ideological bridge—but there were also the questions of "national necessity" and continuing "partnership in the culture," and beyond that the anxiety over the slump in domestic reform. All of these considerations—the requirements of national interest (which in truth occupied few of them), the human impulse to stay in the mainstream of events, the opportunity to rescue a faltering progressivism, and the transcendent vision of a new world order founded on democracy and social justice—accounted for their decision in 1917 to support intervention. John Dewey offered a capsulization of their reckoning in an article that appeared four months after the President's message. In announcing "what America will fight for," Dewey wrote that "a task has to be accomplished to abate an international nuisance, but in the accomplishing there is the prospect of a world organization and the beginnings of a public control which crosses nationalistic boundaries and interests."[29]

The ongoing dialectic that liberals conducted with an unfamiliar, disarranged world between 1914 and 1917 often saw them groping, stumbling, and reeling their way toward some new understanding. On the trail to Armageddon they abandoned old and cherished illusions, picked up new ones, shuffled their values and priorities, and in general experienced a period of intellectual vagabondage. By 1917, with confidence in Wilson and satisfaction in America's purpose, they had reached something of a destination, but in many instances it found them uncomfortably far from their prewar roots. A case in point is the evolution of Walter Lippmann, the tough-minded realist of 1915.

In *The Stakes of Diplomacy* Lippmann had chided Americans who viewed the war in simple abstract terms and urged upon them patience and humility. Into 1916 he was still admonishing crusader types who relied on "angels to the rescue." "Schemes are put forward every day," he wrote in the *New Republic*, "which require an amount of virtue that exists only at the conclusion of orators' speeches. Difficulties are evaded by calling upon brotherly love, citizenship, patriotism, public spirit, and all the other glowing abstractions which mask an incompleted analysis." "Realistic statesmen," he said, "do not cover a rocky path with a silk rug." By 1917, however, he and his *New Republic* colleagues had lost their own grip on reality, and, with the crusade bid, were themselves talking "glowing abstractions" and summoning angels to the rescue. By April Lippmann was reiterating Wilson's war message. Forgotten was his cold, dispassionate analysis of the primacy of power politics, the inefficacy of moral arguments, and the pitfalls of democratic diplomacy.[30]

In an address before the American Academy of Political and Social Science in Philadelphia, Lippmann parroted the preacher-poet-patriot against whom he had railed two years earlier. "There are times," he said,

> when new sources of energy are tapped, when the impossible becomes possible, when events outrun our calculations. This may be such a time. The alliance to which we belong has suddenly grown hot with the new democracy of Russia and the new internationalism of America. It has had an access of spiritual force which opens a new prospect in the policies of the world. We can dare to hope for things which we never dared to hope for in the past.

Ignoring the economic and territorial "stakes of diplomacy" which in 1915 he considered paramount, he now delineated the conflict in terms of its spiritual significance. He noted the movement of ideals "toward a higher degree of spiritual unanimity" and a change in the nature of the Allied commitment from a military agreement among diplomats to a "union of peoples determined to end forever that intriguing adventurous nationalism which has torn the world for three centuries." "Frontier questions, colonial questions," he said, "are now entirely secondary. The whole perspective is changed to-day.

. . . The scale of values is transformed. . . . The war is dissolving into a stupendous revolution."[31]

Lippmann's derisive comment in 1915 about the unthinking masses who flock to a demagogue—"like sheep in a shower we huddle about the leader"—was cruelly applicable to himself in 1917. Why did Lippmann the consummate pragmatist and realist turn idealist? Heinz Eulau, who in a series of incisive articles has examined Lippmann's formative intellectual years and exposed his "ambivalence" and "personal conflicts" throughout the 1910-1920 decade, called the Philadelphia speech "a strange performance" in light of his earlier pronouncements. Eulau concluded that Lippmann, out of a visceral need, had to align himself with "strong men" and "purposeful activity"; in 1917, this meant Wilson and the crusade. Robert Osgood has perceived the subtle interplay between realism and idealism in Lippmann's thought and suggested that Lippmann never lost his grip on reality; rather, in capitalizing on the new turns which the war had taken, Lippmann the publicist cleverly "called idealism into the service of realism." No doubt he was moved also by the elemental impulses of anger and exhilaration which drove other liberals to support the war.[32]

Whatever the case, committed to the cause, Lippmann took leave of the *New Republic* in June 1917 and joined the War Department as a special assistant to Newton Baker. In his new post, the arch-realist of 1915 would play a major role in the strategy of idealism—helping to prepare the American position at the peace talks, serving as secretary to the Inquiry, and, with supreme irony, drafting the Fourteen Points memorandum itself. Roaming far from his prewar roots and flirting with new ideas and adventures, Lippmann, like so many of his liberal colleagues, was already well into the first round of what Eulau termed the "prophylactic cycle of hopes and disappointments."[33]

With all the fanfare surrounding Wilson's message and the stampede to the barricades, it is easy to overlook those liberals who remained unrelentingly cynical and antiinterventionist in 1917. A relatively small but significant minority resisted the pressures and the attractive rhetoric and refused to cross Wilson's ideological bridge. Despite the defection of influential members like Stephen Wise and David Starr Jordan, there remained an active and dedicated nucleus of pacifists headed by bellwethers Jane Addams, Lillian Wald, Norman Thomas, John Haynes Holmes, and *Survey* editor Paul Kellogg. The Rand School bookstore operated by Jack Karpf continued to distribute antiwar material, arrange debates, and sponsor meetings. Scott Nearing kept up a hectic schedule of lecturing and pamphleteering. Although many moderate socialists like Russell and Walling melted into the progressive camp behind Wilson, the Socialist party's official position was antiinterventionist, and at an emergency convention in St. Louis on 7-9 April 1917, they branded the war declaration a "crime against the people of the United States."[34]

Perhaps the most unflinching stand and most searing disapproval came from Randolph Bourne and his *Seven Arts* group. In his celebrated essay "War and the Intellectuals," Bourne castigated the "socialists, college professors, new-republicans, practitioners of literature" who could rationalize going to war. "To those of us who still retain an irreconcilable animus against war," he fumed, "it has been a bitter experience to see the unanimity with which the American intellectuals have thrown their support to the use of the war-technique." Bourne ridiculed the crusade venture as a colossal conceit. "An intellectual class, gently guiding a nation through sheer force of ideas into what the other nations entered only through predatory craft or popular hysteria or military madness! A war free from any taint of self-seeking, a war that will secure the triumph of democracy and internationalize the world!" He saved his most trenchant criticism for pragmatists like Dewey and the *New Republic* editors and their effort to mask the struggle in a virtuous guise by portraying its significance in positive social terms. Bourne contended they were subverting James's philosophy into an expedient, opportunistic system that substituted pure action for thought and conscience and was totally devoid of morals or values. "The American intellectuals," he observed, "seem to have forgotten that the real enemy is War rather than imperial Germany."[35]

Bourne's attack had its merits. But he and the other pacifists who censured warrior liberals for cowardly submitting to the martial spirit and irresponsibly turning the conflict into a crusade for democracy were persisting in their own hollow illusion that the war could be avoided altogether—that it would wind itself down in time, that a liberal peace would somehow be immaculately conceived, and that in the meantime more good could be accomplished by "analytical detachment" than by military involvement. In a somewhat pained analogy Bourne remarked, "It is difficult to see how the child on the back of a mad elephant is to be any more effective in stopping the beast than is the child who tries to stop him from the ground." The point was, of course, that the mad elephant had to be stopped, and that America with its superior arsenal of manpower and supplies could exert considerably more leverage *in* the war than out of it. Harold Laski punctured the pacifist argument with the rebuttal, "One can not stay at Armageddon to philosophize upon the abstract injustice of war."[36]

1917 *was* Armageddon for America. Liberals could no longer enjoy the luxury of being spectators. Willy-nilly, they were locked into the struggle. The majority of liberals understood this, and acknowledged the necessity to intervene. Unfortunately, however, once they decided affirmatively, they typically plunged in as crusaders and saviors, transforming the war into a messianic mission, into something larger than life and with titanic stakes. That they supported American intervention under the duress and very legitimate concerns of the moment is understandable and wholly justifiable. That they went in with their hearts and their mouths instead of their minds is yet another instance of their boundless capacity for self-delusion.

Instead of wading in and adjusting their sights, the liberals went in ceremoniously with the flourish of an Aeschylus hero fashioning his tragic fate. They spoke, theologically, of "unrepentant" Germany, "redemption," "judgment," and "salvation." They dressed their leader Wilson in Solomonic robes. They invoked Lincoln's name repeatedly to extol his example of high purpose and scrupulous conduct in an earlier apocalyptic struggle. In the words of a *New York Times* commentator, it was enough to "make Don Quixote wish he hadn't died so soon." The business ahead required careful attention and analysis (Bourne was correct here) and a cushioning sense of humility, but their approach was blind and impetuous. Debunker Laski did not spare them his contempt. "I confess," Laski wrote to Holmes on 18 April, "I would feel a little happier if the statesmen generally did not promise us a heaven after peace. I can't help remembering the talk in '89 and '48. It's well to go into these things with open eyes. The difficulty is that our democrats go in with an open mouth."[37]

To spin the microfilmed issues of the *New Republic* or *Nation* for the period February-June 1917 is indeed like watching a montage of a Greek tragedy. All the classical conventions are present: the hubris of the protagonists, the grand but flawed vision, the frequent but fleeting premonitions of doom, and, all the while, the inexorable advance toward disillusionment. At every turn the liberal protagonists courted disaster. They misplaced their faith in the Allies' intentions, in the "plain people's" intelligence and earnestness, in Wilson's charismatic powers, and in the efficacy of ideals and moral persuasion. They misconstrued events in Russia, overestimated the readiness of the German people to embrace democracy once rid of their militarist leaders, magnified the impact that American intervention would have on the peace settlement, and in general miscalculated the possibilities for a new world order.

The *New Republic* had found it outrageous of the belligerents to think "in terms of an exclusive and jealous national sovereignty." Liberals were convinced that the imperialist mentality was limited to a few irresponsible and sinister leaders; that the "popular objects" and "ultimate issues" of the war were arbitration, no annexations, peaceful restorations, and a league of nations. Always when things looked bad it was the "people" who they expected would rise to the occasion. University of Chicago historian Andrew McLaughlin wrote in August 1917, "There is nothing upon which we can more safely rely than the plain sense of the plain people." Lippmann remarked in his April speech in Philadelphia that the war would throw the German government back into the arms of the German people, "marked and discredited as the author of their miseries. It is for them to make the final settlement with it."[38] People were rational, they were enlightened, with no passions, no infirmities, no trace of vindictiveness! The Americans who rallied to Wilson's commission would do so with a philosophical calm! The Germans, once defeated, would remodel their government with a chastened and levelheaded pursuit! Liberals simply ignored the huge obstacles that would have to be surmounted if the war were to be prosecuted on their inspired terms: the enormous task of educating and ennobling public opinion, the historic rivalries that would have to dissolve overnight into a commonwealth of nations, and the fundamental limitations imposed by human nature and the psychological realities of people at war. In the face of these hurdles the talk of high purpose and scrupulous conduct was hopelessly pompous and unavailing, as if the force of the liberals' own entry could break down the store of antagonisms and catapult the world toward the millennium.

Back in 1915, when liberals were either paralyzed with fright or buzzing with bold predictions, the *New Republic* men had sketched a wonderfully discerning and timely article on "mental unpreparedness" in which they called for education and understanding in place of prophecy or preaching, a "foundation of stern realism on which to build our new ideals," an outlook formulated in concrete rather than metaphysical terms. By 1917, what they, and the others, had done instead was—to use a phrase of their own—screw their ideals a notch higher. Croly later said that they "manufactured a great national uprising as a necessary emotional and technical corollary of their decision to enter the war."[39] Whether they actually believed their words or "manufactured" them in an artful sophistry, whichever the case, the crusade gambit was an emotionally hazardous and eventually self-deceiving undertaking. As Lippmann had realized at a more sober juncture, by summoning "angels to the rescue" they could win only imaginary victories, and ultimately bring upon themselves only a painful and crushing disillusionment.

5 THE WAR, 1917-1918

AN ACID TEST

There is no episode in the life of a nation more exhilarating or consuming than that initial burst into war when cowards discover secret courage, shirkers assume grave responsibilities, and ordinary men become martyrs. The crucible of war—especially a war publicized as a war to end war—brings together a strange assortment of patriots. "Whatever their position toward U.S. intervention had been," observes Wolfgang Helbich, "now that America was in the war, liberals of all shades tried to make the sacrifice for the nation worthwhile and to obtain maximum benefit from it." Early recruits like Ray Stannard Baker stepped up their efforts. "As the war progressed and the issues grew clearer," Baker wrote, "I became more and more sincerely convinced of the necessity . . . that the Germans and all they stood for be defeated. . . . With this new perception of the issues of the war, came an intense desire to help the good cause along, without knowing where I could take hold or what I was fitted to do." Indomitable pacifists gradually made their own commitment to the cause. "I am made ill when I see or hear anyone suffering the slightest pain or anguish," Samuel Gompers announced in a speech before the American Alliance for Labor and Democracy, in September 1917, "and yet I hold that it is essential that the sacrifice must be made that humanity shall never again be cursed by a war such as the one which has been thrust upon us."[1]

The "sacrifice" was made relatively easy for them. A war of the sort forged by Wilson and the *New Republic* was more an exercise in social service and spiritual conversion than a military engagement. Liberals located the war theater more in men's minds than on the bloody battlefields of Europe. Newton Baker, the secretary of war and a man of avowed pacifist convictions, became a busy articulator of the crusade theme. He told an Independence Day audience that "all mankind" must choose whether "the nations of the earth" are to be autocratic and militarist or democratic and just. In an address in December to the New York Southern Society, entitled appropriately "The Embattled Democracy," he promised a "joy in store . . . in the introduction of a new and higher era."[2] Numbing themselves to the slaughter in Europe, liberals followed a friendlier war on the home front, watching agreeably the progress of the domestic campaigns: public information, industrial mobilization, and social and economic reform spurred by the need for wartime reorganization. Charity organizer Edward T. Devine was ecstatic about the whirl of activity and social consciousness spawned by American intervention. "Enthusiasm for social service is epidemic," he exclaimed. By July a "luxuriant crop of new agencies" had sprouted. "We scurry back and forth to the national capital; we stock offices with typewriters and new letterheads. It is all very exhilarating, stimulating, intoxicating."[3]

Through 1917 and 1918 many liberals could think of the war less as a main event than as a rehearsal for peacetime social reconstruction. Horace Kallen marveled at the process of nationalization sweeping America and noted that "if it is an advantage for the wastage of war, what may it not mean for the creativity of peace! Its form and technique need only to be studied, perfected, and extended." "What we have learned in war we shall hardly forget in peace," Walter Weyl wrote in 1918. "The new economic solidarity, once gained, can never again be surrendered." Norman Angell perceived the war's collectivizing tendencies as making socialism a real possibility for the first time in America. The captain of the social reconstructionists, John Dewey, took a planetary view and foresaw the whole world more highly organized as a result of the war, "a world knit together by more conscious and substantial bonds." The million or two young men returning from France would "jolt" America's intellectual isolation, said Dewey. And Europe would learn more about America as well. "The shrinkage of the world already effected as a physical fact by steam and electricity will henceforth be naturalized in the imagination."[4]

In a sense the war became a sort of laboratory for frustrated progressives seeking some new impetus and technology for lagging social reform and international cooperation. Bourne and other persevering pacifist critics accused them of using the war as their plaything while condemning younger Americans to die needlessly. Jane Addams later insisted that it was "an old man's war."[5]

What about the young men? What was their reaction to the war they were expected to fight? *Was* it an "old man's war"? In the light of postwar literature, it is tempting to portray the younger, more idealistic types as antiwar and antiintervention and the older progressive types as opportunists with more of an interest in machinery and efficiency than in human life; the facts, however, are more complicated.

There were, of course, those young recruits who were predictably alienated and morbid about the whole thing. F. Scott Fitzgerald told his mother in November 1917 to spare him "either tragedy or Heroics. I went into this perfectly cold-bloodedly. . . . To a profound pessimist about life, being in danger is not depressing." Malcolm Cowley later wrote that the war was a "relief from boredom," and that he and the others went about their tasks with a "spectatorial attitude"—an interest in collecting "souvenirs of death" and a "monumental indifference toward the cause for which young Americans were risking their lives." Max Eastman, at one point totally unaffected by the crusade fervor, declared the war a bore and added that he personally cared more about being allowed to lie on a bench in Washington Square than about having permission to ride on a British vessel through the submarine zone.[6]

Surprisingly, however, many sensitive and aspiring young men, reared in a suffocating, genteel environment about which they constantly complained, were eager to go to war and to participate in a new experience. In a lecture at the University of Virginia, Cowley recalled that few of their number were actually draft dodgers, and that a prevalent mood among them was to volunteer. The motive often was not patriotic. Dos Passos, graduating from Harvard in the spring of 1916 and spending an uneventful summer at home, was driven by a "hellish curiosity." "The breathless July days, the dusty roads, the cornfields curling in the drought seemed hideous to me that hot Virginia summer," said Dos Passos. He wanted to see the world, "paddle up undiscovered rivers . . . climb unmapped mountains." Matthew Josephson remembered that many of his friends volunteered purely "for the excitement of the thing . . . to enjoy a front seat at the greatest and bloodiest show in history."[7] Others were pacifists at heart who wished to contribute to the humane efforts of the Red Cross or ambulance corps.* At a session of the American Historical Association that examined the "European Intellectuals and the Coming of the War," Roland Stromberg and Peter Stansky were agreed that, as a group, the young college students and literary aspirants who were excited by the war approached it more as a personal than as a national experience.[8] If true of European intellectuals,

---

*The ambulance corps became the most popular outfit for young men like Cowley, E. E. Cummings, Dos Passos, and Walt Disney (he was seventeen in 1918), who relished the excitement and spectacle but whose pacifist convictions prevented them from joining as combatants. It was a remarkable lure. Cowley dropped out of Harvard in the middle of his sophomore year to enlist as an ambulance driver. Altogether, 325 from Harvard enlisted in the ambulance service, 187 from Yale, and 181 from Princeton. For a detailed listing of schools and their delegations and a catalogue of their experiences, see Charles A. Fenton, "Ambulance Drivers in France and Italy: 1914–1918," *American Quarterly* 3 (Winter 1951): 326–43.

Stromberg's and Stansky's observations apply even more emphatically to young American intellectuals who, their country not immediately endangered, could more easily remain aloof from the military necessities of the war. Thus Walter Millis, nineteen and preparing to go overseas as a raw second lieutenant, could picture himself as "a story-book soldier."[9]

Undeniably, there was a strong current of existential romanticism and a spirit of adventure that carried these young Americans from their confining pastures at home into the more thrilling arena of the European war. What is more interesting, however, is that as they became involved in the conflict, whatever their personal reasons, they often became conscientious soldiers and patriots, moved by much the same concerns—and illusions—that occupied their progressive elders. Eastman, reporting rather than fighting but sharing the romantic and Marxist inclinations of his friends overseas, became an admirer of Wilson and believed that he could "do more than one man has ever done since Napoleon to constitute and create a future of the world." William Bullitt, who was to become something of a cult hero for his walkout at the peace conference, was fired with enthusiasm over the prospect of a new dawn in human affairs. Bullitt was less interested in Dewey's social and political reconstruction than in the possibilities for "spiritual conversion," but he was no less aroused and "glad to serve":

> I suppose it is the sort of feeling that Wordsworth talks about in his poems on the French Revolution in which he says "Bliss was it in that dawn to be alive but to be young was very heaven" or something of the kind. I haven't got Wordsworth handy. I feel as if there might be a dawn after this war. Not a dawn of new international political machinery; but a new dawn in men's hearts. I feel as if there might be after this war, if it comes out right, a sort of spiritual conversion in the hearts of Americans and Englishmen and Frenchmen and Italians and Russians and Germans and all the worried peoples of Austria-Hungary.[10]

Perhaps the best example of the romantic-patriot soldier was Alan Seeger, America's premier war poet. Harvard-educated Seeger settled in Paris in 1912 as a student-writer and, like many other young Americans who volunteered their services before their own country intervened, enlisted in the French Foreign Legion the third week of the war. Called "Seegerette" next to his bigger, athletic brother, he may have volunteered to prove his virility. He became wildly exuberant about the war, although fatalistic about his chances of surviving it. His letters to home reveal an incurable romanticism quickened by a sense of duty. "I hope you see the thing as I do," he wrote his mother in September 1914, "and think that I have done well . . . in taking upon my shoulders . . . the burden that so much of humanity is suffering under and, rather than stand ingloriously aside when the opportunity was given me, doing my share for the side that I think right." Seeger regarded the war as an intimately personal, almost mystical experience, but he was alert to the larger significance of the struggle and preceded Wilson and the progressive crusaders in avowing the necessity to intervene. While Dewey and Kallen and the *New Republic* editors dragged their feet, Seeger was writing home in June 1915 that "everybody should take part in this struggle which is to have so decisive an effect, not only on the nations engaged but on all humanity." "There should be no neutrals," he said, "but everyone should bear some part of the burden." The letters and narratives of literate American recruits fighting in the Expeditionary Force in 1917 and 1918 generally reflect the same determined sentiments. The prophecy of Seeger's most famous poem, "I Have a Rendezvous With Death," was fulfilled on 5 July 1916, when, at the age of twenty-eight, he died from wounds received in battle.[11]

The point of this digression into the attitudes of young radicals and literati is that, despite the literature of postwar disillusionment, the trenches of the Western front were not manned by armies of alienated youth merely serving the illusions of their elders. The war was not "an old man's war," as Jane Addams maintained. The progressive editors and reformers who manufactured the crusade for democracy had no monopoly on illusions in 1915, 1916, 1917, or 1918. Young Americans, many of them volunteer combatants, themselves looked upon the war as a rare opportunity. Whether as glorious adventure or solemn enterprise, the war represented a watershed in their life, and they were as eager as the Deweys and Devines to capitalize upon it. In the struggle for democracy and social justice, their romanticism and the progressives' pragmatism often cross-fertilized one another, creating a tremendous reservoir of faith and emotion that fueled their *mutual* illusionment as they plunged further into war.

Because liberals—both young and old—construed the war in the context of social reconstruction or spiritual conversion rather than primarily as a military encounter, the measure of success and satisfaction during the war was social and spiritual progress rather than the conventional yardstick of military victories. Thus it was possible that as the war progressed quite satisfactorily on the battlefield, liberals could express deepening disappointment at the failures at home and in the

Allied councils. No matter how well the war went militarily, if the crusade for a liberal peace and a new world order foundered, then their efforts were for naught—and, by their own exacting standards, actually criminal.

Symptomatic of the liberal predicament throughout was the shifting character of the American intervention. All along they had been obsessed with the *manner,* the *spirit* in which intervention would be undertaken. John Jay Chapman, in 1914, warned, "It makes a great difference in what spirit you shoot a man. For this treatment will control your treatment of those who are left alive." Charles William Eliot, anticipating American intervention about the same time as Chapman, urged "thinking Americans" to remember "the immense services which Germany has rendered to civilization" and typed out a letter to *The New York Times* enumerating the redeeming qualities of German culture and statehood. In a war prosecuted solely for ideals, restraint and compassion were imperative. Eliot, Russell, Lippmann, and others pointed out time and time again that the fight was with the German military caste and with the "ideas" of militarism and autocracy, not with the mass of the German people. Dismayed as they were with the imperialist, vindictive tendencies of the Allies, American liberals had assumed that at least their own countrymen were equal to the task assigned by Wilson; that the national temper, the national intelligence was such that America could avoid the brute nationalism and jingoistic outbursts that beset most interventions and would inevitably obscure the lofty goals expounded in the President's message. The *New Republic* noted happily the way in which Wilson severed relations with Germany—"the total lack of bitterness, the absence of ugly epithets, the refusal to stoop to bad temper. He has set a high standard of honor and decency for what lies ahead. . . . The sense of the people now is that they will do whatever is required, but they will not wallow in the folly and credulity and panic that accompany wars."[12]

But the *New Republic* had commented prematurely. On the face of it, Wilson seemed indeed to have scored a magnificent accomplishment in marshaling the country's resources and fulfilling liberal hopes for a benign intervention. In the process, however, the great crusade was rapidly changing its complexion. In a few short weeks its tone became more chauvinistic than humane. Americans, as it happened, were acting not with the sobriety that the crusade demanded, but rather out of unbridled hysteria, wallowing in the "folly and panic" to which the *New Republic* had thought them immune. Lincoln Steffens, lecturing through the Midwest in behalf of pacifism, wrote his brother-in-law from Peoria, Illinois, in September 1917 that he was not arrested yet. "Everybody else is," said Steffens. "The war psychology is intense here in the Middle West." "The least word out of tune" brought a "sword of a question" from the audience. Ray Stannard Baker, seeking to promote a popular understanding of the Wilsonian program, joined on with a group of self-styled publicists calling themselves The Vigilantes and was reprimanded because "I declined to take along for distribution a package of pamphlets dealing with German atrocities."[13]

Steffens's and Baker's experiences were repeated almost everywhere. The Creel Committee with its "Red, White, and Blue" pamphlets conjuring up images of the Germans as a race of demons had thrown the war into a brutal perspective. Huns were seen lurking behind every umlaut. Cartoons depicted bodies of children skewered like shish kebabs on German bayonets. Ida Tarbell wrote that "all the paraphernalia of life had taken on war coloring; the platforms from which I spoke were so swathed in flags that I often had to watch my step entering and leaving. I found I was expected to wear a flag—not a corsage." Beethoven was banned. Pretzels were barred from saloon counters. Anthems were tooted on auto horns and played at the beginning and conclusion of all concerts, one participant noted, "with the fervor of novelty" and "a tingle down our spines." In Baltimore, irate citizens changed the name of German Street to Redwood Street in tribute to a native son killed in the early action. Although the propagandizing and atrocity stories had their origin and most extensive development among the English, Norman Angell (who was a frequent foreign contributor to the *New Republic* and who resided in America during the war) confided that "the mob mind in the United States often outdid that of Britain in violence and silliness."[14]

The emphatic statements of Wilson and his liberal followers that there was no quarrel with the German people but only with the forces of aggression had completely bypassed the great majority of Americans, who were engaged in a militant campaign, not the benevolent crusade with broader implications and nobler purposes that the architects originally conceived. Wilson in his famous aside to Frank Cobb of the New York *World* had a presentiment of what the climate would be like. Prior to delivering his war message, he confessed to Cobb that once into war, the people would "forget there ever was such a thing as tolerance. The spirit of ruthless brutality will enter into the very fibre of our national life, infecting Congress, the courts, the policeman on the beat, the man in the street."* Newton Baker

---

*There is evidence that contests the authenticity of the Cobb-Wilson conversation. See Jerold S. Auerbach, "Woodrow Wilson's 'Prediction' to Frank Cobb: Words Historians Should Doubt Ever Got Spoken," *Journal of American History* 54 (Dec. 1967): 608-17. See also Arthur Link's rebuttal and Auerbach's counterreply in the June 1968 issue, pp. 231-38.

shared his anxiety. At a gathering of college presidents in May 1917, in Washington's Continental Hall, he urged them to preach the doctrine of tolerance and to exercise a steadying influence in what was likely to be a period of high emotion.[15] Like other vigilant liberals, Wilson and Baker hoped that the sugar-coating of ideals would sweeten the bitterness of war, and that public discussion and presidential direction would keep the nation on proper course. Instead of raw patriotic instincts and passions being sublimated, however, they became more acute. And the crusade as liberals had projected it hobbled along badly.

In a premonition as haunting as Wilson's, Frederick Lewis Allen sensed the shifting public mood three weeks after the war declaration:

> Already one can see the tide of feeling rising. . . . One sees sensible people honestly suspecting the most transparently honest pacifists of conspiring on behalf of Germany.
>
> What we have seen, it is clear, is only a beginning. Hatred will spring up quickly when American blood has been shed in war. Sensationalism will spread the German spy scare. . . . Reprisals against loyal Americans of German birth will be advocated, and, one fears, frequently effected. We may have our own Liebknechts thrown into prison, . . . our own conscientious objectors punished, our own Bertrand Russells expelled from our university faculties.

Liberals watched with consternation as Allen's words came true. A virtual wave of terror inundated the country during those months in 1917 when the German war machine gave no indication of stalling and tensions stood at a fever pitch. Those opponents of war who voiced their dissent were subjected to cruel abuse. Frederic Howe, who, as commissioner of the immigration depot at Ellis Island, was in a peculiarly sensitive position, found himself becoming "a jailor instead of a commissioner of immigration"; when he protested he was accused by his staff and superiors of pro-German sympathies. Bourne had his bag searched and some scribbled notes for a poem interpreted as a code description of the Atlantic coastline. Oswald Villard, slowly recoiling back into his pacifist posture as circumstances became more disconcerting, recalled years later his experience with the terror: how he was branded a traitor for disputing the stories of Belgian babies with hands cut off, how his children were constantly taunted, and how his dog with the unfortunate name of Fritz was nearly stoned to death. Max Eastman, blowing hot and cold toward the war, suffered through a cold spell in which he was harassed and on one occasion barely escaped a lynching at the hands of soldiers readying for their task with stanzas from "The Star-Spangled Banner."[16]

What was especially disquieting was the spectacle of supposedly incorruptible intellectuals and reformers contributing to the delirium. Harold Stearns recalled how men who had boasted of intellectual integrity "seemed delighted to be able to shed their intellectual harness and scamper and romp gaily in the green fields of emotion." Another observer remembered "historians who were hysterical, philosophers who had no worthy philosophy of life, psychologists and psychiatrists who were rattle-brained." The reformers who donated their talents as publicists to the Creel Committee had performed outstanding services for progressivism, and George Creel himself had been an energetic progressive journalist before the war. Cornell's George Lincoln Burr, the venerable president of the American Historical Association who gave his 1914 invocation to colleagues on "The Freedom of History" and who had long been an advocate of tolerance and objectivity, donned a uniform and drilled with khaki-clad students on the Cornell campus.[17] Granville Hicks in a scathing article documented the overzealous reaction of clergymen.[18]

The most improbable of individuals succumbed to the madness. Jane Addams recalled how difficult it was for the conscientious to keep their senses. "The force of the majority was so overwhelming that it seemed not only impossible to hold one's own against it, but at moments absolutely unnatural, and one secretly yearned to participate in 'the folly of all mankind.' " The normally unaffected Holmes wrote to Laski in June 1917 of his unexplainable pleasure at a sign marked "Damn a man who ain't for his country right or wrong." The president of Columbia University, Nicholas Murray Butler, a member of the Carnegie Endowment for International Peace and a leading exponent of freedom of speech, supervised the dismissal of a number of students and professors connected with pacifist organizations. Brand Whitlock, in calmer days a dedicated pacifist and humanist, came suddenly unhinged. The war impassioned him and brought out a vindictive streak, as evidenced in a response late in the war to a Toledo acquaintance. "I am glad we are in this war," he wrote from Le Havre in France, "and we must never get out of it until we have given the brutal and bestial spirit that so lightly began it the only answer it can ever understand." Moved to tears by the appearance of American troops, Whitlock bade them act swiftly and thoroughly. "I feel exultant to see them coming in a whirlwind of wrath to deal out justice and righteous retribution to those impious ones who have flouted every sentiment of honour and decency in the world."[19]

The dereliction of luminaries like Burr and Butler, respected figures in their own ranks, caused liberals to shudder nervously and prompted angry replies from those who, whether they had backed or opposed American involvement in 1917, by 1918 shared a common concern. Carl Becker, a more composed supporter of the war effort than his Cornell colleague Burr, wrote to an associate in April that his devotion to the cause was as unqualified as anyone's, but "if anything could shake my faith it would be the spirit of frenzied intolerance, masking under the name of patriotism, which seems to be sweeping the country." Horace Kallen, also in April, was distressed that the mass of Americans was reacting so unmindfully to Wilson's leadership. Even the independent journals, Kallen lamented, "writhed and sputtered." Yet never was the President "in greater need of active, considered, intelligent support from his fellow-citizens." Bourne's censure of derelict liberals—"the American intellectuals seem to have forgotten that the real enemy is War rather than imperial Germany"—was echoed now by those who earlier considered him an alarmist. Bourne's chief target, John Dewey, was himself startled by the sudden gyrations by which "wrongheadedness had become sedition and folly treason," and implored "liberals who believe in the war to be more aggressive than they have been in their opposition to those reactionaries who also believe in war." Charles Beard, who had supported the war earnestly from the start, was appalled by Butler's faculty dismissals and resigned from Columbia in protest. Beard still believed in the war effort but realized that many of his countrymen did not share his view. "Their opinions," he wrote Butler, "cannot be changed by curses or bludgeons."[20]

Liberals might have taken a cue from the apparent subversion of national purpose and toned down their expectations for a glorious conclusion to the war and a magnanimous peace. But through all the turbulence most of them stuck to their idealistic course and remained undaunted. The sloganeering and apocalyptic thinking continued unabated, helped along in no small measure by Wilson's promulgation of the Fourteen Points in January 1918. Kallen, who in one breath heaved sighs of dismay over the "hysteria and blindness," in another could whistle in the wind about "considered, intelligent support" for Wilson's program; almost masochistically, he persisted in depicting the struggle in do-or-die terms: "The kind of peace we shall make will determine the kind of future we shall create for ourselves and our children. Win or lose, there is an inexorable alternative before us!" Newton Baker continued his circuit of civic organizations as a roving Administration ambassador, selling the Wilsonian program with unflagging enthusiasm despite personal qualms. "The day is in sight," Baker told a gathering of the Boston City Club, "when peace will be written—permanent peace."[21]

The degeneration of the crusade likewise had no perceptible impact on the pious pronouncements that continued to issue from the Manhattan loft of the *New Republic*, where Croly, running the show virtually alone after Lippmann's departure for Washington, still couched their editorials theologically: the "salvation of democracy," "redemption of Germany's soul," the "deliverance of humanity." Though momentarily flustered by the "war propaganda" and "diplomatic nihilism," Croly and his staff remained outwardly confident through 1918. In their issue of 30 March they replayed a familiar theme: "The thing which the American people are committed to seeing through is not merely the defeat of the German autocratic imperialism. It is the creation of a new world after the war, in which imperialism in all its manifestations cannot live." As late as 3 August, sixteen months after United States intervention, they were still rationalizing the mob violence as a passing phase—"the reaction which an intensely patriotic and essentially political people would naturally pass through during the earlier stages of a war." "The violence," they were sure, "will not last."[22]

Elsewhere, at the national convention of the League to Enforce Peace, meeting in Philadelphia in May 1918, keynote speakers vied with one another in affirming America's purpose and the epic nature of the conflict. "This is indeed a holy war, the holiest in all history," one exulted. "No nation has ever gone into a war with so little love of war for war's sake . . .; no war has ever before in the midst of its passions offered such possibility, such promise, such surety of its being a war against war." Harvard president A. Lawrence Lowell proclaimed that civilization had reached a point "where it must preclude war or perish by war." Richard Heath Dabney, the dean of the Department of Graduate Studies at the University of Virginia, invoked Patrick Henry's "Give me liberty, or give me death." Rabbi Stephen Wise billed his address "Battling for a New World." "That seems a grandiose title," Wise began, "and yet, I make bold to say that nothing less than the creation of a new world would justify the physical horrors, the moral desolations which have been wrought by four long terrible years of war."[23]

It seems incredible that as late as the waning months of the war, in the face of the manifest failures at home, these men could remain so benighted, so implacably committed to a cause that offered so little hint of success. In 1916 many of them had complained that Americans were drifting aimlessly; by 1918 their "aimless" countrymen were reeling uncontrollably in the backwash of hysteria. By their compass, the nation was more rudderless than ever; floundering, wallowing, irretrievably off course. And if America was off course—with their own pilot at the helm in the person of Wilson—how could they expect

Britain or France or any of the Europeans to follow in tow? Mencken, his cynicism for once warranted, read Upton Sinclair's Wilsonian magazine and wrote to Sinclair that he saw "no chance for the Internation you talk of. The end of the war will see national animosities more bitter than ever before. Worse, even the present alliances will not hold up." He looked for "at least 25 years of wars." Baker was asked why he expected "this particular crop of thistles to grow figs when none other in the history of the world has ever done so."[24]

What caused liberals like Sinclair, Kallen, and Wise to persevere in their tired phrases and strained optimism must have been less a case of blind intransigence than wounded pride and professional jeopardy. Here were liberals—humanists and pacifists by both nature and profession—who had compromised every item of their intellectual faith by proposing a *war* to end war. Debunkers like Mencken and fence-sitters like Villard, once the going got tough, could retire to the sidelines with a smug second guess.[25] But the majority of liberals had placed their reputations and consciences on the line with pages upon pages of elaborate reasoning and impassioned exhortation, and they were committed to seeing things through. "Their very self-respect," Robert Osgood has commented, "depended upon the achievement of Wilson's goals, for nothing much short of those goals could have vindicated their personal concessions to the war spirit."[26] Admission of failure or blunder thus required a particularly agonizing and labored confession. It was easier for them, like the blinkered plowhorse, to continue breaking the ground and sowing the seeds for the new world order, although they must have known that a harvest of disillusionment awaited them.

As the remonstrances of Bourne, Kallen, Beard, and other sober liberals went unheeded, and the contagion of intolerance grew to epidemic proportions, doubt and disillusion slowly infiltrated the liberal community, creeping eventually into the salons and sitting rooms of the diehards themselves. Compounding the troubles at home, the Bolsheviks, in November 1917, published the damning contents of the secret treaties, implicating the Allies in a conspiracy to divide the spoils of war and restore the old system of power politics. Early in 1918 the Allies invaded Russia in the first of a series of apparent aggressions. The "great crusade," from all angles, took on the appearance of a colossal masquerade.

Liberals took stock of what had transpired during the months that America was at war and finally performed some hard accounting: at home, the breakdown of national purpose, the wholesale aberrations from stated goals, the corruption of balanced minds and gentle souls; abroad, among their allies, the same wayward behavior, subverted ideals, and squandered opportunities. Ray Stannard Baker admitted that they were "living in a cave of illusion," fooling themselves. "We must readjust our valuations, moral & otherwise." Willard Straight, the patrician reformer and a patron of the "New Diplomacy" (despite his notorious identification with "dollar diplomacy"), wrote his wife from Europe that the war appealed to him "less and less. It's something disagreeable we've all got to go through with and do our damndest in, but . . . I am more and more beginning to hate all it means." "It's terribly unintelligent and unreasonable," Straight fretted. "It must in the end brutalize." George Santayana had been briefly aroused by Wilson's peace program and the Russian revolution, but the actions of "little men" and "helpless minds" blunted his feelings, and he quietly slunk back into private pursuits. "As to the war," he wrote in a letter of 6 April 1918, "I have grown a protective cuticle . . . fallen back on a sort of grey leaden sea of philosophy. . . . Though I take up the paper every morning with a beating heart, I lay it down with [an] inward smile, as if someone said to me . . . 'never mind.' "27

In general, the first to express their resignation were the radicals and younger intelligentsia who, like Santayana, had been disenchanted and uneasy with progressivism *before* the war. For them, the conduct of the war was the acid test of progressivism. Their hopes were temporarily rejuvenated by events in Russia and by what promised to be a great adventure to save the world, but the betrayal of ideals jolted them and they revealed their dismay openly and early. John Reed was among the first of many radicals who expatriated themselves during the war. In a pensive essay written in 1917, he expressed his "turmoil of imaginings," his confusion and disorientation at the rapid turn of events. Bourne, a skeptic throughout but always a frisky one, suddenly became sullen and withdrawn. "I feel very much secluded from the world," he wrote a childhood friend, "very much out of touch with my time, except perhaps with the Bolsheviki. The magazines I write die violent deaths. . . . If I start to write on public matters I discover that my ideas are seditious, and if I start to write a novel I discover that my outlook is immoral if not obscene." Fitzgerald grew ever more morose, ranting about losing his youth as well as any lingering faith. An old hand like Lincoln Steffens shared the youngsters' infatuation with Russia and exasperation with the mass of Americans whom he found consistently unreliable. "It doesn't matter," he wrote his sister in January 1918, "that we Americans misunderstand the Russians, as we came near doing to the Mexicans. . . . We are so cocksure of the rightness of our own false ideas that we are likely . . . to misunderstand every people and every crisis that rises."[28]

Diehard progressives like the Kallens and Deweys held their faith longer and had no intention of abandoning liberalism for Leninism, but they became increasingly brooding and penitent and in some cases renounced their affiliation with the crusade. Villard's *Nation*, after 1917, concentrated on exposing the hypocrisy of Wilson and the Allies. The *New Republic* revived a favorite prewar metaphor of the leaking vessel with disabled engines thrashing through troubled waters. "We stand in fair way," sighed Straight, "of having fought the war, lost thousands of lives and millions of dollars, upsetting everything, and of not getting the peace we started for." Even the imperturbable Croly privately expressed concern over the designs of the Allies. "The indications are increasing day by day," he told Judge Learned Hand near the end of the war, "that our friends abroad have not the slightest intention of writing anything but a punitive peace."[29]

Consoled by the imminent German defeat and buoyed by an abiding trust in the people, Croly and his *New Republic* remained in relatively good spirits. But few progressives managed their resiliency. One of the most crestfallen was Brand Whitlock. Whitlock was racked by personal doubts and guilt. The war confused and embarrassed him. He regretted his chauvinistic outbursts, but was at a loss to explain his actions. "I'm losing my grip, or something," he agonized, "and I can't make speeches to stir up hate. What I have written has a cheap, rhetorical sound. This war has so confused my ideas that I don't know any more. . . . I know that democracy ought to win, must win, but—I don't like the stupendous folly of war." Whitlock unburdened himself in a stream of letters and diary entries that reflected to a remarkable degree the washed-out sentiments of Bourne and Fitzgerald. His forty-ninth birthday, on 4 March 1918, occasioned two such efforts, a letter to a friend in which he wrote, "We were all young then . . . the world is never going to be again what it used to be," and a melancholic diary entry: "I have the terribly depressing sense of the waste of life occasioned by this war. We mark time . . . waiting to be allowed to live again." A week later, in a diary entry of 10 March, he groaned that he had "lived in an atmosphere, for nearly a year, of Tory sentiment and speech." His ideas were "all warped," his liberalism "compromised. I have drifted far out of my course." The war left him "with whitened hair, and the aged feeling," he wrote in a letter of 17 May. He told Rutger Jewett, his editor at Appleton, of a visit with Ray Stannard Baker. They had "a long talk about that world of illusions in which we used to live before the Hun swept down upon us."[30]

The patriarch of the disillusionment among the veteran progressives was Walter Weyl. Always the most scrupulous and compassionate of the *New Republic* trio, the Jeffersonian among Hamiltonians, Weyl was a personality of "paper-thin sensitivity who could be moved to tears by the sight of a European casualty list."[31] He was extremely shaken by his countrymen's callousness. As the crusade deviated farther and farther from the course charted by the editors, Weyl had beseeched Croly and Lippmann to offer new directives and to sever ties with an Administration that he believed was being bamboozled by insincere allies. His patience exhausted, he took leave of the magazine to record his own reflections. In *The End of the War*, published in 1918, he maintained that opportunities were still available for the conclusion of a just and democratic peace, but in a solemn prologue conceded that "Wilson's ideals were sometimes left to hang high in the diplomatic heavens." There had been at times a lack of reality, Weyl lamented. "Here was a great man uttering noble sentiments in noble language, yet missing one chance after another to translate those sentiments into decisive action." He joined Bourne and Villard in reproaching liberals, himself included, who forget "that war is the opponent and remember only a grinning and contemptuous foe." Although he returned briefly to the magazine, the divorce became final when Croly refused to publish his "Tired Radicals" essay. In it Weyl mused on how his generation aspired to construct a whole new society, how they wandered through a "wilderness of altruism," and how they would likely "return to self." With his death a year later, at forty-six, this statement became his legacy to liberalism.[32]

By the fall of 1918 a malaise shrouded the entire liberal community. With the armistice in sight but the new world order still a distant dream, there was scant reason to rejoice. Unremitting repression at home and widening application of the espionage and sedition acts scuttled efforts to restore sanity or purpose. The Bolshevik perversion of democracy, the disclosure of additional secret agreements, and continuing Allied coolness to the Fourteen Points further testified to the corruption of liberal values. John Jay Chapman composed a wistful "Sonnet on Middle Life," dated 7 November but left unpublished. Whitlock scribbled in his diary for 11 October that the war at last seemed won but there was strangely no emotion—only "depression, which I fear will be permanent." Vultures fluttered overhead. A group of intellectuals groomed a successor to the pragmatists' *Creative*

Intelligence. Santayana was deep into a book to be called *Dominations and Powers*—an "attempt to explain how it happens that governments and religions, with so little to recommend them, secure such a measure of popular allegiance."[33]

The war took its toll of liberal casualties. Bourne, fatigued and despondent, died of pneumonia days after the armistice, only thirty-two years old. A few months before, Walter Rauschenbusch, harassed mercilessly because of his German descent and outspoken pacifism, died at the age of fifty-seven—"a troubled man, invaded by an uneasiness he had no time to plumb."[34] Weyl lasted on into 1919. Of those who remained, many were skeletons of their former selves. Of the liberal journals, only the *Nation* and *New Republic* survived the war. The *Seven Arts,* after October 1917, disappeared without ceremony, its sponsors withdrawing support. The *Masses,* hounded by federal agents, closed down a month later.

By any standard, 1918 produced an unusually autumnal season. Whether they had been prointervention or antiintervention, pacifists or pragmatists or adventurous romantics, liberals were chagrined by the outcome of the war. The struggle had confirmed what all feared, and hoped would never be put to a test; that under certain circumstances individuals acted out of brute impulse rather than reason or compassion, and that the triumph of progressivism and the human spirit was not inevitable after all. Those antiinterventionists whose suspicions were vindicated and those cynics who had watched the spectacle with bemused detachment were hardly consoled. They all shared in a sense of loss and mourning. They had been brought up in the exuberance of the prewar years, and the shadowy denouement of the war seemed to mark the twilight of their own intellectual prime.

As Wilson sailed for Paris on the *George Washington,* many liberals stowed their copies of Croly's *Promise of American Life* and Brooks's *Coming-of-Age* and began retreats that already were taking them from Greenwich Village to the Riviera. Some followed the trail blazed by Reed to Russia. But the majority were not quite yet the tired radicals who, Weyl predicted, would "return to self." With Wilson as their ambassador, they were willing to try to salvage what they could out of the smouldering debris of war. For them, Versailles would be a final way station on the track to disillusionment.

6 THE TRAGEDY AT PARIS

ACT I

Versailles, then, represented something of a last stand for the prewar liberalism. A checkered four years of tortuous maneuvering, of false starts and rash advances, of wildly fluctuating moments of exhilaration and despair now came down to one last move. The closing months of the war had served as a decompression chamber in which liberals dismounted from their pulpits, faced the sobering facts of international life, and released their store of regrets and disappointments. They emerged from the war weary and deflated. But most had come too far to give up the fight. They had lost many of their illusions but not their determination. Newton Baker wrote to Whitlock in November, "The scenes are now shifting, and an entirely different act in this great drama is about to be introduced." "I pray earnestly," Baker said, "that we may all be wise and farsighted and that we may remember the long interests of the future in the new order which we seem to have the chance to start."[1] Their self-assigned task at Paris was to impress upon the rulers and peoples of the world, their own countrymen included, the soundness of the principles for which they had been willing to fight—the right of self-determination, the renunciation of indemnities and annexations, the abolition of secret diplomacy, the reduction of arms, the formation of a league to preserve peace—principles that not long ago had seemed to them invincible but in the crucible of war had become severely charred. Those ideals now had to be resurrected.

While Wilson's Inquiry staff readied the government's blueprint for the peace talks, a corps of liberal internationalists regrouped in New York City in a last-ditch effort to gain popular understanding and support for the Wilsonian program. Led by Beard, Croly, Dewey, Felix Frankfurter, and Learned Hand, they formed the League of Free Nations Association.[2] The League's impressive roster listed such notables as John Commons, James Harvey Robinson, Jane Addams,

Harold Stearns, Lillian Wald, Ida Tarbell, and Paul Kellogg. The inclusion of prominent pacifists like Addams, Wald, and Kellogg together with Bourne-crony Stearns underscored the unity of purpose that now fused the liberal community. Not since the prewar days had there been such consensus. No conscientious liberal—pacifist, aesthete, or otherwise—could contest the virtue of the new campaign his colleagues were preparing to wage, nor refrain from hoping for the success of Wilson and his Fourteen Points at Paris. Even the left-wing elements, the young expatriates and the Russian devotees among the socialists, although they more often embraced Lenin's Decree of Peace than Wilson's Fourteen Points, considered the two leaders merely rival prophets of peace and were solidly behind the manifesto for the new order.

Editorials of liberal journals in the weeks before the peace conference reveal this unanimity. They were conceived in a singular spirit and developed around the same fundamental themes: continuing concern for illiberal professions at home and among the Allies, thoughts of resignation overcome by the riveting obsession with the "new order," and a call for liberals of all persuasions to unite. A *New Republic* editorial of 16 November, entitled "The Pivot of History," exemplified the sense of anticipation:

> What we can be sure of is that however we may use or misuse the present opportunity, the downfall of the one government in the world that offered a serious challenge to democracy will exert a continuous and cumulative effect upon the political life of all mankind. For a century all history will pivot upon the great war, and the greater events of the last weeks. The French Revolution ushered in a new era. The European Revolution now under way is ushering in a new world.

The *Nation* on 19 October had been convinced that a peace was still within reach which was "honorable, just, definitive—one to satisfy all true Americans whose souls are not corroded with bitterness and hate and all those abroad as well who have fought the good fight." By 2 November, as the Allied intervention in Russia smacked increasingly of imperialism and dockets at home overflowed with sedition cases, Villard's journal wrote less sanguinely of the peace prospects, but still urged liberals to overlook Wilson's and the Allies' delinquency and "pull together that the new world order may come into existence." The *Dial*, which after the collapse of the *Seven Arts* became the chief purveyor of the cultural radicals' viewpoint, joined in the *New Republic* and *Nation* refrain that liberals must "remain true to the ideals" which inspired the war's acceptance and prevail over those who would "make a mockery" of them. The issue was "immediate and urgent," declared the *Dial*; no American liberal could afford to leave Wilson "to play a lone hand" at Paris.[3]

Amid this thumping chorus of liberal resolution were the familiar voices of moderation and skepticism who, even as they sorely hoped for Wilson's success, cautioned against overexpectation and wondered out loud how such a feat as a new world order could be accomplished. Steffens told his sister on 1 November of his "jolt the other day when Wilson said 'free trade' didn't mean free trade." He did not question Wilson's sincerity, but recognized the insurmountable obstacles facing the President: the vagueness of the liberal program, a poisoned public mind conditioned to war rather than peace, and the "crooks and tories" who were still in the saddle and who "know what they want." Willard Straight had written his wife warily in August that "Downing Street and the Quai D'Orsay will not forget in a year the training of centuries." In October he thought of the myriad problems, and they staggered him. He decided "we should have made our bargain with the Allies when we first came in. . . . Now we will be apt to get nothing—not even the peace we fight for. . . . There are all manner of . . . political squabbles on the way." Brand Whitlock likewise realized that the spiritual bond uniting the Allies during the war was only temporary and that the professed crusade for democracy was only a convenient rallying point. "As I have always thought," he entered in his diary on 7 November, "the Franco-American alliance was a thin thing of silly sentiment for the most part, and has no real reason for existing. The French don't understand us, don't like us, and never will." Further along Whitlock noted "the cold and cruel cynicism of European chancelleries"; "the French Government, for instance, believes no more in democracy than the Kaiser himself."[4]

Walter Lippmann, seduced by Wilsonianism in 1917, was now in a slack period in his prophylactic cycle of hope and disappointment. After helping draft the Fourteen Points, he accepted an overseas position with army intelligence in the spring of 1918. His stay in war-torn Europe and immediate contact with the broken world that was to be "reconstructed" retrieved his skepticism, and by the time of the armistice the vintage Lippmann, cautious and restrained, was registering. In a letter to Mrs. Willard Straight shortly after her husband's death on 1 December, he told her they were looking ahead to the peace talks with apprehension, that with their lingering hopes "was mixed also a fear that what we had meant, and what alone could justify it all, was not the meaning and justification of those who will decide." Lippmann returned to New York and the *New Republic* and arranged his shuffled thoughts in a long essay published in 1919 as

The Political Scene: An Essay on the Victory of 1918. He warned that no absolutely liberal solutions could be achieved at Paris because of Europe's chaotic state. "It calls for imagination," he said,

> to picture just what has happened to Europe and the world by the disappearance of its imperial organizations. We find ourselves in a world where four of the eight or nine centers of decisive authority have collapsed; where hundreds of millions of people have been unwrenched [*sic*] from their ancient altars of obedience; where the necessities of bare existence are scarce, and precariously obtained. These people have lost homes, children, fathers. They are full of rumor and fear, and subject to every gust of agitation. Their leaders are untried, their lands undefined, their class interests and property in a jumble, they cannot see ahead three weeks with assurance.

Lippmann was not completely discouraged—he saw a chance, albeit "a somewhat slim one," for Wilson's success—and he supported Wilson's League proposition as the only available instrument for peace; but he now reverted to the *Realpolitik* idiom of limited goals and proximate solutions, and stated dourly that "no one who has grasped those problems as they press upon mankind can persist in the idea that peace consists in signing a treaty, shaking hands with the Allies, and returning home to gaze in rapt admiration at the Monroe Doctrine."[5]

Lippmann pressed his liberal associates who lacked his firsthand acquaintance with conditions in Europe and his appreciation for the realities of power to brace themselves for compromise. But once again, as in 1914 on the eve of war and in 1916 on the eve of American intervention, the cautioners were discordant voices. Louis Brandeis, at dinner with Steffens in October, imagined not normalcy or reaction issuing from the smoke of war, but revolution and "adventure"—"a world of men who will not be content to return to the sordid, humdrum life we all have lived."[6] The liberals who took to the crusade and who now ushered Wilson to the peace conference were not about to accept half loaves or any further postponement of reform. There was too much invested, too much already wasted. Even among those who had opposed intervention in 1917, although they had not risked as much of their liberal credit or intellectual integrity, men of their stubborn conviction were not prepared to compromise. These were dreamers and bitter-enders, not negotiators. They were planning to return from Paris with their shields or upon them.

Such was the temper of the liberal community as Wilson sailed for Europe in December 1918. Frank Simonds, a liberal journalist and war correspondent for the *New Republic,* explained that for Wilson and his followers alike, "the Paris journey was nothing less than another apostolic adventure." William Allen White, traveling to the peace conference on the *Chicago* with several other newspapermen, was "fired with a desire to see and be a part of . . . one of the greatest adventures that man had embarked upon since he dropped his tail and went to Eden." On the other side of the Atlantic, Harold Nicolson and hopefuls in the British delegation, prior to departing for Paris, were given a small volume on the Congress of Vienna which they studied and put down with the vain resolution to eradicate all vestiges of reactionary rule. "We were journeying to Paris," Nicolson later recalled their frame of mind, "not merely to liquidate the war, but to found a new order in Europe. We were preparing not Peace only, but Eternal Peace. There was about us the halo of some divine mission. . . . For we were bent on doing great, permanent and noble things."* George Herron wrote to Upton Sinclair on 4 December, "The next few weeks will decide whether the world takes a long step forward or goes back into the melting-pot. It is indeed a time for fasting and prayer."[7]

Woodrow Wilson, for his part, interpreted the nature of his mission with customary solemnity. Three days before the *George Washington* docked in Brest, he assembled several members of the Inquiry staff and others in the American delegation aboard ship and told them of his proposed program—his intention to follow through on the League and the principle of self-determination, regenerate a prostrate Europe, and fulfill the mandate of all humanity. "It is to be our business at the Peace Conference," he told his colleagues plainly, "to fight for a new order."[8]

The reception accorded Wilson and the peace argosy hardly diminished the sense of mission. Charles Thompson, an Associated Press correspondent who came to Brest "to see the opening scene in the presidential pilgrimage," recounted "deafening salvos of artillery ashore and afloat . . . a tumultuous demonstration of the vast multitude massed along the quays and terraces." While fleets of allied warships roared their salutes in the harbor, a tremendous groundswell of hope and humanity gathered in Paris. The "suitors and suppliants" had come in streams—individuals seeking to escape

*Nicolson and other British liberals present at Paris were committed to the same broad program as their American counterparts, and their aspirations and disappointments were often conveyed far more vividly; where I have inserted their impressions, it has been to illuminate general currents of liberal thought at Paris and to suggest how truly universal an experience the "liberal disillusionment" was.

the tyranny of overlords, families believing that land and favors were to be dispensed, whole delegations appearing overnight to request territory for their districts. Colonel House later wrote of peacetime Paris that it was a mecca for all the oppressed where "pilgrims came in countless numbers to lay their hopes and grievances at the feet of those in the seats of the mighty." Those who did not make the pilgrimage to Paris hung pictures of Wilson in windows and sang hymns of praise and prayer. Some sent letters and petitions. Whitlock wrote House from Brussels on 28 November, "The President's picture is everywhere, and people speak of him as the great moral figure of the war, and as one of the greatest personages in all history."[9]

In retrospect, Wilson's triumphant arrival was reminiscent of the grand entrance of Agamemnon after his victory over the Trojans, landing amid great ceremony and celebration only to be conspired against and slain. Indeed, the aura of high tragedy that shadowed the liberal effort from the beginning now hovered unrelieved over the drama at Paris. Among Wilson's own party, there were already the forebodings, the bits of fatalism, the Cassandra-like prophets of doom. While Paris rejoiced and young liberals playfully "swapped back copies of the *Nation* and *New Republic* for the *Spectator* or *Round Table*," sensitive men aboard the *George Washington* silently pondered their destiny. James Shotwell of the Inquiry staff wrote ominously in his diary on 9 December that they expected to land in Brest on Friday the thirteenth.[10]

Other Inquiry members, as if sensing the oblivion in store for them, grumbled about their dingy accommodations. "Our dreams of the great state in which we were to travel," noted William Westermann, an expert on Turkey, "were readily shattered. There were four of us in a small room with five bunks." William Bullitt, now a junior State Department attaché who would become intimately involved in events at Paris and would subsequently emerge as a fountainhead of the disillusionment, cast early skepticism at the imperial trappings of the voyage. In his diary, he complained of the "hierarchical arrangement" of the ship, the segregation of smoking rooms, and the arbitrary decision that barred "the brainiest men on the ship . . . from the upper excellent room." In all these faint perceptions there was a hint of the tragedy awaiting them.[11]

Wilson, the prophet of peace himself, foresaw a shipwreck ahead. Just as in another searching moment he conveyed to Frank Cobb his misgivings on the eve of American intervention, he now spoke somberly to George Creel on the deck of the *George Washington*. "It is to America that the whole world turns today," he told Creel. "The hungry expect us to feed them, the roofless look to us for shelter, the sick of heart and body depend on us for cure. All of these expectations have in them the quality of terrible urgency. There must be no delay." "Yet you know, and I know," he said, "that these ancient wrongs . . . are not to be remedied in a day or two with a wave of the hand. What I seem to see—with all my heart I hope that I am wrong—is a tragedy of disappointment."[12]

Once settled in its quarters at the Hôtel de Crillon, the American delegation remained uneasy. Herbert Hoover, one of many delegates who came to the peace conference as liberal internationalists and left as confirmed isolationists, remarked to Wilson on 15 December that the atmosphere in Paris "had suddenly become charged with currents of indescribable malignity." Stephen Bonsal, an interpreter and aide to Colonel House, felt a tenseness in the wind and forecasted squalls and storms. Delegates groused about the weather, about the decrepit condition of the hotel, about a bug in the air. The malaise was contagious. At the Hotel Majestic, British representatives found fault with the communications and the cooking that was "half French and half English with the defects of both and the qualities of neither."[13]

What caused such queer discomfort on the *George Washington* and at Paris was something more profound than whim or crankiness. Here were men who, despite their brave commitment, were suspecting already that they were at the mercy of powerful forces beyond their control and that they were the principals of a tragedy that was now playing itself out. The "currents of malignity" that Hoover spoke of were not merely the scent of bad food or the chill of the Paris air, but something far more foul and disagreeable—the germs of nationalism, imperialism, and militarism. The bad food, the miserable weather, the prostitutes lining the hotel corridors, the stench of hastily buried bodies—all were grim reminders of Old World decadence, and mordant suggestions of new weeds that were sprouting.

Despite the flushed mass of humanity gathered at Paris that looked to Wilson for a "new order," the victorious Allies persisted in talking about "normalcy" and "national interest." National barriers had not dissolved since the armistice, but rather were reinforced. Oswald Villard on his way to the peace conference had trouble securing passage to a British port because of his pacifism during the war and his arraignment of British statesmen for their hypocrisy; a French visa was delayed because of his German ancestry.[14] Postarmistice politics had disclosed a steady drift away from idealism. Lloyd George and a conservative Parliament bent on "hanging the Kaiser" won a sweeping victory in the British elections; the American electorate ignored Wilson's "October Appeal" and returned Republican majorities to both houses of Congress; in France, Clemenceau was granted a vote of confidence by the National Assembly, with the implicit commitment to restore the old balance of power and pursue national advantages. Of Clemenceau's vote of confidence by a four to one majority, Colonel House wrote in his diary that it was "about as bad an augury for the success of progressive principles at the Peace Conference as we could have coming on the heels of the English elections, and taking into consideration the result of recent elections in the United States, the situation strategically could not be worse."[15]

Idealism seemed to have faded irretrievably, and the champions of the "new order" sensed defeat even before they got into the arena. As winter approached, as bleakly as the peace conference, the cryptic diary notations of the men aboard the *George Washington* were amplified by increasingly glum editorials of liberal journals. The *Manchester Guardian*, Britain's leading liberal newspaper, commented on 19 December, "President Wilson can not long have breathed the diplomatic air of Paris without discovering certain strange discrepancies" between professions of principle and actual demands. The "luminous outlook of a universal peace, founded on mutual confidence and friendship of nations, is more and more becoming reduced to a new equilibrium of forces," the Paris *L'Oeuvre* observed. In America, the *Nation* chafed in a 21 December editorial that the stage was apparently set "for a peace congress of the time-honored Vienna-Berlin type." The *Dial* concurred on 14 December: "The high hopes which the world has entertained for a peace settlement that will make future wars impossible do not seem likely to be realized. . . . The bald facts are frankly disquieting." Only the *New Republic*, with characteristic optimism, remained hopeful, buoyed by the popular reception accorded the President. "If the diplomats are too shortsighted to make a just and stable peace, the peoples are capable of taking the work into their own hands."[16]

The *New Republic* refused to recognize that the masses, too, were shortsighted. The victims of oppression, the "suitors and suppliants," were intent on doing big things, but among the victorious peoples the cathartic aftermath of war left citizens with little willingness to "take the work into their own hands." Lippmann reported a conversation with an Italian celebrant who had been entranced with Wilson in 1917 but then at war's end "paid a visit to the old haunts, met the old cronies, and felt most awfully bored with the everlasting morality of the Fourteen Commandments." Nowhere was this "slump in idealism," as Ray Stannard Baker called it, more evident than in America. The *New Republic* editors themselves detected a strong strain of normalcy, admitting that with parcels of real estate certain to jump in price, stock values to be had for a song, and Broadway theaters offering rich diversion, "it is difficult to give large space in one's mind to so vague a conception as reconstruction."

Where reservoirs of political energy did exist in America, they were channeled into Red-baiting and witch hunts. Radicals heard Wilson pronounce that "everything for which America fought has been accomplished" and "it will now be our fortunate duty to assist by example in the establishment of just democracy throughout the world," and then discovered that censorship and espionage laws were being tightened instead of relaxed. Eugene Debs, denied an executive pardon, began serving a ten-year sentence in federal prison. The *Masses* staff was finally tried in October, and although no convictions were obtained, the trial was a dress rehearsal for the kangaroo hearings of the "terror winter" of 1919–1920. Among the few who continued to speak out against the government was John Reed, the expatriate who had voluntarily returned to the United States in April to face charges related to the *Masses* case. "Well," Reed harangued at a Brooklyn rally on 10 January, "the war is finished, comrades, and where the hell is the democracy? Now in New York City free speech is suppressed; Socialists are not allowed to meet; the red flag is banned; periodicals are barred from the mails; all the evidences of Prussianism appear." It was a brave speech, and for it he was arrested, for at the very time that the wares of democracy were placed on display in Paris, its agents at home were peddling censorship and repression.[17]

Such were the currents of malignity, the strains of complacency and intolerance, the slump in idealism that Hoover, Bonsal, and the others sensed in Europe and in the prevailing climate of opinion that stretched across the Atlantic. Such was the larger meaning of Shotwell's metaphorical diary entry, "This old world is badly germridden." Nationalism, in all its vicious manifestations, was still rampant. "I see very clearly here," Steffens informed his sister from Paris in late December, "how it is not merely a class division, but an issue which divides every human heart against itself. Every little peasant and workingman wants both his revenge upon the foe, his share of the recompense for injury done *and* no more wars." Subconsciously, intuitively, conference-bound liberals were capitulating to Steffens's and Lippmann's gloomy prognosis. The vaporous ecumenical spirit that greeted them in Paris would never penetrate the steeled chambers of council. And by the eve of commencement they were openly conceding as much. On the first day of the new year, two weeks before the opening session of the conference, Villard wrote home to his wife that they would get "a nominal League of Nations, enough for Wilson to boast about, which will not be worth the paper it is described on." Even irrepressible William Allen White was resigned to defeat. He told Colonel House that liberals were agreed that the rumored League plan was "bunk," and on 10 January, in his first news dispatch from Paris, he cabled that Wilson's program did not "stand a dog's chance."[18]

"Having locked ourselves in our little extraterritorial spots," Vernon Bartlett later quipped, "we set about making peace, based on the Fourteen Points."[19] The Council of Ten, the principal decision-making body in the early stages of the conference, met for the first time on 12 January. As if preconference portents were not foreboding enough, the council's initial step was a decidedly backward one retreating to the "old diplomacy." The Ten, consisting of the two ranking delegates from each of the five big powers (the United States, Britain, France, Italy, and Japan) and invested with virtually sovereign authority, issued a statement on publicity advising that press representatives were to be admitted only to the plenary sessions—a transparent move to bar the press effectively from the real negotiations and a seeming contradiction to Wilson's pledged "open diplomacy."[20]

White and others who were edgy going into the conference seized upon the publicity clampdown as the first concrete sign that liberal principles were to be given mere lip service. Villard cabled the *Nation* that it was inconceivable that Wilson should "have yielded on this vital point . . . essential to victory on other issues." The *New Republic* accepted the edict more realistically. "There is here a violation of the spirit of the first of the President's fourteen points," it conceded, "but it is difficult to see how it could have been otherwise. With the public opinion of the world in its present condition of super-excitability, would the diplomats care to expose their preliminary bargaining demands in the full light of day?" The *New Republic* was harder pressed to explain the conspiracy of silence that existed outside of the council chamber, as the top-level secrecy filtered down to the embassy level and made even the delegation headquarters graveyards for correspondents. The news blackout was especially acute at British headquarters, where one nettled journalist reported that "the emptying of the wastepaper baskets was a highly important business" and Bartlett remarked that "lady secretaries were supposed to be carefully herded about by 'chaperones,' less to protect their morals than to avoid risks of indiscreet talking."[21]

More unsettling, however, than the procedural clampdown on publicity was the handling of the first substantive business of the conference—at Wilson's insistence, the matter of a League of Nations.

The League question was fundamental; its resolution would cast either a glimmer of hope or a lengthening shadow over the future of the talks. Inquiry experts and liberal publicists had worked long and hard to develop Wilson's prize package, and they expected success despite the rumbles of pessimism and the acknowledged hazards. At the second plenary session on 25 January, a commission was appointed to produce a covenant that would be agreeable to all parties. Among the several fiercely contested issues were the disposition of the German colonies (France and Britain hoping to realize the promises of the secret treaties and demanding outright annexation, and Wilson pressing for a modified mandate system), the location of the League headquarters, the representation that smaller nations would be allotted in the League Assembly, and the inclusion in the covenant of racial and religious equality clauses. The League debate consumed the first month of the conference. The Byzantine nature of the negotiations is a familiar and well-documented affair.[22] What emerged was essentially a compromise, with Wilsonianism on the long end. Wilson got his cherished League, but not without sacrificing many of the liberal demands: the equality clauses were pigeonholed; the representation plan relegated small nations to the role of mere apprentices rather than full partners in the new association; and in order to gain the endorsement of the Italians, he was forced to cede them the Brenner Pass with its 250,000 Germans and Austrians—a blatant violation of the principle of self-determination.

Ray Stannard Baker, chief press officer at Paris, felt it remarkable that Wilson achieved what he did, considering the prevailing nationalism. "The 'old order,' " he enthused, "came into the conferences at Paris quite confident of itself. But the President by a series of bold and skillful strokes had snatched the reins of leadership." Charles Seymour, head of the American commission's Austro-Hungarian division, agreed that "considering the difficulties which he faced on arrival . . . the carrying through of the League of Nations was a great triumph for him, and . . . really a great piece of diplomacy." Baker and Seymour were probably too faithfully Administration men to be objective, but Wilson's achievement, by any fair estimate, if not remarkable, was at least statesmanlike. Unsurprisingly, however, few liberals saw it that way. Most of them, demanding perfection, construed the tainted result as tantamount to a wholesale betrayal of the liberal program. In acquiescing to a watered-down covenant Wilson had, by their exacting standard, demolished the very cornerstone of the "New Diplomacy," and some of them were comparing the proposed League to Tsar Alexander's Holy Alliance. The preconference talk of "bunk" and a "nominal" League seemed to them substantiated. The *New Republic* continued its patronizing ways, droning on about time and patience, but the *Nation*'s acerbic reaction was more typical. "Scrutiny of the proposed constitution," read a 22 February editorial, "fails to show that as now planned the League will incorporate a single new principle beyond those already tried and found wanting."[23]

The publicity blackout and the patchwork that passed for a solemn covenant were the inevitable products of a conference with no genuinely uniform purpose or consensus. In an atmosphere of intense historic rivalry, the peacemakers resorted to the tested apparatus of secret transaction, manipulation, and compromise. The diplomatic exchange of the first month—the partisan wrangling, the devious bargains, the desultory compromises, the betrayal of professed principles—dramatized the durability of the old diplomacy. The much-heralded doctrine of open diplomacy and the League covenant were but two casualties among many liberal principles that suffered. Bartlett, in the following passage, recounts the tremendous letdown of those opening weeks:

> The long-promised "open diplomacy" dwindled down to a few very carefully-staged plenary sessions, apparently arranged for the benefit of garrulous South Americans. We saw more greed and jealousy and compromise than at any time during the war or before it. . . .Things drifted on from day to day, each delegation becoming more and more national, less and less tolerant and unselfish. And the greatest Peace Conference the world has ever seen reminded one strongly of the quarrelling crowds of beggars who hover around the entrances of the cathedrals of Italy. No, Paris was not all one had hoped it would be.

Lost in the diplomatic shuffle were the aspirations of small nations and supplications of the conquered. Villard tells in his memoirs of his consternation as he scanned the room at the start of the first plenary session. "Great territories involving the lives of millions of black men were to be turned over to new masters, yet there was hardly a dark skin visible. Worst of all, for the first time in modern history, a great peace was to be written without a single representative of the defeated peoples in the council chamber."[24]

Among the unkindest cuts at Paris was the rebuff suffered by the liberals themselves. Despite their premonitions of failure, they dutifully drafted proposals, volunteered for burdensome assignments, and assisted tirelessly in the arduous work of compiling data and statistics; and yet in the final decision making they were consistently ignored. Shotwell mentions in several diary entries that Wilson discarded the advice of Inquiry experts much the same as he did the opinions of Lansing and others of his official party.[25] Even the *New Republic* men, accustomed to being in the Administration's good graces and in the vortex of political affairs, were confined to the sidelines: Willard Straight, the magazine's founder, complained that he was being used in Paris to give "little parties"; Walter Lippmann, who collaborated on the Fourteen Points in a more comradely moment, found himself thanklessly "shunted aside."[26]

Straight died in December of pneumonia aggravated by severe depression. Lippmann could tolerate his oblivion for only a month, and returned to America in February to publish his soured *Essay on the Victory of 1918*. Others stayed on, but like William Allen White came to regret it. White was appointed on 10 February to head a mission to bring representatives of the warring factions in Russia together with Allied representatives, a meeting that liberals considered essential to a universal and permanent peace settlement; the proposed Prinkipo conference, however, never materialized, sabotaged by the French refusal to recognize any Bolshevik regime. White was relieved of his assignment with a longing to be back home in genial Emporia and away from the skulduggery of the Old World.[27]

It was all very frustrating. The corridors of power were closed to liberals at a time when liberalism cried out for a desperate last hearing. White, Villard, and the others could knock at the chamber doors with all the muscle of their liberal conviction and not gain admission; inside, the Council of Ten sat as if quarantined, the sores of the old diplomacy festering away untreated. Liberals had half expected it to turn out that way—they wrote the scenario themselves on the way to Paris—but they were unconsoled. Harold Nicolson retrieved his volume on the Congress of Vienna. Vienna . . . Paris . . . suddenly there was little to distinguish the two. Like others removed from influence, Nicolson went about his routine tasks with a dedication steadily sapped by an overwhelming sense of futility. "Again there opens before me," he wrote his father, "a thick week of committees, drafts, articles, proposals, counter proposals, statistics, compasses, rulers, tracing paper, coloured inks—and dossier after dossier to read." He felt "quite dead with it all . . . so dispirited. It is as though four architects had each designed an entirely different house, and then met round a table to arrive at an agreement."[28]

General Tasker Bliss, a member of the official American peace commission and thus a relative insider, experienced much the same frustrations. A man of great sensitivity despite his military occupation, Bliss was a fluent writer and linguist, a scholar of Greek and

Latin, and expert in such uncommon fields as geology and Oriental botany. In Ray Stannard Baker's *Woodrow Wilson and World Settlement* he emerges as one of the ablest and most perceptive men at Paris, an impression borne out by his private correspondence. He was an energetic and enthusiastic peacemaker, solidly behind the Fourteen Points, but increasingly overwhelmed by the enormity of the job. Five weeks after the armistice he first wrote his wife of his concern. The American peace commissioners had had a preliminary meeting and he came away "disquieted to see how lazy and vague our ideas are." As the conference dragged on he became, like Nicolson, impatient and despairing over the interminable drafts, bogging details, and merry-go-round of consultations and committee work that promised little reward or relief. He wrote Mrs. Bliss again on 21 January:

> But, oh my dear, if you could see my room, you would not expect much letter writing. Tables, chairs, lounges, are piled up high with papers, marked "important," "urgent" and all that sort of thing. And then the people that waste my time with foolish talk! Two or three are waiting to see me now. A Persian delegation is coming, a Chinese one has just left, Poles- Czechs- Yugoslavs!! I wish there had never been a war—or else that it lasted longer—for peace seems to be worse than war.

A month later, on 26 February, weary of the whole business and as exasperated with the parasitical "small nations" as with the sinister doings of the Council of Ten, he was "beginning to think that the world is in for another 30 years' war. . . . The 'submerged nations' are coming to the surface and as soon as they appear, they fly at somebody's throat. They are like mosquitoes, vicious from the moment of their birth."[29]

Bliss decided that the best option for the United States would be to make a speedy peace with Germany and then go home and leave Europe to Europe. "I think that the most humane thing we could do," he wrote an old army friend, "would be to say that when we have signed peace with Germany we are going home and will let Europe settle her own problems in her own way."[30] In a few short weeks, visions of a new world order had turned to thoughts of Vienna, the Thirty Years' War, and old-fashioned isolationism. Indeed, after a winter of peacemaking, Paris was not all one had hoped it would be.

7 THE TRAGEDY AT PARIS

ACT II

Making the best of a worsening situation, Woodrow Wilson presented the completed League covenant to the third plenary session of the peace conference on 14 February, and on the fifteenth sailed for home—not in retiring isolationism, as Bliss had suggested, but to deliver personally to the American people the patched blueprint of the new international community. The month he spent away from Paris was a costly one. Among his countrymen, disgruntled liberals attacked the covenant for its omissions and outraged conservatives for its commitments; back at the conference, with men of slight vision and slighter scruples holding the reins, diplomacy degenerated to its most primitive state. One participant wrote that the militaristic and nationalistic forces seemed to come instantly to the front when Wilson departed. When he returned to Paris on 14 March, his position and the position of the whole liberal cause, to the extent that it could still be salvaged, had weakened drastically.[1]

As Wilson entered the harbor of Brest for the second time, the historic monuments lining the Breton coast, with the crumbling walls of the castle built by Caesar and rebuilt by Napoleon, must have seemed suddenly imposing. Even without the embarrassment suffered in the domestic reaction to his program and the mad jockeying among European diplomats in his absence, he had already previously lost much of his authority. Most of his initial prerogatives and advantages were exhausted in the fight over the League. Implicit promises had been made to get the League through the deadlock of debate, and delicate matters such as the fate of Fiume and Shantung had been merely postponed. Moreover, the future issues with which the conference would deal—boundaries, reparations, and disarmament—could not be disposed of as expeditiously as the League, on which everyone could agree at least in principle. To make matters worse, on 24 March the Council of Ten was supplanted by the more manageable but craftier "Big Four" as the supreme ruling body of the conference. Thus, little over a week after his return, with his prestige diminished, his aces played, and pressures to conclude a peace mounting, Wilson found himself entering the ring with the opportunist Lloyd George, the imperialist Orlando, and Clemenceau, "the man of 1870," to resume the struggle for the new order. It was these sessions, conducted in what Ray Stannard Baker called variously "that double-doored, sound-proof" and "that hermetically sealed" room, that epitomized the treachery of Paris and dealt liberalism a final crippling blow.

There was, of course, no way that the liberal program could emerge from such a confrontation intact. Wilson's experience with the fuzzier-thinking Council of Ten and the bitter League debate had already demonstrated that. There were simply too many insoluble aspects to the whole affair, as Steffens and Lippmann had warned at the outset and as Bliss and Nicolson were realizing belatedly. A key point in the liberal program, for instance, was the equalization of military and economic power, but could anyone realistically expect the "have" powers to sacrifice their economic advantages or military capability to enable the "have-nots" to approach their level of wealth and security? Likewise, could private and national interests be expected to surrender overseas investments and concessions to international control? Could the great powers, the United States included, be expected to submit their sovereignty to a world government?

And then there was the overriding condition of a peace being negotiated on the smouldering ruins of the battlefield, with the passions of the moment kindling already long-standing grievances. England had lost almost a million men, Italy more than half a million. Clemenceau, accused by liberal internationalists of being unnecessarily selfish and mulish, had to account for his actions to a French people who had just suffered losses of more than one million men and who were still young enough to remember Sedan. How could they forget such tremendous casualties and historic enmities? How could they be expected to become farsighted and selfless in the wake of enormous personal losses and the opportunity for handsome revenge? "A bona fide application of Wilsonism," wrote the historian George Bernard Noble, "would have required the rapid and almost miraculous birth of good will between peoples who had only tentatively laid aside hostilities."[2]

Clemenceau, ruthlessly logical, whittled away at the pretentiousness of the liberal program. Brand Whitlock recalled that as Wilson spoke of ideals, Clemenceau would listen politely, then say, "And now gentlemen, let's get down to business." Steffens drew a superb vignette of the Frenchman ensnaring the American president in the web of his own contradictions. At a meeting of the Big Four Clemenceau asked his colleagues what they meant by "permanent peace." He stressed that France most of all, more than insular England and the remote United States, would be interested in such a plan. It would be expensive, he said. "If we are to prevent war, we must give up our empires and all hope of empire." The English would have to come out of India; the Americans would have to leave the Philippines and Puerto Rico. At that point Wilson protested that he did not mean all that, that was not necessary, not all at once. "Then," said Clemenceau, "you don't mean peace. You mean war. And the time for us French to make war is now, when we have got one of our neighbors down; we shall finish him and get ready for—the next war."[3]

Noble writes, "The confusion of purposes and conflict of policies were too great. The lack of clarity as to real war aims was too obvious." The principle of self-determination was perhaps the biggest farce of all the liberal pretensions. Nicolson complained to Valentine Wilson, a correspondent for the London *Daily Mail*, that it was "appalling that these ignorant and irresponsible men should be cutting Asia Minor as if they were dividing a cake. . . . Isn't it terrible, the happiness of millions being decided in that way?" Compromise and expediency, however, were often necessary where a baffling mélange of nationalities presented an impossible calculus of self-determination. As one of the experts later expressed the problem, "It seldom if ever happens that the racial frontier, the economic frontier, the natural geographic frontier, and the historical or political frontier coincide in any given district." There were, to be sure, a number of flagrant and indefensible violations of the self-determination principle—notably the disposition of the Brenner Pass and Shantung territories—but the decisions in most cases were made conscientiously and many of the shortcomings were the result of petty bickering among the nationality groups themselves. Many around Wilson felt the self-determination principle to be not only impractical but hypocritical as well. Clemenceau made the point brilliantly in the Steffens vignette, and Wilson's own Secretary Lansing, a blushing realist, remarked that if the principle were applied scrupulously it would have meant that the Southern secession from the Union in 1861 was wholly justifiable.[4]

In defense of the Big Four it must be added that the burden of the postwar situation weighed heavily upon them. Chaos and urgency confronted them at every turn. The interim blockade of Germany prevented the entire continent from regaining its economic footing. Sporadic fighting continued over the spoils of the disintegrating Hapsburg and Ottoman empires and threatened to unleash a new round of continental warfare. Further, there were the specter of the Bolshevik menace and the politically acute domestic pressures for demobilization. The reality of the situation was simply that Europe needed peace and a start toward reconstruction before it could be bothered with the perplexing requirements of self-determination and social justice. Charles Seymour, an earnest but levelheaded liberal at Paris, referred repeatedly in his correspondence to the importance of speed and order, even at the sacrifice of principle. "The Conference," he explained on one occasion, "is working under difficulties far greater than those of the Congress of Vienna, for conditions in Central Europe are in such a state of flux, to say nothing of Russia, that it is impossible to know what the latest developments are." It pained him to witness some of the territorial arrangements, but he did not flinch. "Europe cannot wait very much longer," he said.[5]

The effort to restore a semblance of social and economic order and to fulfill their obligations to their own people thus required the statesmen to make and implement peace with dispatch. In this light it is understandable that the claims of the small nations could not be heard at length; that some secrecy and expediency were necessary; and that on the larger issues facing the conference compromise was inevitable. Steffens realized the bind they were in, that the statesmen did not have the luxury of freethinking that he and his fellow liberal critics enjoyed. He felt he could "understand Wilson and what happened to him." They "had to act," he later wrote Whitlock. "They could not go around open-headed as I could."[6]

Most liberals, however, overlooked all this. They chalked up the failures to betrayal and deceit instead of to the imperatives of postwar politics, and they watched the developments with growing bitterness and misplaced anger. They fulminated rather than reflecting on the true nature or depth of the problem. "Unfortunately," Lewis Mumford wrote twenty years after Versailles, "in 1919, the world was full of pert young men who believed that in less than six months, immediately on top of a war of unparalleled brutality, rancor and violence, a perfectly just and generous treaty could be composed."[7] Instead of accepting the plain facts gracefully and closing the book on a liberal peace, they stuck to their fairy-tale script to the end, unfairly skewering Wilson and the peacemakers and needlessly prolonging their own disillusionment.

Nicolson wrote home on 23 March, "The Conference is deteriorating rapidly and I am depressed," and to Valentine Wilson on 24 March, "It will be too awful, if after winning the war we are to lose the peace." By the end of March, the *New Republic* was cringing at the prospect of "a colossal bargain" and finally willing to concede, "It is extremely doubtful, in fact, whether the power to make peace still exists at Paris." Colonel House conferred with Robert Cecil, the British delegate who collaborated with Wilson on the League covenant, and wrote in his diary, "We both see the world crumbling about our feet."[8]

The scanty reports on the German settlement were not encouraging. Liberals had insisted on the inclusion of Germany in the League, no indemnities, fixed reparations, and German retention of the Rhine territories which, they maintained, were irrevocably hers by the principle of self-determination—terms, as the *Dial* put it, that would show the peace to be "the child of President Wilson's idealism" and make Germany "eager to adopt and defend the faith." Bliss warned Wilson that terms must be offered "which a responsible Government in Germany can expect to be able to carry out" and asked "why Germany, if she accepts the terms we consider just and fair, should not be admitted to the League of Nations." But Clemenceau demanded both ironclad security and a measure of retribution. Where Wilson offered the paper security of the Covenant and a guarantee to station Allied troops along the border to protect France until peace was firmly established, Clemenceau held out for a more binding military pact and the crippling of Germany militarily and economically along the Rhine frontier. The result was a critical stalemate, with Clemenceau holding the upper hand this time.[9]

Bliss wrote home dejectedly on the same day of his memorandum to Wilson, "Things here seem to grow blacker and blacker every day. . . . I don't wonder that the world is going Bolshevik. It is the last despairing cry of people who have lost all faith in their government." Interpreter Bonsal penciled in his diary on 1 April that the conference was in the doldrums. "Our delegates are whistling for wind from a favorable quarter, or merely to keep up their courage." Wilson had clearly lost command, and it was as evident across the seas as in the council chamber. Reinhold Niebuhr, five years out of theological seminary and practicing the Social Gospel in a Detroit ministry, followed the proceedings attentively from his faraway perch. He entered in his notebook that Wilson was losing his battle. "He would have done better to stay at home and throw bolts from Olympus. . . . What seems to be happening at Paris is that they will let Wilson label the transaction if the others can determine its true import. Thus realities are exchanged for words."[10] The President himself was so disgusted and helpless before Clemenceau's intransigence that on 7 April he summoned the *George Washington*, docked in New York, to sail for Brest and take him home.[11]

Finally, on 9 April, "the Tiger" relented, and the famous "German accord" was reached: Clemenceau would surrender the Saar Valley to a plebiscite; Wilson would accede to his reparations proposal and demand for an Anglo-American security pact.* Once again, Wilson had been backed into a corner and forced to participate in the maneuvering native to European diplomacy but anathema to the squeamish liberal mind. Bonsal offered a realistic and sympathetic appraisal of the President's predicament. "The President must realize today that he has lost the ideal peace he dreamed of. What should he do? Wash his hands of the whole matter and go home? In this case there would be no treaty, . . . the predatory powers would pitch in and take what they want, and the democracies we thought to help . . . would be despoiled." "Or," Bonsal continued, "should the President consent to a treaty that will reveal some compromises in principle but at least one that will contain the Covenant," a source of hope and guidance in the troubled times ahead? Bonsal showed Colonel House an excerpt from a Gladstone speech which the colonel promised to give to Wilson: "Men ought not to suffer from disenchantment; they ought to know that ideals in politics are never realized."[12]

House and Wilson perhaps could be heartened by such generous sentiments, but not the majority of liberals who had treated the German settlement as the final test of Wilson's mettle. Down to the eighth of April Wilson had at least held the "new order" line,[13] however tenuously, but the critical concessions of the ninth and of the following week they found intolerable. New crises developed over the Fiume and Shantung issues that added to the liberal choler, as did expanding Allied operations in Siberia,[14] but it was the resolution of the German question that signaled the breaking point. Anticipating the outcome, Oswald Villard had already sailed home on 4 April to launch personally the *Nation's* attack. Marshaling all his fury, Villard wrote the first systematic indictment of the peace conference for the 26 April issue. "It has, of course, been everything but a peace *conference*," he railed. "So far as the word is concerned, it is a palpable fraud upon the world. A small executive committee, first of ten men, then of five, then of four, has been parcelling out the globe in sessions so secret that their closest associates, the members of their own delegations, have not known what was going on." "A democratic peace," he concluded, "it can never be; a lasting peace it can be only if heaven shows an unexampled favor. . . . The struggle is ending at Paris with bitterness and hatred as well as with colossal hypocrisy."[15]

Back in Europe, Whitlock noted sadly, "The President's excursion into European diplomacy has been rather disastrous." George Her-

*A record of the French claims, the Wilsonian reaction, and the "dark period" of negotiations and eventual compromise is in Baker, *Woodrow Wilson and World Settlement*, v. 2, pt. 5.

ron, one of Wilson's diplomatic agents, predicted confidentially to Upton Sinclair, "There will be a period of complete chaos in Europe for a time, during which the old regime will come back into power in Germany, and Germany, or at least Prussia, as the only centre of order, will proceed to reorganize Europe and to Germanize it at the same time." Charles Seymour hurried off to a performance of *Faust*, stopping to write that "what remains to be done in the peace settlement will have to be done by the few big men at the top, and I think they may want us out of the way in order not to embarrass them by obtruding our consciences when they feel it necessary to make a deal." Alone in a Paris hotel James Shotwell pondered the events of a particularly trying day. Toward midnight he looked out over the roof of the Crillon and saw against the sky the dark figure of a sentry, walking back and forth with his gun on his shoulder. "It gave a queer sense of a beleaguered city, in the midst of the unsettled social forces of Europe today," he jotted in his diary. As if cued by Villard, he finished reading *The Friendly Road* and on the evening of 3 May opened a book entitled *A Far Journey*.[16]

The drama was played to its conclusion. On 7 May the Germans were presented with a draft of the treaty and given two weeks to review it. The interlude provided a timely opportunity for final accounting. In an address before the International Law Society delivered at Paris on 9 May, Wilson confessed disappointment, admitted some failure, and asked for yet more patience. Unrelenting, liberals filed their verdicts with a coroner's finality. Harold Nicolson's diary became a stiffening chronicle of embitterment. Of the Austrian settlement, which was begun while the Germans inspected the treaty, Nicolson recorded cynically that Hungary was partitioned while the water sprinkled on the lilacs outside, Balfour slept, and Lansing drew hobgoblins on his writing pad. "They began with Transylvania, and after some insults flung like tennis balls between Tardieu and Lansing, Hungary loses her South. Then Czecho-Slovakia, and while the flies drone in and out of the open windows Hungary loses her North and East. Then the frontier with Austria. . . . Then the Jugo-Slav frontier. . . . Then tea and macaroons." Nicolson's compatriot, John Maynard Keynes, wrote his mother on 14 May that he was "utterly worn out, partly by work, partly by depression at the evil around me. I've never been so miserable as for the last two or three weeks; the peace is outrageous and impossible and can bring nothing but misfortune behind it." Keynes resigned three weeks later. Several of the young Americans submitted letters of resignation to Lansing, although, with the exception of William Bullitt, they were persuaded to withdraw them.[17]

The story behind Bullitt's resignation is an instructive one in its illumination of the truly tragic aspects of the Paris conference. Twenty-eight, eager, and impressionable, Bullitt exemplified the adventurous breed at Paris and throughout Europe and America that was ripe for disillusionment. He had reported the war for the Philadelphia *Public Ledger* before joining the State Department in 1917. At Paris he was assigned to the post of intelligence chief, functioning as a sort of "clearing house of information" for the American delegation. He performed his duties patiently, and before long gained an opportunity to do more constructive work. On 22 February, accompanied by veteran muckraker Steffens and Captain Walter Pettit, an army intelligence officer, he was sent secretly to Moscow to determine the Russian position on the matter of rapprochement and incorporation into the new European order—an attempt, initiated by Colonel House and Lloyd George and unbeknownst to the French, to revive the stillborn Prinkipo parley. Elated by his good fortune and thrilled with a sense of mission, Bullitt made his way along the Arctic Circle, according to Steffens, the two of them like rollicking bear cubs. Upon reaching Moscow, both he and Steffens were favorably impressed with the enthusiasm of the Russian people and, after a conference with Lenin, with the good intentions of the Russian leaders. After obtaining certain promises, he returned with his group to Paris in late March, confident that his recommendations would be acted upon with dispatch and secure in the belief that he had made an eminent contribution to the cause of peace. But in the muddle of persistent anti-Bolshevik sentiment and preoccupation with the German question, Bullitt's report was ignored; when he pleaded for attention, Wilson refused to see him, and Lloyd George, in order to avoid political embarrassment, denied authorization or even knowledge of the mission. Weeks went by, the whole affair was eventually forgotten, and Bullitt was left ignominiously in the cold—a tragic victim of the intrigue and subtleties of high politics.

On 17 May, "writing and packing bags at the same time, in a white heat of indignation," Bullitt drew up his letter of resignation. It was addressed to Wilson, and it spoke for all the others of his generation who felt they had been victimized at Paris. "I was one of the millions who trusted confidently and implicitly in your leadership and believed that you would take nothing less than 'a permanent peace,' " he wrote the President. "But our Government has consented now to deliver the suffering peoples of the world to new oppressions, subjections, and dismemberments—a new century of war." "I am sorry," he said, "that you did not fight our fight to the finish and that you had so little faith in the millions of men, like myself, in every nation who had faith in you."[18]

Bullitt departed Paris a polestar. On the same day that he tendered his resignation, the *New Republic* completed its own grudging surrender, asking plaintively on its 17 May cover, "Is it Peace?" The *Dial*, which had followed the proceedings with much the same guarded optimism as the *New Republic*, flatly stated that the peace was lost, and suggested "the proper mood for the reception of President Wilson on his return be that of the old Puritan day of fasting, humiliation, and prayer." The *Nation*, its verdict already in, had anticipated a "rigorous" peace but not one "of undisguised vengeance . . . which openly flouts some of the plainest dictates of reason and humanity . . . , flies in the face of accepted principles of law and economics, and makes the very name of democracy a reproach." "In the whole history of diplomacy," the *Nation* bellowed, "there is no treaty more properly to be regarded as an international crime."[19]

The Germans presented their own case against the treaty on 29 May. On 30 May General Jan Smuts, who worked with Wilson and Lord Cecil on the League covenant, sent a desperate letter to Wilson that reiterated the German contentions, and poignantly expressed the conviction that solemn obligations and trusts had been betrayed and that "there will be a terrible disillusion if the peoples come to think that we are not concluding a Wilson peace, that we are not keeping our promises to the world or faith with the public." It was all to no avail. The terms remained fixed. Smuts's letter, with the petitions of Bliss and Bullitt and the countless other recordings of anxiety, vexation, and regret, littered the field of Paris like the flotsam of a great shipwreck. "I ought to let you know," Keynes wrote Lloyd George on 5 June, "that on Saturday I am slipping away from this scene of nightmare. I can do no more good here. I've gone on hoping even through these last dreadful weeks that you'd find some way to make of the Treaty a just and expedient document. But now it's apparently too late. The battle is lost." "If I ever had any illusions," Bliss wrote home, "they are all dispelled."[20]

On 28 June an imposing curtain slowly descended upon the stage of the peace conference. In the Hall of Mirrors in the Palace at Versailles the principal characters assembled for the finale: the Germans were ready to sign. So scarce were tickets for the historic performance that only sixty-seven members of the American delegation were permitted to attend. A vacancy was created when Steffens, offered one of the precious invitations, declined, explaining apologetically that he "had to take a bath at that very hour." Herbert Hoover was present, but had difficulty keeping his mind on the events. "It was constantly traveling along the fearful consequences of many paragraphs which these men were signing with such pomp, and then it moved back to the high hopes with which I had landed in Europe eight months before." Colonel House watched the ceremony and sympathized with the Germans "who sat there quite stoically." "It was," House observed, "not unlike what was done in olden times, when the conqueror dragged the conquered at his chariot wheels." Even "the Tiger," Clemenceau, was mellow. His parting remark to Hoover was that "there will be another world war in your time and you will be needed back in Europe."[21]

For the prewar liberals who had taken in the "dumb show" in 1914, witnessed the foundering of the great crusade in 1917, and now experienced an abortive six months of peacemaking, the signing at Versailles constituted a final symbolic act. "The disillusionment is complete," tolled the socialist journal *Humanité*. That evening, in the Hotel Majestic, Harold Nicolson closed his diary: "Celebrations in the hotel afterwards. We are given free champagne at the expense of the taxpayer. It is very bad champagne. Go out on to the boulevards afterwards. . . . To bed, sick of life."[22]

8 REFLECTIONS

THE WAR AS A WATERSHED

A small book appeared in 1922, entitled simply *Disenchantment*, which captured perfectly the sense of utter futility that gripped liberals on both sides of the Atlantic following the peace. "So we had failed—had won the fight and lost the prize," wrote its English author. "The garland of the war was withered before it was gained. . . . There had been that illogical hope . . . that could move mountains in 1914 and seems to be scarcely able to shift an ant-hill to-day." Everywhere one looked, idealism was in hasty retreat. The Fourteen Points lay either spoiled or in limbo. Europeans busily staged a fresh round of aggressions over the remains of the Hapsburg and Ottoman empires. The newly formed nations, presumably the sole vestiges of a Wilsonian peace, were themselves engaged in aggressive, illiberal activities, moving General Bliss to remark, "The child-nations that we are creating have fangs and claws in their very cradles and before they can walk are screaming for knives to cut the throats of those in the neighboring cradles."[1] There was no new order, no elevation of the human spirit, no expanded public control or responsibility, no perceptible increase in social cooperation or class harmony or humanitarianism. All of the Olympian ideals had spilled into the gutter of normalcy.

With few exceptions, liberals recognized the entrenchment of the old order. Ray Stannard Baker observed that during the winter of 1918–1919 Italians had named cities and squares after Woodrow Wilson and four months later were taking down the signs and renaming them after Fiume or D'Annunzio, the poet-patriot. Bullitt acknowledged the durability of the old politics in a review of Keynes's *The Economic Consequences of the Peace*. The blockade of Soviet Russia would be lifted, he believed, but only "because Europe needs Russia's wheat and flax, not because the Governments sympathize with the suffering Russian people." Peace would be made with the Russians "not because of any liberal tolerance or love of peace among the Governments, but because the Soviet Government will not fall, and finally because Mr. Lloyd George will become more afraid of the Red Army and the British Labour Party than of Lord Northcliffe and the

Tory majority in the House of Commons." Back home in Kansas, William Allen White could tell Republican National Chairman Will Hays in August 1919 that the country wanted a man with vision to follow up the treaty and would never elect a Lodge or a Harding. But a year later, with the nominations of Harding and Cox and with the "solemn referendum" shaping up unavoidably as a vote for isolation, White was so low he "wouldn't laugh at Charlie Chaplin throwing a custard pie at Cox or Harding or both."[2]

In America especially, the illusions that were dimmed by the wartime experience and extinguished at Paris were buried in the return to normalcy. Robert Herrick wrote in the *Nation* in December 1921 that "three years after the bloodiest conflict known to mankind, the greatest convulsion humanly and socially the world has ever experienced . . . one may buy almost any magazine or book on the stalls, and except for an occasional remote allusion . . . it is impossible to guess that anything momentous has happened to the world, to life itself since 1914." Liberals who had viewed the war as a golden opportunity for social reorganization and "democratic collectivism" watched helplessly as the reform engines were dismantled. Tentative plans for public housing and social insurance were summarily scrapped. Gains made by women, labor, and the young proved ephemeral. The cornucopia of new agencies was swallowed up by apathy and retrenchment. "By 1920," writes Allen Davis, "there was little left from wartime social reform except prohibition, immigration restriction and racist hysteria."[3]

Those liberals who wanted to carry on the banner found their audience lost to prizefights, miniature golf, crossword puzzles, and confession magazines. The *New Republic* lapsed into a circulation decline that would plunge its readership from a wartime high of 37,000 to a low of 12,000 a decade later. Villard tried to keep his *Nation* focused on public concerns, but young staff members like Mark Van Doren, Joseph Wood Krutch, and Freda Kirchwey spurned the reformer's beat for private digressions into art, poetry, and cultural politics. The disregard for serious matters and reckless pursuit of personal whims and amusements prompted one commentator to compare the aftermath of war with the aftermath of the Black Death.[4]

The postwar years would only widen the gulf between ideals and reality and increase the anonymity of earnest men. Walter Weyl had foreseen their predicament in his "Tired Radicals" essay when he wrote that those who "aspired to overturn Society" would end by "fighting in a dull Board of Directors of a village library for the inclusion of certain books." Malcolm Cowley shuddered at the thought of Carl Sandburg "traveling around the country with his guitar, a great poet hired as an entertainer for business men's luncheon clubs." By

1925 William Allen White would be beside himself with frustration: "God, how I would like to get out and raise hell for righteousness! Instead of which I sit in my office and write unimportant editorials and go to my house and write unimportant books." Brand Whitlock replied to him in a letter from Brussels, "I often feel . . . that I can't write at all any more, that the show is over, and the lights out, and that there remains nothing but the hollow noises of the weary scene-shifters, packing up their tawdry and artificial properties."[5]

The world would never again be so congenial or fertile, and everywhere they sensed their impotence, their obsolescence in a marketplace in which business and pleasure would be patronized more than the craft of social engineering. It was all rather pathetic. The old world was not dead, the new one was powerless to be born.

When liberals looked back on the war experience with the benefit of perspective, when they looked back on the time, in Steffens's phrase, "when we were fixing the world that has since fixed us," they marveled at the vanity of their illusions. Ida Tarbell, who had come to France in January 1919 as a reporter for *Red Cross Magazine*, remembered her brother writing from the States then that "the job the Conference seemed to have set itself was as big as creating the world"; in 1939, she observed "men were not big enough for that, and one was aghast that they felt so equal to it." Lewis Mumford wrote in 1940, "Our actions were sound when we went into the first World War; but our dreams were vain ones; for they were founded on the belief that one single high act would enable us to live happily ever afterward, without further duties, further burdens . . . a childish dream indeed." John Dos Passos allowed, "We easily fell prey to the notion that by a series of revolutions like the Russian the working people of the world could invent out of their own heads a reign of peace and justice. It was an illusion like the quaint illusion the early Christians had that the world would come to an end in the year One Thousand."[6]

Throughout the years 1914–1920, and for that matter for years before that, liberals fell prey to foolish notions and grandiose illusions—about the peace conference, the war, the Russian Revolution, about progressivism and their own "American promise." They consistently overexpected and miscalculated, their illusions seemingly gathering momentum as their plight became more desperate. Initially, they thought war impossible; when war broke out, they were convinced that it would be short; when it became protracted and necessitated American intervention, they rationalized it as a crusade for democracy and a vehicle for social reconstruction; when the crusade degenerated into chauvinism and brute nationalism, they counted on the peace talks to produce a new international order. All along, as Lippmann noticed the trend early in the war, they were "feeding on maps, talking of populations as if they were abstract lumps, and tuning . . . minds to a scale unheard of in history."[7]

When the war was over and the dust had settled into normalcy and the human race had seemed to take a step backward, liberals had to come to grips with their failure. As they plumbed the significance of these years it was natural for them at first to blame the failure on deceptions and betrayals—on bungling diplomats, hypocritical leaders, a misled public, conniving capitalists—rather than on their own erroneous assumptions. Young Reinhold Niebuhr, his German ancestry and priestly vocation permitting him to support the war only after great deliberation, asked himself how he could "ever again believe anything" after comparing "the solemn pretensions of statesmen with the cynically conceived secret treaties." Upton Sinclair, one of Wilson's staunchest backers, wondered how he could have been "trapped into supporting" the war. "I thought that Woodrow Wilson really meant his golden, glowing words," Sinclair winced; "I thought he was in a position to know what I couldn't know, and would take the obvious steps to protect us against diplomatic perfidy. I knew nothing of the pre-war intrigues of the French and Russian statesmen against Germany . . . nothing of the secret treaties which bound the allies." George Herron, who had undertaken several confidential missions for Wilson and met with the same exasperating fate as Bullitt, wrote Sinclair in 1924, "Every passing event between the nations shows me how I was bridled and saddled and ridden to opposite ends from those to which I intended to go. My own good faith was used to accomplish the opposite of what I believed in and worked for. In this the British Government used and betrayed me even more shamefully than the American Government."[8]

Randolph Bourne perceived during the war the confused plight of liberals like Sinclair and Herron who would be abandoned by the captains of government—"like brave passengers who have set out for the Isles of the Blest only to find that the first mate has gone insane and jumped overboard, the rudder has come loose and dropped to the bottom of the sea, and the captain and pilot are lying dead drunk under the wheel." Fred Howe later wrote that, "like children when first punished," they did not understand. Because they had been largely snubbed at Paris, because their program had not been given an attentive enough hearing, because their best brains on the Inquiry staff were reduced to messenger boys (even though, Nicolson noted, "the *George Washington* creaked and groaned across the Atlantic under

the weight of their erudition"), liberals felt they had been betrayed—
not defeated or discredited, but *betrayed*. Thus Harold Stearns in 1919
explained the liberal failure "partly because our leaders were not genuinely liberal in principle . . . partly because the peoples of the world
were duped from beginning to end." The betrayal contention filtered
through Bullitt's letter of resignation, Villard's savage indictment in
the *Nation*, and a spate of postwar editorials which charged "fraud"
and "hoax." It was the source of Bullitt's bitter and spiteful testimony
before the Senate Foreign Relations Committee in September 1919; of
the decision by the *New Republic, Nation*, and *Dial* to advocate categor-
ically the rejection of the treaty even though, Lippmann conceded, it
meant supplying their enemies with ammunition; and of the disillusioned tracts of Fitzgerald's "lost generation." It was the source,
too, for much of the historical revisionism that followed the war and
shifted war guilt to the Allied side. Historians like Harry Elmer
Barnes, who blasted the "melodious rhetoric" and "sordid and selfish
plans of unscrupulous diplomats and foreign ministers," were generally men of tender conscience who had actively promoted the war
effort and who could postpone their own moral accounting by taking
the leaders to task.[9]

The chief villain in the piece, invariably, was Woodrow Wilson.
Wilson became a convenient scapegoat for the fiasco. In his exalted
leadership resided the hopes of all liberals in Paris and at home, and
even in moments of despair there was the trust that somehow he
would deliver. With failure, the leader of the great crusade was un-
masked as a Pied Piper. "His rhetorical phrases," snapped the *Nation*,
"torn and faded tinsel of a thought which men now doubt if he himself ever really believed, will never again fall with hypnotic charm
upon the ears of eager multitudes. The camouflage of ethical precept
and political philosophizing which for long blinded the eyes of all but
the most observing has been stripped away, and the peoples of the
world see revealed, not a friend faithful to the last, but an arrogant
autocrat and a compromising politician." Walter Weyl, five months
before he died, found Wilson to be at once "celestial and subterra-
nean," standing "on the mountain top and in the cellar," surrender-
ing the role of prophet and accepting the lesser role of opportunist
politician. Keynes granted in his famous postwar treatise that Wilson
was "generously intentioned," but added that he was all too ordinary
to be "a hero or a prophet." Max Eastman, who had praised Wilson
in 1918 for his "poise and fluency of mind," wrote a year later that
"he is extremely gullible . . . he has been 'made a fool of.' " The
editors of the *New Republic* admitted dispassionately, "he was not like
Lincoln the finely tempered and thoroughly unified instrument for

the accomplishment of a great human purpose."[10]

In an assortment of evasive postmortems, Weyl blamed Wilson for "maladroitness" and "insincerity"; Stearns blamed Wilsonian liberals for their abandonment of "pragmatic analysis"; David Starr Jordan deplored "the long delay between armistice and peace"; and Villard challenged the decision to go *to war* to achieve the liberal aims.[11] At their worst, liberals vindictively pilloried Wilson and the war rhetoricians; at their best, they argued over matters of timing and strategy. Some bothered to question the wisdom of their methods—their choice of means. But few liberals contested the reasonableness of their *ends*. Few questioned their fundamental assumptions about people and progress. The backbiting served merely to sidestep paramount issues and to postpone a more troublesome reckoning. Christopher Lasch concluded in his study *American Liberals and the Russian Revolution* that after the war there was "no real questioning of basic assumptions, no real loss of illusions." "What they attacked," wrote Lasch, "was not liberalism itself so much as Wilson's 'betrayal' of it. They criticized Wilson for sacrificing his Fourteen Points to Allied greed, but they never criticized the Fourteen Points themselves." "If they became 'disillusioned,' " said Lasch, "it was only because they began to despair that the measures in question would ever be undertaken by the American government, not because they were uncertain as to what the measures themselves would accomplish."[12]

Only as the initial numbness wore off and petty faultfinding gave way to mature judgment did a new awareness slowly emerge. After they had disowned Wilson, liberals reviewed their own role in the crusade. Gradually, they came to realize that Wilson was not the *author* of their hopes but merely the *translator*, and that his shortcomings and failures were also their own. The real culprits at Paris were not "insincerity" or "diplomatic perfidy" or "broken promises," but inflated optimism, overdrawn goals, and the manifest irrationality and self-interest of men and nations. It was not a tragedy of betrayal, but of self-delusion. Ideals were defeated, John Dewey wrote even before the Paris conference, "because we took into the war our sentimentalism, our attachment to moral sentiments as efficacious powers, our pious optimism as to the inevitable victory of the 'right,' our childish belief that physical energy can do the work that only intelligence can do, our evangelical hypocrisy that morals and 'ideals' have a self-propelling and self-executing capacity." Carl Becker wrote a lengthy mea culpa to fellow historian William Dodd in June 1920, in which he confessed that what really irritated him was that he "could have been naive enough to suppose, during the war, that Wilson could ever accomplish those ideal objects." "A man of any intelligence who has been studying history for 25 years," Becker chided himself, "should have known that in this war as in all wars, men would profess to be fighting for justice and liberty, but in the end would demand the spoils of victory if they won." In another letter to Dodd, in February 1923, Becker recanted an earlier criticism of Wilson. "I had had a moment of optimism," he explained, "had experienced a faint hope that Wilson might do as he wished to do. When he failed, I was angry because I had failed to see that he must fail; and took it out on Wilson. But that is all over. . . ." Likewise, General Bliss, for all his disappointment at the outcome of the peace, did not deny Wilson's sincerity or the heroism of his effort. Bliss wrote Mark Sullivan in November 1922 that the President had done what was practical. "If it had been Homer's 'Gods in Council' perhaps it would have been different. But even they had their differences. And Olympian Zeus himself had sometimes to yield."[13]

When Stearns and Villard persisted in blaming the liberal failure on Wilson and on the contingent of liberals who stuck by him, Herbert Croly countered that a more fundamental error was the prewar illusion they *all* shared about the limitless possibilities of progressive change. "When the Great War came," Croly wrote in December 1920, "it revealed with awful emphasis and finality the lack of integrity in the authoritative moral standards of modern civilization." The miscalculation in his own case, said Croly, consisted in falsely assuming that the American people, once engaged in the struggle, would keep their composure. Lippmann, in a review of Stearns's book, expressed admiration for "the conservatives" who were "infinitely more resourceful" and "knew how to go past the fragile reason of men to their passions." "So long as liberalism is content to be above the battle," he wrote six months after the peace conference, "it will be one of the graces of a cultivated gentleman but never a force in actual affairs." Santayana reviewed *Civilization in the United States*, the collaborative work of Stearns, Bullitt, and some thirty other disaffected intellectuals who harped on the betrayal theme. Their intellect, he scoffed, "is shy and feminine; it paints nature in water-colours; whereas the sharp masculine eye sees the world as a moving-picture—rapid, dramatic, vulgar. . . . The spirit of these critics is one of offended sensibility."[14]

Some of the most searching efforts at self-examination were initiated by the famous *Survey* symposium of 1 February 1926, which brought many of the liberals together to discuss what had gone wrong with the great crusade and the defects of their movement in general. Norman Thomas reflected on the prewar reformer's "uncritical faith in the wisdom of political democracy, and the power of moral sentiments." Liberal economist Stuart Chase, who had gone through the reform movement "from settlement house to socialist party," agreed they were "too moral, . . . too sure. They knew little about the realities of production and distribution, and nothing about the springs of human behavior." Ray Stannard Baker said they were just like all the other politicians: "We were more interested in bossing our neighbors into our own little plans for goodness, or efficiency, or justice." "The fact is," sighed Ida Tarbell, "the pre-war radical was often not a wise man—an experienced or patient man. He knew little about human beings, and what as individuals and herds they can be counted on to do under certain circumstances."[15]

Liberals had put their trust in progressivism's too facile environmental and institutional solutions. What they had aspired to do in 1917—democratize the German, internationalize world citizenry, create a League or World Government that would effectively arbitrate differences among federated world states—was no less an ambition than to whitewash the globe and remodel it with a total disregard for the consciousness of history and the realities of power. Repeatedly they made the mistake of operating in a vacuum of ideals. The *New Republic* men, in a rare moment of illumination during the war, explained why they had failed to foresee the outbreak of fighting in the first place:

> We had inadvertently washed the colors out of our maps, and left only geographical boundary lines between the peoples. . . . We persistently thought of democracy, universal suffrage, equal rights, social legislation, as benevolent diseases which were spreading through one after another of the nations of Europe. . . . We studied the forms of social politics in the different countries, scarcely stopping to analyze the motivations which made laws in Baden mean something wholly different from the same laws in France. . . . All the "problems of power," the conflict of national interests, we deprecated as unreal.

Such "unreality" fogged their perception all the way to Versailles. Continually, they insisted that reform was possible on an international scale, that the salvation of the world lay ultimately in the universal extension of democratic politics, and that the peoples of the world, their own countrymen included, would, given a chance, embrace democracy readily and responsibly—the assumption, William Allen White later remarked, that "liberty could be passed around as alms or material benefits."[16]

Undoubtedly, the liberals' most grievous error was their gross overestimation of the human character. From the beginning, as the *Survey* symposium underscored, they had placed an exorbitant hope in people's good sense and good will. Samuel Gompers was convinced back in 1909 that if the "profitmongers" contrived to do battle, "the working people of the countries of the world would stop work simultaneously, if necessary, in order to prevent international war." They had had an almost paranoid concern over the designs of capitalists, kings, ministers, and others in power, but, as is evident in the conclusion to Brand Whitlock's 1913 autobiography, there had been the overriding conviction that "always the people remain, pressing onward in a great stream up the slopes, and always somehow toward the light." During the war it was the people they had counted on to transform the conflict into a struggle for democracy and social justice. A speaker at the Philadelphia convention of the League to Enforce Peace had been certain that after *this* war a new international order would emerge: "The peoples are behind it; and when the peoples are awake, there is no combination of autocratic systems or any other power which can keep them from the complete fulfilment of their aim." Even when the crusade foundered and the people deserted them, they nourished the illusion of a postwar enlightenment. Throughout they ignored the frailty of the human condition even in its most sublime moments. It took an inveterate cynic like Mencken to indicate to Sinclair "the error of overestimating the sense and decency of the actual proletariat." Mencken reminded Sinclair that the soldiers, in most cases, were proletarians, conscripted against their will and forced to fight in a war that few of them could understand. "Well, what did they actually do?" he asked. "They succumbed instantly to the most ridiculous blather, and began raiding and beating up the very men who were trying to save them from another such war."[17]

In the end, as General Smuts realized, it was "not Wilson, but humanity" that failed them. "In the end," conceded Jane Addams, "not only the leaders but the people themselves preferred a bit of booty here, a strategic frontier there, a coal field or an oil well, an addition to their population or their resources—to all the faint allurements of an ideal." Walter Millis, twenty years after the debacle, was moved to reflect on the real lesson of the war experience. "There were greed and bitterness, silly nationalism, paltry personal ambition and plain unwisdom at Paris," Millis said, "and the Treaty of Versailles certainly was not perfect." "But," he added, "for me, and I imagine for a great many of my generation, it was not the Treaty, not anything which happened at Paris, that produced the real disillusion. It was what happened afterward." The statesmen, he said, may have been greedy and unwise, but it was nothing compared to the greed and folly of the people who were to pass upon their work. "It was not simply that the ideal had been betrayed by politicians or sold by evil men; it had been abandoned by the whole society of which we were a part." Not Wilson, but humanity had failed them. This was the heavy revelation that completed their reckoning and crowned their disillusionment.[18]

For the majority of liberals, the years after Versailles were a time of intellectual trial. What the phenomenon of "postwar disillusionment" consisted of precisely—its intensity and the form(s) it took—will be discussed in the epilogue. It is sufficient for now to say that there was a general mood of despondency and/or alienation prevailing throughout the liberal ranks following the war and that this trauma lasted well into the twenties, for many into the thirties, and for some right up until they died in the forties and fifties. Ideals had been the prewar liberals' staple, and with their depletion nothing remained to sustain them. And so it was quite natural for them after the war to grope for some new lifeblood—whether it might be the self-gratification of the business culture, the opiate of cynicism, or the fresh elixir of communism. In any case, whether they emerged as conservatives or cynics or communists, they emerged disillusioned; they emerged divested of a faith or illusion they once had. In Harold Nicolson's words, those once "fervent apprentices in the school of Wilson" appeared to leave Paris as "renegades."[19]

A vital question for this study, and a major problem for historical scholarship, is "To what extent was the First World War truly the source of the liberal disillusionment?" To what extent was it in fact a watershed, the pivotal experience between an earlier period of optimism and the era of disillusion which seemed to follow as a direct issue? Did the liberals become "renegades" only after Paris, or had they in fact been leaning one way or another into apostasy before the war even began?

It has always been tempting for intellectual historians to fasten upon the First World War as a watershed separating the main currents of twentieth-century life and thought. In the case of America, the war seemed to mark a natural divide between progressivism and the lighthearted reformist mentality that preceded the war and the conservative reaction and more tough-minded brand of liberalism that ensued. Historians emphasizing the profound impact of the war have been able to draw upon countless letters and memoirs of men who personally underwent the transition from kindly liberal to crusty conservative (or mild progressive to embittered revolutionary) and who traced their conversion directly to the war experience. Niebuhr wrote in 1928 that the war created his entire world view: "It made me a child of the age of disillusionment. When the war started I was a young man trying to be an optimist without falling into sentimentality. When it ended . . . I had become a realist trying to save myself from cynicism." Speaking for the young intelligentsia—the Bournes, the Eastmans, the Fitzgeralds who had been rebellious but generally exuberant before the war and who surfaced in the twenties as history's "lost generation"— Malcolm Cowley looked back from the vantage point of 1937 and concluded similarly that the war was responsible for their alienation. "Before 1917," Cowley wrote, "the new writers had felt, even though they were rebelling, that they were still in the main current of American life—the world was going in their direction, the new standards were winning out, and America in ten or twenty or fifty years at most would be not only a fatherland of the arts but also a socialist commonwealth. Then suddenly all these aspirations seemed ingenuous and the new generation felt itself to be isolated from society." As late as 1967 Cowley still spoke hauntingly of the "Big Words" which had intoxicated them and then, unfulfilled, left them in emotional and ideological ruins.[20]

Certainly the war provided a convenient hinge on which historians could turn a new chapter and disillusioned liberals could hang their conversion. In revisionist investigations of the late 1950s and 1960s, however, unimpressed students of the period began to minimize the significance of the war and to accent the concept of *continuity* through the prewar, wartime, and postwar years; continuity in "reform," which received the most frequent historiographical treatment,[21] and also continuity in "disillusion." Dismissing memoir accounts like Niebuhr's and Cowley's as myopic or embellished, they found the "great disillusionment" to be a much broader, more sustained phenomenon with roots at least as far back as 1910 and, some contended, in the industrial and technological upheavals of the 1870s and 1880s.

In two seminal works of the 1940s, Lloyd Morris and Max Lerner suggested for the first time that the disillusionment ran deeper than a simplistic "war" explanation, Morris citing the fundamental, ongoing disparity between "culture" and "society."[22] In the next two decades the influential studies of Eric F. Goldman (*Rendezvous With Destiny,* 1952), David W. Noble (*The Paradox of Progressive Thought,* 1958), Charles Forcey (*The Crossroads of Liberalism,* 1961) and Arthur S. Link (in his multivolume history of Wilson and progressivism) virtually ritualized the "continuity" interpretation. These historians explained the liberal collapse in terms of internal intellectual and political factors which, they argued, were operative *before* the war: a flagging Wilsonianism, a demoralizing turn to conservatism in both popular and official thinking, the achievement of many of the progressives' goals and subsequently a willingness to retire or surrender on the remaining issues, and a preoccupation with means and techniques at the expense of ends and values (Goldman's concept of "moral relativism") which, they maintained, vitiated liberalism's purpose and certainty.

Henry May and Christopher Lasch were foremost among those who applied the continuity thesis to the artists and writers and more radical elements of the prewar liberalism, the alleged rebels and debunkers of the twenties. Their argument was, essentially, that the alienations and disillusions customarily associated with the postwar period were apparent before the war, more so than Cowley would admit, in the conflict between the cultural custodians of the genteel tradition and cultural liberationists such as Bourne and Ezra Pound. Lasch insisted in *The New Radicalism in America, 1889–1963* (1965) that the so-called tired radicals, although they recorded a literature of disenchantment in the twenties, were estranged from American society years before when it had already turned oppressively impersonalized and materialistic. Even a relative oldster like Lincoln Steffens, Lasch wrote, by 1910 "was already well advanced toward 'disillusionment.' " In a similar vein, Henry Dan Piper noted that between 1910 and the outbreak of the war, Fitzgerald at Princeton, Bourne at Columbia, Reed and Dos Passos at Harvard had already formed a "cult of disillusion." Larzer Ziff discovered a "lost generation" in the 1890s unable to cope with a surging industrialization and materialism. The "continuity" interpretation suggested that for young and old alike the war was no watershed between innocence and rebellion.[23]

In 1959, speculation over "the end of American innocence" framed the title of an important work by Henry May that remains perhaps the best expression of the continuity thesis. May stated the thesis succinctly in an earlier article. "It is obvious that America's first major venture into world tragedy, with its rapid cycle of national exaltation, exhaustion, and revulsion played a very large part in the emotional life of the postwar rebels," May wrote. "[Yet] the period 1912–1917 was itself, for some, a time of doubt and fragmentation, of upheaval in ideas, of the disintegration of tradition. . . . Nearly every phenomenon of the twenties from Freudianism to expatriation or the abandonment of politics was present before the war." May went on to elaborate in his fuller study that Freudianism was popular in the salons as early as 1913, that the disillusioned tracts of the twenties had prototypes in both theme and technique in the prewar outpourings of Eliot and Pound, that the cynicism and political indifference of the twenties had their antecedent in the irrationalists' prewar attacks on both progressivism and socialism, that free love, jazz, and drug consumption were practiced in Greenwich Village a decade before the war, and that the various "movements" of the twenties were all preceded by manifestoes of 1910–1917. May was supported by a wealth of evidence in both primary and secondary sources. In his encyclopedic social history of the Americans, J. C. Furnas noted that cigarette consumption, one of the many mischiefs thought to be the legacy of the war, had increased by 500 percent between 1900 and 1914. Thomas Beer, writing in 1930, stated bluntly that "at least two of the naked mixed swimming parties since so much used in moral films . . . took place in a private pool near St. Louis before 1911. The most alcoholized dance I have ever seen among polite people occurred in 1912. To get very practical and flat, it is a matter of official record that more than a half of the senior boys in a big midland high school habitually carried contraceptuals in 1911."[24]

What sort of conclusions, then, can be drawn from these diverging interpretations? What of the implicit assumption of this study that the prewar years were indeed years of innocence and illusion and that the war—like a "baleful meteor from outer space," in Mumford's phrase—introduced fresh tensions, brought into play new forces, and provoked unprecedented agonizing and disillusionment? Several deductions can be made.

1. The phrase "postwar disillusionment" is misleading. Trite and uncomplicated, it causes one to overlook the subtle but authentic currents of disillusionment that existed in American society in the decade (and decades) preceding the war. Although for most liberal reformers and intellectuals the prewar years were a time of unparalleled hope and confidence, there were, among others, visible traces of depression, disaffection, and fatigue brought on by an increasingly hostile environment. Fitzgerald's letters to his mother, the early expatriations of Pound and Gertrude Stein, before that the troubled confessions of Henry Adams and naturalistic novels of Dreiser, Crane, and Norris provide ample testimony to the span of the disillusionment. Nor was the prewar anomie limited to the *enfants terribles*, the younger cultural rebels. It touched Steffens, as Lasch has shown, and it touched such staunch progressive faithfuls as Walter Lippmann and Carl Becker. Lippmann at one time was a classic example of the watershed impact of war in converting a liberal, optimistic mind to cynicism, but Heinz Eulau demonstrated how his "journey from conviction" began as early as 1912 and how his postwar emergence as cynic and antidemocrat was foreshadowed in his prewar writings. Becker, the presumed progressive-turned-relativist in the twenties, also had his pessimistic moments before the war.[25]

2. If the war was no absolute watershed between illusion and disil-

lusion, between innocence and rebellion, it most certainly was a crucial event. For many unquestioning prewar optimists, for Pollyannas
like Whitlock and William Allen White, the war experience was no
less than a revelation—*the* source of their disillusionment. For others
like Steffens, Lippmann, and the young radicals whose progressive
faith was flickering before 1917 the war perhaps did not have so shattering an effect, but it was nonetheless a major episode in their intellectual trials. However anxious or alienated they had been prior to
1917, the American intervention and crusade for democracy offered a
momentary hope that spiritual values were not exhausted; the disap-
pointing outcome clinched their disillusionment. Allen Davis has
written that discouraged progressives were "rescued by the excitement of the wartime social experiments," then irrevocably demoralized by the liberal collapse. Even May, although he disputed its
watershed significance, acknowledged the powerful effect the war
had on the young radicals. "The war . . . was not the cause of the
cultural revolution of the twenties," he said. "It played, however, the
immense part that the Civil War played in the economic and political
revolution of the mid-nineteenth century, speeding, widening and al-
tering in kind a movement already under way. The experiences of
1917–19 darkened and soured the mood of the rebels. . . . Many who
had been rebellious optimists became despairing nihilists and those
who had already been preaching the futility of conscious effort
preached it with different emotional corollaries."[26]

The case of Steffens is instructive here. Lasch dwells on his prewar
disillusion—on his unmitigated contempt before 1914 for municipal
politics, capitalism, and American democracy. His *Shame of the Cities*
and several letters to friends do reflect a simmering strain of cynicism
in the prewar years, but elsewhere before the war Steffens displayed
an almost transcendent faith, if not in human intelligence then in the
basic goodness of human intentions. Another rendering of Steffens's
letters suggests that Lasch underestimated his prewar optimism; that
although Steffens was skeptical of "cures" he was still a confirmed
believer in democratic progress. He wrote Theodore Roosevelt in June
1908 that he did not think representative government would correct
all evils. "I do think, however," he added, "that fighting for it, consciously, will uncover not only the principal evils, but their common
source, and that when we see that, we shall make . . . intelligent
progress." About a year later, he consoled Tom Johnson, the reform
mayor voted out by the people of Cleveland:

> You and I used to agree upon one article in the creed of a demo-
> crat: we believed in the people. The people of Cleveland may
> have shaken your faith. I doubt it. They may have made you sick,

as they have me. But they have not disturbed my confidence that in the long run the people will go right more surely than any individuals or set of individuals. I believe, for example, that they will re-elect you at the next election.

As late as June 1914, he wrote John Reed in a burst of progressive enthusiasm that Wilson was "doing, doing, doing, and it is really wonderful what he is getting done. . . . The conviction he is spreading that good and beautiful ideas and ideals work" is his biggest achievement. "His inspiration," said Steffens, "is not enough stated. He doesn't talk enough."

When the war came Steffens was too sophisticated to become "a patriot" and followed the crusade with clinical detachment, but in his letters and even his autobiography, when one filters through the sarcasm one intuits that Steffens did have a subliminal faith in Wilson and a lingering measure of illusion. His hope was that the people would stop "feeling" and start "thinking," and he seemed to believe a liberal peace was possible if Wilson could somehow educate the people and beat down the imperialists. As the peace conference approached and the prospect for a liberal peace faded, however, he gave up on "the system," as he liked to call it, and became convinced that progressivism was bankrupt after all. The mission to Moscow with Bullitt impressed him greatly, and he wrote to the wife of Fred Howe his famous line which he would repeat many times afterward, "I have seen the future; and it works." Thus did Lincoln Steffens become a communist. As with so many others who had been drifting away from the mainstream of American liberalism before 1914, it was the war experience that marked the final break. His prewar disillusion notwithstanding, it was the war experience that resolved Steffens's skepticism and permanently estranged him.[27]

3. In the final analysis, one concludes that the war was a pivotal event because liberals *made* it a pivotal event. The *New Republic* unabashedly titled an editorial "The Pivot of History." and predicted prior to the peace conference, "For a century all history will pivot upon the great war. . . . The French Revolution ushered in a new era. The European Revolution now under way is ushering in a new world." Newton Baker told an audience in December 1917, "The new date line of this central and pivotal event in the history of the human race will have made memories of a lot of things which have been prejudices heretofore."[28] The war arrived at a singularly impressionable juncture in the nation's history, in the infancy of America's international experience and in the prime of her domestic progressive experience, and so it captured men's imaginations and riveted their minds with an extraordinary sense of expectation—whatever their

prewar misgivings or alienations. Pragmatists like Dewey envisaged the war revolutionizing social organization. Liberal economists like Weyl expected that it would tear down barriers to world trade. Internationalists like Nicholas Murray Butler were prepared to witness the dissolution of the old balance of power and the triumph of a new politics and diplomacy (in 1916, Butler had interpreted the war as a climactic "catharsis"). Socialists like Sinclair and Herron anticipated a sweeping away of privileged institutions. Young romantics like Dos Passos and Cowley regarded the struggle as a supreme adventure and an almost mystical initiation into manhood. Even pacifists like Jordan and Gompers were captivated by the prospect of a "war to end war."

For all of them, the war was a traumatic experience because they attached to it an epic significance, because it became for them an intensely personal affair which placed them squarely at the crossroads between an uncertain past and a summoning future. They counted on the war to resolve certain critical questions—about themselves, about society, about the course of human history—and so whether they looked to it to confirm nagging suspicions or fulfill drawing-board aspirations they shared a tremendous emotional, in some instances professional stake in its outcome. For the prewar skeptics, the war was an acid test; for the optimists, it was a baptism of fire. For all of them it was an ordeal.

Whatever the long-term dynamics of the liberal disillusionment, then, whether one argues that the disillusionment had its source in the war itself or in the longer span of 1910–1917 or in the 1890s (indeed, May's innocence-rebellion concept can be carried back as far as the Jacksonian period with its incipient industrialization and accompanying loss of innocence), there is no denying that the First World War was a pivotal event. If it did not hatch the disillusionment, it nourished and diffused it. If it did not create liberalism's tensions and dilemmas, it intensified them and in the end resolved them with sledgehammer finality.

The "journeys" of the twenties and thirties—the expatriations, the conversions to cynicism or communism, the withdrawals into private life or the business culture—may have had their beginnings before the war, but it was the convulsing experience at Armageddon and at Paris that launched them for good. Whitlock wrote to Steffens from Brussels in February 1919, "As you say, we have all been changed with this war. No human being, and certainly no intelligent human being, could go through it without having been changed in many particulars, and lucky are those who have not been changed by it for the worse." Steffens himself wrote to his sister and brother-in-law from a seaside resort three hours outside Paris and four weeks after the signing at Versailles. "My old tentative theories didn't stand up under the crisis of the war," he said. "Unexpected facts have come up to tear holes in them." Other prevailing philosophies, "the practical man's and the socialist's and the pacifist's, have all gone down more or less with mine. We must think it all out again in the new light."[29]

9 EPILOGUE

JOURNEYS TO
AND FROM CONVICTION

Popularizing historians and indulgent memoirists have peopled the postwar stage with a cast of wooden figures—babbitts, bohemians, cynics, debunkers, escapists, "lost generation" youth—all in one way or another products of an overwhelming disillusionment of cosmic proportions. In fact, the "great disillusionment" was a far more subtle phenomenon. It was not all-pervasive in the sense that it touched everyone, nor did it irrevocably alter the spirit or philosophy of all those it did touch. Soulful biographers such as Cowley and jilted idealists like Bullitt no doubt exaggerated the postwar malaise out of remorse or rage. Few of the young artists or writers were as "lost" as Fitzgerald and the band of expatriates made them out to be. Of the prewar progressives, one of their own number wrote in 1926, they "are not all gone any more than the pre-war Scotch—though both are much diminished."[1]

What, then, *was* the extent of the postwar disillusionment? As with all intellectual currents, disillusionment is a difficult matter to calibrate—especially in the frenetic twenties, when reformers dropped in and out of movements like horse players, hitching on to new causes as they were repenting old ones. The *Survey* symposium of 1926 furnished an updated profile of the "pre-war radicals"* at a time when the disillusionment should have been fairly well distilled, but the responses of a wide range of contributors revealed considerable disagreement as to whether their ranks were depleted, reinforced, or holding steady. Some insisted that disillusionment claimed virtually all of the prewar group. Basil Manly, director of the People's Legislative Service and a member of the War Labor Board, wrote that "the

---

*The question "Where are the pre-war radicals?" was posed by Fred Howe in his 1925 autobiography, and instantly attracted the attention of fellow reformers. The *Survey* offered them a forum in its issue of 1 February 1926. By "radicals," Howe was referring to the prewar "movers and shakers," whether they be progressives like himself or younger, more insurgent types like Eastman and Bullitt.

radicals of ten years ago have for the most part gone to seed. Only a few hardy perennials remain." Norman Thomas, confirming Weyl's glum prophecy, found the old reformer a "Tired Radical," drinking with his sons and daughters at the fountain of Mencken's *American Mercury*. Stuart Chase delivered a coroner's report, proposing that a wreath be placed on the "Uplift Movement." "The avowed Socialists," Chase moaned, could fill "a roomy new house, the muckrakers have joined the breadlines, . . . Mr. Eastman writes triolets in France, Mr. Steffens has bought a castle in Italy, and Mr. Howe digs turnips in Nantucket." Others took exception to Chase's obituary and insisted that the "tired radicals" were still circulating, still gainfully employed, and as determined as ever. "Roger Baldwin never sleeps in his work for old-fashioned Jeffersonian freedom," Norman Hapgood noted. "Victor Berger is in Congress and is trying to have Russia recognized. I do not know that Ray Stannard Baker was ever any better employed than now that he is in large part studying other sources of progress than political ones." Seconding Hapgood, Benjamin Marsh, secretary of the People's Reconstruction League, traveled the country and concluded "the real radicals are not exterminated nor dead. They are working as hard as ever and there are more of them than ever." In Ida Tarbell's judgment, the group was not seriously depleted, "and if less vociferous still in their own way useful." Most of the contributors hedged. Charlotte Perkins Gilman suggested they were still at large, but with rigor mortis setting in. Journalist and publisher John S. Phillips detected some of them "modified by money or natural ambitions," some "fallen by the wayside through love or marriage," and a hardy few yet singing the old tunes, but in "meager chorus" and "quavering voices, . . . an unnoticed droning to the elders and a discord to the young."[2]

The *Survey* symposium's mixed reflections on the course of liberalism in the twenties indicates the vagueness and complexity of the phenomenon of postwar disillusion. The prewar "radicals," to use the *Survey*'s term, encompassed old-stock progressives like Croly and Whitlock, pragmatic liberals like Dewey and Lippmann, older radicals like Steffens and Sinclair, younger ones like Eastman and Bullitt, and cultural radicals like Dos Passos and Fitzgerald. Because of differences in age, temperament, and slant of commitment, all did not follow the same intellectual trail after the war, just as they had not before the war. The nature of disillusionment, like the nature of the prewar "illusionment," differed appreciably from one group to another. To be sure, for all of them the postwar years were a time of profound reckoning—as Whitlock and Steffens wrote after Versailles, they *all* had to think it out again in the new light—but such soulsearching did not lead in every case to disillusion, or to the same degree or pattern of disillusion. Herbert Croly, Walter Lippmann, Lincoln Steffens, F. Scott Fitzgerald were all victims of disïlusionment, but each in a different way. Some of the prewar radicals changed hardly at all in the twenties; others recoiled into conservatism or became retiring cynics; still others proceeded leftward on the reform spectrum and became revolutionaries. It followed that, depending upon which "prewar radicals" one was talking about, the twenties could appear as a treadmill of continuing reform efforts, a graveyard of radical demise, or a seedbed of resurgent radical activity. Thus, in the same 1926 survey, Basil Manly could speak of the prewar radicals "going to seed" and Benjamin Marsh could say that there were "more of them than ever."

The disillusionment, then, was a very relative, highly personalized experience, and its extent and precise nature must be analyzed in this context. Although it is futile for this reason to attempt any definitive classification, it is possible to isolate three general routes taken by prewar liberals in the years following Versailles.

The first tendency was, quite simply, no disillusionment at all. A number of liberals, possessed with indomitable faith, a gift for endless rationalization, or immense ego, persevered in the same flabby convictions and hopes that characterized the prewar spirit. Refusing to concede a thing to the Jeremiahs, they proceeded through the remainder of their careers with the same crusading fervor that they had brought to progressivism and the war effort. Mostly they included diehard optimists like Jane Addams, wistful socialists like Charles Edward Russell, and bullheaded types like Oswald Villard, but there were also more reflective individuals such as John Dewey. For all of them, the war posed few challenges to their cherished assumptions about democracy and progress. Except for an occasional concession, they managed to dismiss or outwit the arguments of disillusioned liberals that their estimations of people and progress were inflated; in any case they remained vigorously active in both the reform and internationalist movements of the postwar years.

The second tendency represented essentially a "journey from conviction." Arthur Schlesinger, Jr., used the term to describe Walter Lippmann's course in the twenties.[3] Lippmann is perhaps the most obvious example, but there were many others who took this route, some of them on a vacation from the exhausting pursuit of ideals, others on a pilgrimage back to their fathers' more conservative faith, still others on a nomadic, never-ending path of meditation and soul-searching. Whether they wound up, as Lippmann did, behind the desk of a venerable newspaper, or in some secluded country village, or in the anonymity of the business culture, they all eventually confessed a loss of faith in that "promise of American life" in which they believed so staunchly in 1914. Their liberal philosophy could not survive the wartime brutality and hysteria, and when the perversion of liberal principles at Versailles compounded their disillusionment, they shunned the crusading causes of the twenties and embarked on their journeys from conviction. They were the type Basil Manly said had "gone to seed."

A third group of prewar liberals, by contrast, undertook what might be called "journeys *toward* conviction." These included rebellious members of the younger intelligentsia such as Eastman and Floyd Dell, Cowley and Dos Passos (and probably Randolph Bourne, had he lived into the twenties), as well as a handful of grizzled muckrakers like Steffens who had soured on progressivism very early. This group had been disenchanted with the American system and the quality of American life *before* the war, and although they shared abundantly in the illusoriness of those prewar years, theirs were the illusions of a brave new world far more exhilarating than the middle-class utopia of Croly's American promise. When the war confirmed the rottenness of the system and heightened their disenchantment with American society (Christopher Lasch says they experienced a "second disillusion"), their course in the twenties became one of further estrangement—journeys *toward* conviction. They characteristically moved leftward on the political spectrum into expatriation, revolutionary exile, or communism, most of them to suffer yet another disillusionment in the thirties with the betrayal of Marxism.

There were, then, three major routes traveled by the prewar liberals—three major patterns or syndromes of disillusionment. Historians charting the intellectual direction of the twenties have generally emphasized one tendency at the neglect of the others. Thus Clarke Chambers in *Seedtime of Reform* has chronicled the resumption of reform in the twenties (understating the disillusionment), Arthur Schlesinger has focused on the journeys from conviction (overstating the disillusionment), and Lasch has portrayed the journey toward conviction (correctly in the case of prewar malcontents like Steffens, but his description is hardly applicable to someone like Croly or William Allen White). The full complexity of the disillusionment can be understood only through a multidimensional approach that recognizes in effect three distinct postwar reactions: no disillusionment at all; a disillusionment with primarily conservative manifestations (journeys from conviction); and a disillusionment with primarily radical manifestations (journeys toward conviction).

It is my purpose in the remaining pages of this study to trace these three tendencies and suggest the outlines of what promises to be a continuing investigation. I survey the approximate interval 1920–1940, not out of any hopelessly ambitious attempt to write the intellectual history of liberalism during these years, but in order to project the currents of disillusionment—to chart the "journeys"—roughly to their conclusion. I am mainly interested in the immediate postwar reaction, and it is with that period that the bulk of the remaining pages deal; but the contours of the disillusionment are not complete without at least a mention of the remarkable gyrations of the thirties that brought disillusioned Marxists like Eastman and Dos Passos full circle to conservatism and vacationing reformers like Fred Howe back into the reform movement under the banner of the New Deal.*

NO DISILLUSIONMENT

In a metaphor as misleading as his "Great Barbeque" description of the Gilded Age, Vernon Parrington likened the state of reform after World War I to an empty whiskey flask. Violently tossed, seriously depleted, perhaps, but the flask was not empty. There were many in the liberal community who carried on with the same intemperate convictions, the same intoxicated illusions, that fueled the prewar binge.

Certainly the internationalist movement continued unabated in the twenties. Stalwarts like Villard, Nicholas Murray Butler, Rabbi Wise, Jane Addams, James Shotwell, and Norman Thomas stepped up their pacifist efforts, strengthened by the confirmation that war was a futile pursuit. "The post-Wilsonian decade," Robert Osgood writes, "was really a continuation of prewar trends toward a broader international outlook. A strong body of internationalists kept their faith in the League and worked quietly to educate the American people to a more cosmopolitan view of foreign policy. The organized peace movement continued to expand." The Carnegie Endowment sponsored a 140-volume *Economic and Social History of the War* under Shotwell's general editorship, detailing the cost of the struggle in terms of lives and treasure and hoping to impress upon people the folly of militarism. Ironically, pacifists like Villard and Addams, because they were not taken in by the Wilsonian rhetoric (or so they said), now sneered at the Wilsonians' naïveté and proudly deemed themselves the

---

*I have selected several representatives for each of the three tendencies. Certain protean individuals fit more than one syndrome, and so there may be an instance or two of overlapping. As throughout the study, I am more concerned with an understanding of the phenomenon than with the tidy arrangement of the intellectual spectrum.

"realists." Addams, referring to liberals who crossed Wilson's ideological bridge, spoke derisively in 1922 of the "pathetic belief in the regenerative results of war," overlooking the pacifists' own feeble trust in disarmament and international law and morality. Realist or idealist, Addams's own philosophy remained unchanged. In 1921 she attended the Women's Peace Congress and joined in their assertion that war was an "abnormal" activity and that "it is a natural tendency of men to come into friendly relationships with ever larger and larger groups." Butler, who, with Wise, had supported the war, retrieved his doctrinaire pacifism and stumped the country during the twenties with speeches on "The Gospel of Hope" and "All Is Not Wrong With This World." He dedicated *The Path to Peace* to Aristide Briand, whom he called "master builder" for proposing a pact to outlaw war. On Armistice Day 1931, Butler pleaded that the apparatus of war "be consigned to the museums of history."[4]

Social Gospelers like Thomas, A.J. Muste, and Sherwood Eddy remained determined pacifists in the twenties. The *Christian Century*, their principal organ, ran a series of articles in 1927 and 1928 under the heading "What the War Did to My Mind." Paul Jones wrote of his loss of confidence in leaders and "organized schemes" but unflagging faith in "the individual who embodies dynamic conviction," referring to the conscientious objector. For Eddy the war had served to purge and clarify. "The chief result of the war upon my mind," he said, "may be summed up in the single word—liberation." Such liberation did not wash out belief in the millennium. "May not the decade following 1918," Eddy wrote in the *Survey*, "break the back of the prevailing war system of the world, just as a single decade saw the great battle won against slavery?" These are not times for an easy optimism, he granted, but "it is no time to retire from the battle. The desperate need of our country offers larger opportunity than peaceful farming or the solace of personal meditation."[5]

Domestic reform also counted its veteran crusaders in the twenties. Men like John Dewey, Upton Sinclair, and Charles Edward Russell were as convinced as ever of the orderly progression of democracy toward social justice. Historians have discovered recently that the reform movement was not adjourned after the war. "Out of defeat was born the desire to seek out new paths of reform, new roads to Zion," Clarke Chambers observed. "The high enthusiasm with which some had predicted immediate reconstruction . . . proved not justified, but neither were the years of the twenties the wasteland for reform that they have frequently seemed."[6] The road back, however, as Chambers indicates, was led by new men with new techniques and new, more specific goals—men like Robert Wagner and Fiorello La Guardia in New York. The Villards and Russells, with their cavalier style and grand pronouncements, seemed anachronistic—clownish, pathetic figures, to the twenties what Bryan was to progressivism. Most of their kind were casualties of the war. Villard might have been expected to decline along with his readerless *Nation*, as Croly did with the *New Republic*. But he and a handful of the old guard persisted— those "most unwearied hopers," Florence Kelley called them.

John Dewey was born in 1859. He died in 1952, into his nineties and into yet another era of international tension and liberal eclipse. Along the way, he swerved intellectually hardly at all. To the end, he remained a sure believer in progress, democracy, and the creative capacity of human intelligence. Sidney Kaplan, who has traced Dewey's thought through the twenties and thirties "in search of a new idea," concluded that it is "a thankless task." After the war, Dewey served as an editor and frequent contributor to the *New Republic* while churning out a steady flow of reassuring articles and books (*Human Nature and Conduct*, 1922; *The Public and Its Problems*, 1927; *Individualism Old and New*, 1929) and working actively for organizations like the League for Independent Political Action. He was concerned about a number of infirmities that the war had uncovered—prejudice, ignorance, and the increasing reliance on sentiment rather than discussion and rational planning—and at one point seemed to agree with Lippmann's critique of democracy in *The Phantom Public,* in which Lippmann advocated restraints on public decision making and a general pruning of the democratic process. But he believed that the "sick world" could be cured, and with his patent remedy, education. While Lippmann was on the verge of resignation, preparing chapters entitled "The Acids of Modernity" and "The Loss of Certainty," Dewey was coolly developing a fresh blueprint. In *The Public and Its Problems* he titled his chapters "Search for the Public," "Discovery of the State," and "Search for the Great Community." He assailed democracy's critics for their "exhibition of querulousness and spleen" and "superiority complex," and declared, "The cure for the ailments of democracy is more democracy." The public had its problems, but with education and the application of intelligence he felt they could be solved. The "amorphous mass," he was still hopeful, could yet become the "responsible public."[7]

It was characteristic of Dewey's persevering optimism that in 1929 while others—Lippmann, Joseph Wood Krutch, John Chamberlain—were writing existentialist pieces on their loss of faith he published *The Quest for Certainty*, outlining a philosophical system which could give "solidity and confidence," "maturity," and "authoritative guidance" to modern life. In the thirties Dewey became a

close friend of labor and unionism and urged a thoroughgoing socialization that placed him to the left of Roosevelt and the New Deal,
though a safe distance from communism. In *Encore For Reform* Otis
Graham suggests that his socialism involved a "turning," but through
all the turbulence of the thirties Dewey remained true to the pragmatism and essential optimism of his prewar days. By 1940, Max
Lerner found him strangely silent—"Dewey is scarcely heard
from"—perhaps forgetting that the patriarchal progressive was in his
eighties. No doubt he was still sanguine. As Kaplan remarked,
"Plainly Dewey had little new to suggest and the war might never
have happened for all the change it had . . . made in his former position."[8]

Upton Sinclair was twenty years younger than Dewey, a more mer-
curial personality with a more volatile brand of politics, but there was
the same consistency of thought. In a frantic prewar career, Sinclair
vaulted into national prominence in 1906 with the publication of *The
Jungle*, organized a communitarian colony near Englewood, New Jer-
sey, was arrested and briefly imprisoned in 1917 for protesting the
massacre of striking coal miners in Ludlow, Colorado, and became a
zealous leader in the prohibition movement. There was a lot of
flimflam to Sinclair; he was an eccentric, a food faddist, an ESP en-
thusiast, and something of a puritan despite his left-wing politics and
a scandalous private life. But from his prewar days until his death in
1968, he was consistently a socialist, and a utopian socialist at that.
After supporting Wilson unstintingly through the war, he emerged
disappointed and angry with him for not producing the liberal peace;
unlike others who felt betrayed, however, he remained the benign,
critical but uncynical, tough but nonvindictive reformer. Unimpressed
with communism, committed as ever to democratic socialism, he
supported the farmer-labor causes of the twenties while continuing
his exposés and protest novels. He seemed to get more tenacious with
age. In 1934 an aggressive end-to-poverty (EPIC) campaign nearly
propelled him into California's governorship. In 1962, at the age of 84,
Sinclair published his autobiography. It was a record not of embarrassment, humility, or disillusionment, but of success and fulfillment.
He wrote that by the age of twenty he had acquired a messianic complex. More than sixty years later he still believed in the democratic
millennium.[9]

Another reformer who did not have to adjust his sights was Charles
Edward Russell. Russell had been a member of the Socialist party and
the author of numerous books on socialist themes, notably *Lawless
Wealth: The Origin of Some Great American Fortunes* (1908). Like Sinclair,
he bolted from the party to back the war effort, and in 1917 was re-

warded for his patriotism with an appointment to the special American diplomatic mission to Moscow. Russell was the quintessential crusader. Between 1914 and 1919 he believed that the world was experiencing a titanic struggle between the forces of order and change. He insisted "the conflict was not essentially among peoples but between ideas," blamed the competitive, capitalist "system" for corrupting the Germans as well as the Allies, and urged new "forms" and "institutions" (e.g., a republic in Germany, an overhaul of capitalism in the United States, a League of Nations) that would be more conducive to peace and progress. "After the whirlwind," as he called his 1919 commentary, Russell foresaw "a noble growth" and felt that on balance there were a number of blessings for which to be thankful: Russia had achieved its liberation after centuries of despotic neglect; the Germans were reconstructing their government; women and labor had obtained some measure of social equality. "The gain of the sacrifice in this war," he concluded loftily in 1919, "is a new light in all the world, a new hope in men's hearts." He was one of the very few whose optimism survived the war fully intact (even Dewey and Sinclair were briefly shaken). Even when the "noble growth" failed to materialize, he could still say, as late as 1933, that another generation might look upon the war as "a turning-point of regeneration . . . terrible, stupid, mad, and yet with compensations."[10]

Russell remained an avuncular critic of American society and international capitalism, too doughty to give up the fight and too gentle to become a communist. He faithfully supported a legion of organizations such as the Farmers' Alliance and the Public Ownership League and liberal causes in Russia, Ireland, and the Philippines. Although he considered himself a radical he continued to tread the mainstream, and farther-ranging left-wingers like Steffens criticized him for the flabbiness of his socialism and stubborn opposition to Bolshevism. Otis Graham says he preferred "to comfort the casualties of a capitalistic Western world while others tended to the revolution." Not altogether unjustly, Russell, for his part, scolded the revolutionaries and cynics for their impatience. "The common error and cherished delusion of reformers," he wrote, "is to think that if the particular organization to which they belong goes ashore, all is lost. Reform is not so simple as that. . . . It is not to be had with the naïveté of a single push." In 1933, entering the last decade of his life, Russell published his autobiography and drafted an article for *Scribner's* in which he pondered the "mad-house world." Although he titled the autobiography *Bare Hands and Stone Walls*, it contained mostly fond recollections and the sturdy conviction that the world "grows always better."[11]

Oswald Villard plodded through the postwar years with his mugwumpish progressivism, a champion without a cause or even much of a sword, as his magazine was virtually expropriated by a cadre of younger editors. Villard joined in the internationalist and civil libertarian movements of the twenties, but was suspicious of the New Deal and resisted all the ideological frills of the thirties. With the coming of the Second World War he insisted that American intervention would solve nothing as it had solved nothing in 1917, and that in any case the United States had nothing to fear since its position was impregnable and neither Germany nor Japan would dare attack. Villard resigned from the *Nation* in June 1940, when differences between him and the editors over the matter of war and intervention became insurmountable. In his very last piece for the magazine, long on memory and short on prescience, he revived the old betrayal theme. "America is to be safeguarded," he said, "not by guns and warships . . . but only by greater economic and industrial wisdom, by social justice, by making our democracy work. That the United States has the genius, the power, the resources, and the vision to accomplish this I cannot question if only it is not again betrayed in the White House and by the politicians." He refused to admit discouragement. "We have much with which to reproach ourselves in the frequent failure of our leadership [and] our own weaknesses," he said, "but not as to our aims."[12]

Ten years after Villard's valedictory, another aging and unreconstructed warrior delivered a farewell message at New York's Astor Hotel. Stephen Wise, honored on the occasion of his seventy-fifth birthday, recounted the accomplishments and disappointments of a lifetime of causes and brought the gathering to its feet with a closing chant, "I'll fight! I'll fight! I'll fight!"[13]

When one examines these "most unwearied hopers" one wonders if indeed there was a "liberal disillusionment" at all. Osgood, impressed by the persistence of idealism and pacifism in the twenties, restricts the disillusionment to those liberals who had staked their liberalism on the outcome of the war and committed themselves emotionally and professionally; those who had opposed American intervention, and never expected anything good to come out of the war, says Osgood, were not disillusioned, but rather fortified in their pacifist convictions. Thus, "strictly speaking, Villard was not disillusioned, since, from his point of view, he had never really shared the illusions that were alleged to have victimized more gullible liberals." The same could be said of Addams, Thomas, Scott Nearing, and the other nonbelligerents.[14]

Osgood's distinction breaks down when one notices that Dewey, Sinclair, Russell, Wise, and others who actively *supported* intervention and who were thereby "victimized" were not in the front ranks of the disillusioned following the war. More fundamentally, Osgood fails to recognize that the war was a shattering experience for the pacifists and noninterventionists no less than the prowar liberals. People like Villard, Addams, Fitzgerald, and Steffens who did not approve of the war effort or succumb to Wilson's rhetoric may not have been, strictly speaking, "disillusioned," but they were surely chagrined at the outcome. The conduct of the war and the peace negotiations did nothing to enhance their faith in progress or humanity. Moreover, even from the sidelines they could hardly refrain from the excitement of the great crusade and at moments must have, at least privately, participated in its hopes and spirit—and subsequent despair.

Villard, for instance, the indefatigable internationalist, could write his wife from Paris in March 1919, "I could go to Russia in a responsible position and do a whole lot of things. But it's home for me. I have had all I want of Europe for some time." Fitzgerald, already a brooding existentialist in 1917, cared not one iota who won the war; nonetheless, he was racked by the madness of it all. In September 1920 he wrote his friend, Irish author Shane Leslie, "My ideas now are in such wild riot that I would flatter myself did I claim even the clarity of agnosticism." Walter Weyl in *The End of the War* observed that the war had disillusioned *both* the prowar and antiwar liberals: the martial liberal was disillusioned because he believed that war could be noble and heroic, a departure from the monotony of industrial life and an instrument for social progress; the pacifist was disillusioned because he believed in the inherent goodness and rationality of man. [15]

The point here is that the disillusionment ran deeper than Osgood or a cursory examination of the postwar careers of Dewey and company suggest. Whether such persons supported the intervention or not is irrelevant. It was, after all, Steffens, who had not been victimized by Wilson's rhetoric, who remarked that all of them were shaken by the experience. And despite their brave front and remarkable resiliency, not even those "most unwearied hopers" got through the episode totally unscathed. Osgood himself notes that although pacifists and internationalists in the twenties continued to operate on the happy assumption that war was preventable, they were forced to acknowledge that it was no longer unthinkable or impossible. "There was little of the old confidence that war, like the duel, had become obsolete; the buoyant optimism that infused American idealism before the war never returned." [16] There were, then, at least marginal changes in the outlook of even those liberals who seemed to undergo no disillusionment following the war.

Dewey, for example, changed in one important respect that Sidney Kaplan neglected to mention: he became an isolationist. Dewey had abandoned his instinctive pacifist position to support the war on the pragmatic grounds that war could be utilized as an instrument for peace and social reconstruction. During the war he was denounced by stunned protégés like Bourne who had regarded him as their intellectual idol. Afterwards, though he disagreed with Bourne's categorical indictment of force, he granted that "the pacifists who were converted to war are obliged to undertake an unusually searching inquiry into the actual results in their relation to their earlier professions and beliefs." "Were not those right," he asked, "who held that it was self-contradictory to try to further the permanent ideals of peace by recourse to war?" Dewey's process of rationalization convinced him that the inherent wickedness and decadence of European politics were responsible for the failure at Paris, and that American democracy could only become infected by further intercourse with the Old World. In March 1920 he wrote, "We owe monuments to Clemenceau, Sonnino and Balfour" for making Americans realize the treachery of European imperialism. Although he recognized the infeasibility of isolationism, Dewey advised that the United States "tread warily." "We should avoid all general commitments, and confine ourselves to the irreducible minimum," he said. He was skeptical of the "outlawry of war" schemes, but preferred to endorse those efforts rather than American membership in the League, which he feared would lead to reentanglement. Clearly, Dewey was gun-shy. For all his reconstruction work at home in the twenties, he was not about to go on another international crusade: "The notion that we have only to offer ourselves as universal arbiter— and paymaster—and all will be well is childish in the extreme."[17]

Nicholas Murray Butler offers another example of a qualitative change. His international outlook unclouded in the twenties, Butler was chastened instead by the disappointments at home. He became distrustful of democratic reform and displayed an increasing elitist tendency after the war. Alarmed by democracy's unreliability, he declared at a convocation of Columbia freshmen in September 1931 that totalitarian systems often produce men of greater intelligence and stronger character than free elections. Like Dewey in his retreat to isolationism, Butler had been scratched by the war experience. Beneath the steely exteriors of these happy warriors there were wounds—scars and abrasions, minor perhaps, but testimony to the impact the war had had even on tough hides. No one save perhaps a Russell came through wholly unscathed. Even as dogged a reformer as Villard, to the end confident of the eventual triumph of his cause, was forced to concede at the conclusion of his memoirs that "much of the great promise of my youth has been dispelled." "I feel as though I have lived too long," Villard wrote William Allen White in 1939. "I had hoped for another kind of world which I hoped we would reach through another corridor."[18]

Villard mentioned in his memoirs that after the war, "anyone with a brain must have moved during those years to the Left or to the Right."[19] With some grudging adjustments but mostly mindless optimism, Villard and his group moved really very little at all. The jockeying by Dewey and Butler still found them lodged in the same rut, committed to the same overblown ideals and nursing the same worn-out illusions. Villard's concession came twenty years too late at the tail end of a wasted career. These were good men, well-intentioned and self-sacrificing for the most part, but events had passed them by. They were out of tune, out of touch. The Carnegie Endowment's postwar survey, intended to be a primer for peace, became a manual for another war; Sinclair's EPIC program was defeated by the very people it was intended to help. While the "most unwearied hopers" stalled in the middle of the road, more restive liberals were pursuing other alternatives, taking to other "corridors," logging their journeys to and from conviction.

JOURNEYS FROM CONVICTION

Charlotte Gilman commented in the 1926 *Survey* symposium that she knew "many who are discouraged by the war and its effects, who feel that social advance is hopelessly checked, at least for the present, and who have taken refuge in a more personal philosophy."[20] For every persevering Dewey or Russell there seemed to be a score of liberals who could not come to terms with the war. Most liberals who bothered to question their prewar assumptions, without resorting to rationalization or charges of betrayal, came away deeply disturbed. To honestly confront the events of 1914–1920 involved a confession not merely of error, but of failure and impotence. No wonder, then, that while the Deweys and Russells regrouped around the same crusades, many of their former associates quietly withdrew or headed in other directions to pick up the pieces.

Fred Howe, commissioner of immigration during the war, devoted a chapter in his 1925 autobiography to his "unlearning." Ellis Island had disclosed hysterias and hatreds of which he thought democracy incapable. The State Department formulated policy in terms of "oil in

Mexico, gold and railroads in Haiti and Santo Domingo." "Our alleged ideals did not operate at home, they could not operate abroad," he explained. "Until we, ourselves, were ready for renunciation, we could not ask other peoples to begin the process." Howe retired to a remote hideaway and invited to his "Walden" others who "were interested in finding themselves, who wanted to understand life and its meanings." In a desperate search for the qualities that the war had seemed to destroy, he cultivated an attachment to the locomotive engineers, who were "always conscious of and responsive to their tremendous responsibility." "Their daily life is necessarily heroic," he wrote, "and rarely is there record of any betrayal of responsibility."[21]

Not all the prewar liberals who performed Howe's painful reckoning were so morose. In a sardonic account of his loss of innocence, Fremont Older, progressive editor of the *San Francisco Call,* seemed more bitter than dejected. He recalled that before the war he believed that "there was a biological difference between the poor man and the rich man, and that somehow the poor were more altruistic, had more compassion and pity for their fellow men than the wealthy." He was not sure where he got the idea, "possibly from reading one of Jane Addams' books," but the war taught him an important lesson. "Practically the only difference between the poor classes and the rich classes was that one had money and the other had not," he said. "I have only lost my faith in man, not my pity for him. That is stronger than ever." Ray Stannard Baker, apparently as resilient as Russell, considered himself more mature, more sophisticated, but not "disillusioned." He replied he could answer "Here" to the *Survey*'s roll call of the prewar radicals. His fundamental beliefs had not changed. Where he was mistaken, he said, "was in thinking that what I wanted could be had by adopting certain easy devices . . . by short-cuts. What I have gained since is the knowledge that though the thing is true the time appointed is long. There are no miracles in progress." Baker acknowledged they were "no longer so sure . . . or so noisy," but promised, after a period "to ask questions" rather than answer them, they would be heard from again. Norman Thomas agreed. He thought it would "take time for a new crusading zeal to grow up, older and soberer in its expectations, with greater grip on reality." He hoped that the "present doubts and disillusionments" would be a "useful schooling" for a "newer radicalism . . . a wiser and truer idealism."[22]

For most of these liberals, however, the process of revelation was paralyzing. Brand Whitlock apprehended as early as 1918 that "the world could never again be what it had been—that all those who survived would be themselves *mutilés*, with wounds that would never heal."[23] Most of them would *not* be heard from again, their voices of conscience engaged more in introspection than exhortation. Sobering up generally did not lead to a "newer radicalism" or a "wiser and truer idealism," but to abstinence and asceticism. Most of these men had lost both faith and commitment, and for them the aftermath of war called for soul-searching rather than soul-stirring. This was their occupation in the twenties, and, for many, long after that.

The journeys from conviction often took liberals on physical re-treats—to the Riviera, to Spanish isles and Italian villas, to hamlets in New England and the Adirondacks. Seeking serenity and asylum from the traffic of ideals, many became fugitives. Howe sequestered himself on Nantucket. Francis Hackett, the *New Republic*'s literary editor, left the magazine in 1922 for the comforting seclusion of the Pyrenees. Whitlock, after vacating his Brussels ambassador post in 1921, played out his days in semiretirement at Cannes, with summers on the Belgian coast, writing and reading and content with a life of gentlemanly resignation. He had become exhausted with a "peace in its way quite as wearing as the war," found that he could no longer "bear the hour of twilight . . . its mystery, its sadness, its terror," and decided to take a "holiday" in the south of France. The holiday be-came an extended furlough, then a sabbatical, and finally a perma-nent occupation.[24]

Whitlock never did recover his energies. He complained chronically of "lethargy," "incurable laziness," "procrastination," "debility," and "an ankylosis of mind and body." When a Michigan well-wisher wrote to him suggesting that he run for governor or senator as a steppingstone to the presidency, the formerly ebullient reform mayor graciously declined. He did not mean to underestimate the positions' importance, but they no longer had the attraction "they might once have had when I was younger and had more illusions." Again and again he would shy away from politics. To Rutger Jewett, his editor, he wrote emphatically, "I am hoping to get to my writing again and to devote the rest of my life to literary effort. No more politics for me of any kind!" To Marshall Sheppey, a Toledo crony: "No more poli-tics for *me*! Sixteen years of unappreciated and wasted effort have at last taught me the futility, the folly, of that, at any rate." He greeted the nomination of the unheroic Harding with grateful relief. Harding was "in no sense brilliant," but there had been "enough of brilliant genius in the White House, after Roosevelt and Wilson." The presi-dency, in his opinion, now called for "solid, mediocre men," pro-vided they had "good sense, sound and careful judgment, and good manner."[25]

Whitlock's weariness concealed a deeper strain of alienation. He had become disillusioned with democracy. Before the war, although he had always been more urbane mugwump than populist, he was convinced of the basic good sense of the people and construed Wilson's election in 1916 as an indication that "the people in their mass judgment are oftener right than wrong, and . . . can discern truths, realities and principles even in . . . whirlwinds of passion." By 1920 he was appalled by the public's ignorance of world affairs. They knew less of geography than a Belgian schoolboy, he said. Just prior to leaving Brussels he wrote in his diary that he had no desire to return to America because the things he had liked and admired were no longer respected there. Instead, "the spirit of vulgarity" prevailed. His cynicism surfaced completely during the stay at Cannes. Deploring the provincial Main Street mentality, the "mob morality" and "tyranny of majorities," he wrote Jewett that "the world has been made safe for democracy, but not for gentlemen," and that they would have to take a back seat to "the bounders and the cads." A favorite expression became, "Democracy runs to mediocrity just as water runs into the gutter."[26]

Whitlock maintained an abiding affection for the "old America of Lincoln and Washington" (he was at work on an intellectual biography of Jefferson at the time of his death in 1934) and he faithfully and sentimentally attended memorial services for American soldiers buried in France and Belgium. But he had become an expatriate, a conservative one, running away from democracy rather than from capitalism precisely. The titles of his two postwar novels, *Uprooted* and *Transplanted*, written in the twenties on the Riviera, symbolized his journey from conviction. When Allan Nevins drafted a biographical introduction to the *Letters and Journal* he inserted a friend's poignant account of Whitlock's metamorphosis:

> I saw Whitlock in Brussels the spring after the Armistice. He was quite reminiscent. He had lost faith in social reforms, he said. . . . He had some beautiful dogs. His house was filled with honors from the Belgian Government. About his tables were members of the aristocracy. . . . That particular setting and that particular life seemed to satisfy him. It was all very understandable after what he had been through.
>
> I next saw him some years afterwards at an hotel on the Riviera. He was scrupulously dressed; careful in his habits; detached in his emotions. . . . As to whether he was disillusioned or not I don't know, but I think he was. Living was the thing to be finished off in a refined, artistic, and understanding way, possibly unsoiled by what was going on in the world about.[27]

One did not have to take flight to journey from conviction. Among those who stayed at home there were the sometimes more distant emigrations of the mind. Herbert Croly and Walter Lippmann, their *New Republic* declining rapidly, ranged far from their prewar roots. As one writer has said, they "could leave no dynamic legacy of liberalism to the next generation because the heart of their philosophy—the culmination of progress in an evolutionary, middle-class Utopia, created by rational and good men—was shattered."[28] Lippmann took leave of the magazine a year before Hackett's departure and went immediately to work on the long chain of books—*Public Opinion* (1922), *The Phantom Public* (1925), *Men of Destiny* (1927), *American Inquisitors* (1928), capped with the most recent and most emphatic *The Public Philosophy* (1955)—that would chronicle his loss of faith in the common man.

Although Lippmann had braced himself for a Wilsonian failure, he was still disappointed at the outcome. He wrote Colonel House of his hopes "to the very last for a Treaty which would in a measure redeem our promises to the world." 1919 was a confusing year for him. "At times," writes Francine Cary, "he strenuously attacked Wilson, the Fourteen Points, the Treaty of Versailles and the League. At other times he admitted that Wilsonism was not 'pure buncomb,' and might have been realized. His attempt to find a reason for the failure, his almost frantic effort to assume a detached, disinterested view of the issues, only ended in more confusion." Harold Laski spent a weekend with him early in 1920. "We talked the universe over," Laski reported. "I rather gather that he finds the paper [the *New Republic*] a little difficult just now. Croly has the religious bug very badly. . . . But he talked wisely and movingly . . .; he is one of the few Americans I've met who realizes that two hundred millions are on the verge of starvation in Europe largely because the Senate has gone back to its splendid and tragic isolation."[29]

Lippmann vented his frustration on several targets. He blasted officials in Washington who "refused to look ahead, refused to think, refused to plan, refused to prepare for any of the normal consequences of a war"; fumed at "leaders of the community" who had "the habit of wrapping themselves in the American flag"; and faulted the newspapers for distorting the news and playing up the German atrocities for public consumption. Most of all, like Whitlock, he soured on democracy. As Harold Nicolson would do, to a large degree Lippmann blamed "democratic diplomacy" for the breakdown at Paris, and in his first post-Versailles publication, *Liberty and the News* (1920), he called for an elaborate plan of press censorship. Before the war Lippmann had fretted over the intelligence of the masses—in 1915 he wrote, "It would be sheer hypocrisy . . . to suppose that any large section of the American people is informed, or interested, or thoughtful about international relations"—but in the twenties he became a confirmed cynic. He supported John W. Davis in 1924 when liberals with even an ounce of the old faith, including Croly, were huddling around the La Follette candidacy. He did back American membership in the League, though he expected "nothing spectacular."[30]

Lippmann's postwar trek took him to the archconservative New York *Herald Tribune* where he began his "Today and Tomorrow" column in 1931. From behind his columnist's desk and safely above the arena of reform, he pontificated on the evils of demagoguery (for fear of which he distrusted Roosevelt and voted for Landon in 1936), glorified "the old liberalism of natural laws and individual rights that once he had so effectively satirized,"[31] and generally questioned the viability of democracy in an uncertain and malevolent world. In a Phi Beta Kappa oration delivered at Columbia on 31 May 1932, he spoke of the preoccupation of democracy with the present moment, its tyranny of emotion over reason, and warned his young audience that the scholar can have little influence in such circumstances and can best serve by remaining detached. The world would go on best, he said, "if among us there are men who have stood apart, who refused to be anxious or too much concerned, who were cool and inquiring, and had their eyes on a longer past and a longer future." Columnist Heywood Broun, a classmate of his, remembered the Lippmann who had been a Harvard radical (class of 1910), a regular at the Dodge salon, a stringer for Steffens's *Everybody* magazine, and secretary to the socialist mayor of Schenectady before his stint with the *New Republic*, and he shook his head. "I have been watching the mind of Walter Lippmann for more than a quarter of a century, and my eyelids are a little weary," Broun wrote in the *New York World Telegram*.[32]

With publication of *The Good Society* in 1937, Lippmann had come full circle from socialism and progressivism to an espousal of laissez-faire elitism. He questioned if "the good society" could ever be achieved, but was certain the New Deal, with its brutalizing collectivism and mass democracy, was the wrong approach. He urged instead a retrieval of the old wisdom that progress would come from emancipation and self-help rather than from regulation—what in 1914 would have been tantamount to his approving "drift" over "mastery." Though he remained a strong voice in international affairs,[33] Lippmann had abdicated on the issue of social reform. In the 1950s, Heinz Eulau found the erstwhile "mover and shaker" "shopworn" and "unimaginative," "a staid conservative genuinely worried about wars, revolutions and the confusion of human affairs." His condescension invited caricature. Art Buchwald quipped that God was not dead "but alive and appearing twice a week in the Washington Post."

In 1970, at the age of eighty, he was admiring Theodore Roosevelt, Eisenhower, and de Gaulle, damning Lyndon Johnson, and praising only faintly Franklin Roosevelt, Truman, and Kennedy; noticeably, he declined to comment on Wilson. "We're learning, I think," Lippmann said in a birthday interview,

> that the ideal which the people of my generation . . . grew up with—that you could somehow or other educate everybody at a college level and make them fit to govern the mass society—is not going to happen. Some problems are not solvable by living people. They can get on; they can compose their differences a little, but they can't solve them. People die off, and they outlive their problems. One of the great solvers of problems in history is death.

His own came at eighty-five, while he was at work on a book about "the ungovernability of mankind."[34]

Herbert Croly stayed on with the *New Republic*. Whether it was his antediluvian faith in the efficacy of education or stubborn pride as the architect of the American promise, Croly managed to maneuver through the twenties with some of the old bounce that eluded Lippmann and Whitlock. After his death, a colleague wrote of his postwar perseverance that there were several "easy temporary courses" he might have taken. Where others "held their noses and voted for Harding," or condemned the shallowness of American culture, or "ran to the fringes of utopian radicalism," he rejected all such escapes. In a long, discursive piece in October 1920, Croly acknowledged "the contemporary eclipse of progressivism" but outlined a bold new plan of action. He advised liberals to abandon the old mugwumpish approach to reform with its emphasis on citizenship and clean politics and to turn their attention to guttier social and industrial issues. In what amounted to a flirtation with radical politics he deserted his middle-class liberalism for the farmer-labor movement and enthusiastically supported La Follette in 1924. In international affairs, he was chastened enough to avow "no more dashes into a political jungle . . . no more intervention without reservations, without understanding and . . . specific and intelligent political preparation," but he remained a determined believer in the possibility of "permanent pacification" and envisaged a world community under the auspices of the League. "That idea is far from dead," Croly wrote after the solemn referendum of 1920. "The American people are recovering from their war neurosis. As the memory of it fades away they are regaining some of their vision." He hailed the Washington Conference as "a rare and a good opportunity." Harding and Hughes, he felt, "hold strong cards and if they play them well they can make the

Conference a success." The substitution of conference for war was "an entirely possible achievement."[35]

The old gusto, the old illusionment, in Croly's case, had clearly outlasted the war. But the inconclusive results of pacification and of his other commitments, the termination of many long friendships, and the defection of much of the *New Republic*'s audience to the maverick *American Mercury* eventually took their toll, and his mind turned increasingly in the direction of Lippmann's, toward private speculations and an interest in the individual instead of society. The war had demonstrated the malignity of nationalism and centralization, and even as he flirted with socialism Croly was talking about reconstruction in terms of revitalizing local communities and recovering the virtues of self-reliance and independence. Edmund Wilson, another of his colleagues, said after Croly's death that in the days following the war, despite his apparent reinvolvement, "he despaired of politics and really never quite took them seriously again." Charles Forcey notes that "the collapse of the farmer-labor movement in 1924 drove him more and more within himself." As the reform arena no longer beckoned, Croly groped for answers elsewhere. Ethics and religion, always interests for him, became preoccupations. When his search for new directions became too trying, he permitted himself an escape and hired a bearded Englishman named Alfred Orage to teach him the mysteries of yoga.[36]

Nothing seemed to work for Croly. In 1928, he suffered a crippling stroke. Two years later he was dead—retaining more of his conviction perhaps than Lippmann, but nonetheless a shell of his former self. Because of his process of readjustment in the twenties and his death within a decade of the war (which prevented him from distilling his thoughts as Lippmann was able to do), it is difficult to evaluate the precise nature of his disillusionment. He was vague, inconsistent, and toward the end mystical. Sidney Kaplan says, "It is doubtful that even his most loyal admirers have been able to unravel a coherent strain of thought from the variety of editorials, articles and reviews that appeared over his name in the *New Republic* from the end of the war to his retirement in 1928."[37] What is clear is that despite the residue of his old progressive faith he was a deeply troubled man. In his hopeless confusion of values and abortive struggle to discover some new gospel, some new "promise," Croly demonstrated how dark and inscrutable the world of the twenties had become to many of the prophets of 1914.

William Allen White's experience paralleled Croly's closely. He was a year older than Croly, forty-six when the war broke out. Before the war he had been widely recognized as a spokesman for Middle

America, like Croly an incarnation of the progressive paradox—a nationalist, an individualist, cool to labor and the Negro but a robust apostle of democracy. Also like Croly, he supported and believed in the great crusade and emerged from the war, tired and confused, to resume a checkered career. In the twenties White bravely continued in the reform and internationalist movements, following Croly into farmer-labor politics though retaining his fundamentalist predilection for prohibition, sexual puritanism, and orthodox religion and education. He crusaded against the Ku Klux Klan in Kansas, defended labor's demands for higher wages and better working conditions, and championed the civil liberties of radicals. In foreign affairs he endorsed the League without reservations (though it was "obvious that I was fighting for a lost cause"), like Croly was enthusiastic about the Washington Disarmament Conference, and urged recognition of Russia. Less philosophical than Croly, White was not so tormented by failure. He could admit "life is disillusion," but still muster "hope for progress and eager zest to see the next act of the show." "Why retire gloomily into recantations of youth?" he asked. "Better is the fine frenzy of the man who chases the rainbow than the misanthropy of his brother who rocks on his coat tails and nurses his grouch between his knees."[38]

But the aging editor could not escape his own haunting sense of impotence and was enormously frustrated by mounting inactivity and insignificance, as when he wrote Theodore Roosevelt's son of his toiling on "unimportant editorials" and "unimportant books." The thirties only introduced more confusion. As Croly might have been expected to be had he lived on, White was boxed in between his crumbling middle-class progressivism and an ascendant but unpalatable welfare state. "Lord, I don't know," he muttered to Allan Nevins in 1934. And two years later, to Harold Ickes: "It is so hard to know what a man ought to do." He decided to vote for Landon in 1936. With the specter of another war, he became somber and reflective. The fifteenth anniversary of the armistice occasioned a brooding editorial in which he wrote, "The next war will see the same hurrah and the same bowwow of the big dogs to get the little dogs to go out and follow the blood scent and get their entrails tangled in the barbed wire. And for what?" Russia was ruled by "proletarian tyrants," Germany governed by "paranoiac sadists." "The boys who died just went out and died." Although he headed the Committee to Aid the Allies and became resigned to fighting Germany, White harbored no illusions this time. Seven months before Pearl Harbor he wrote Oswald Villard that he hoped he would never see another war and that he surely would never encourage another one. "But if it comes, this summer or next summer . . . I see nothing to do but to fight it with all our might." "That's not a pleasant prospect," he said, "for a man who realizes the utter futility of wars in the past and who can only hope rather vainly that, out of this war, men may learn wisdom in the end."[39]

Although Carl Becker had never shared Croly's or White's penchant for prophecy before the war, he had been a cautious optimist. As a professor of history at the University of Minnesota and then (after 1917) Cornell, Becker had supported the American intervention and the Wilsonian program, less hysterically than a number of his colleagues in the profession but earnestly enough to have contributed two pamphlets to the Committee on Public Information. Almost from the beginning Becker had misgivings about a war prosecuted in the name of ideals, and as the crusade degenerated he flagellated himself for compromising his realism. In a furious backlash after the war he rejected summarily and totally the Enlightenment notion of progress. He wrote William Dodd that he had always suspected "the futility of life," and was always easily persuaded to regard history "as no more than the meaningless resolution of blind forces which struggling men—good men and bad—do not understand and cannot control, although they amuse themselves with the pleasing illusion that they do." "The war and the peace," he said, "have only immensely deepened this pessimism." Becker evidently was so disillusioned by the war experience that he preferred to forget his more effervescent moments prior to the war when he seemed to swallow the progressives' belief in progress as an observable fact rather than an Enlightenment theory. David Noble, in a brilliant chapter in *The Paradox of Progressive Thought*, portrayed the paralyzing effect of the war on Becker's philosophy. "Becker was stripped of history," Noble wrote, "he stood naked and afraid in a century hopelessly cut off from the supporting warmth of the past."[40]

Like Whitlock and eventually Croly, Becker lost interest in politics and told Dodd it was "a matter of complete indifference" to him whether he voted or not. In the twenties he became an admirer of Mencken and, says one of his biographers, developed a greater appreciation for Henry Adams than for Thomas Jefferson. In his classic study *The Declaration of Independence*, published in 1922, Becker conceded Jefferson's "felicity of expression" and respected his "clear, alert intelligence," but questioned, in perhaps another fit of self-incrimination, "Jefferson's placidity, the complacent optimism of his sentiments and ideas [which] carry him at times perilously near the fatuous. One would like more evidence that the iron had some time or other entered his soul, more evidence of his having profoundly reflected upon the enigma of existence, of having more deeply felt its tragic import, of having won his convictions . . . at the expense of some painful travail of the spirit." Although he remained a man of liberal sentiments—he became really more a quietist than a cynic— Becker marveled at the Deweys and Wises who could continue in the uplift movement. "I admire your valiant championship of the oppressed, your courageous defense of lost causes, and only wish I had the generous spirit and the intelligent optimism which inspires your action," he wrote Felix Frankfurter in 1927.[41]

In the thirties, he wrestled with the challenge of the New Deal and at times seemed to be impressed. But his prewar search for certitude and a "genuinely scientific definition of progress" had deteriorated into a relativism which scarcely left him even able to talk about the subject of progress—since there were "no more stable standards of value for measuring it than the infinitely various and ever-changing judgments of individual men." "What, if anything," he asked, "may be said on behalf of the human race? May we still, in whatever different fashion, believe in the progress of mankind?" "Judged by my private values," he chanced his opinion, "very little." In his celebrated presidential address to the American Historical Association in December 1931, Becker told his colleagues that politics could be transformed but never solved. Man could be understood only tentatively, since he and his world were "still in the making, something as yet unfinished." Gone was the assurance that history, however "unfinished," was everlastingly progressive.[42]

Newton Baker returned to Cleveland and his law practice after the war. He busied himself with civic activities, devoted time to the National Consumers' League and the Institute of Human Relations, and argued forcefully for membership in the League of Nations and World Court. He, too, however, was seasoned by failure. Surveying the international scene in 1930, Baker, one of the more vigorous spokesmen for Wilsonian idealism during the war, offered an ironic judgment on the weakness of Hoover's policy. Hoover's statements were incredibly naive, he wrote Whitlock. "His present troubles are largely caused by the comparison of his promises with conditions which he promised to control but which, of course, were in fact incorrigible. As a consequence, Mr. Hoover seems to me not only disappointed and saddened but mystified, as a good child might be to discover that abounding good intentions on his part were not good enough to make everybody else in the world good and happy." He grumbled to fellow peace promoter James Shotwell that their work seemed like "chasing butterflies on a battlefield." Baker died in 1937. To the end he kept his hand in Democratic politics—he was a serious contender for the party's presidential nomination in 1932—but he found the New Deal's breakneck pace menacing and counseled that constructive change would have to be accomplished over several generations. The man who was once an ardent Wilsonian and trumpeter of the new order had lost much of his enthusiasm for reform and rather than seek fulfillment of the good society in his own lifetime was content to "help along the slower fundamental processes which form the future." Becker would have said that the iron had entered his soul.[43]

Most of the liberals who undertook journeys from conviction after the war were already well into middle age when Woodrow Wilson returned from Paris. Howe was 52, White 51, Croly and Whitlock 50, Becker 46, Baker 48, and so on. These were men whom the war had aged even beyond their years and whose lives in mid-passage one could expect to wind to a close with stoic calm and good grace. That they failed to regain their vigor or conviction is not surprising. Weyl's "tired radical" built his home in the country and tilled a different kind of field. John Phillips said the prewar radical became "wiser, more tempered and more hopeful of individual salvation than of mass conversion." Whitlock conceded in an interview in 1922 that the revolving years made them more patient, "perhaps a little wiser." "As one grows older," he said, "one loses a good many illusions, but the main thing is to keep one's ideals. To lose both illusions and ideals is the worst of all tragedies."[44]

Tasker Bliss, in his sixties when the war ended, dedicated the last ten years of his life to the ideal of peace, visiting college international relations clubs and delivering commencement addresses, but he had been reduced to "an ancient pedagogue . . . preaching the lessons of experience to youth." Edward W. Bok, the peace publicist, asked him to speak on the subject "Stopping the Next War Before It Begins." He liked the subject but not the title. "Everybody will think that I am going to give them a cut-and-dried plan. But I have none such." "With all due deference to your views," he wrote Bok, "I think that the great trouble now is that the people of all the world have settled down to wait till someone evolves a plan in all its details which will appeal to all and all will accept. . . . They wait for the next plan which they hope will be perfect only to have their hopes again disappointed." In more phlegmatic moments Bliss would confide that he was intent on going back to his classics. When asked to become a member of the Williamstown Institute of Politics, he declined. "There are other things I would rather do in whatever time is left me than trying to regulate the zigzag spirit of this very wobbly old world."[45]

These were mostly veteran crusaders who were playing out their days quietly, gracefully, with a sense of proportion and ripened wisdom. But there were young men, too, who had gone to seed. There was Lippmann—only 30 in 1919—a precocious radical a decade earlier and in the aftermath of war an entrenched conservative. And there was the withdrawing shadow of an even younger man—someone who had hardly acquired conviction before he was losing it, and who before the end of his career would provide perhaps the most articulate expression of their collective experience.

In 1919 Reinhold Niebuhr was still a novice minister, twenty-seven years old and five years graduated from Eden Seminary. Schooled in the Social Gospel, Niebuhr had supported the war only after great deliberation and even then had reservations. In a notebook entry in 1918 he wrote that he hardly knew how to bring order out of the confusion in his mind. It was "easier to talk about the aims of the war than to justify its methods." Because of his German descent Niebuhr felt he had to take a stand: "If I dissociated myself only slightly I would inevitably be forced into the camp of those who romanticize about the Kaiser. And the Kaiser is certainly nothing to me. If we must have war I'll certainly feel better on the side of Wilson than on the side of the Kaiser." Like many others who were crushed by the war's outcome, Niebuhr impulsively charged the statesmen with betraying the liberal program at Paris. Further reflection, however, convinced him of his own culpability. In 1928 he explained that before the war he had taken the universe for granted. "The love of God and the virtue of man were fixed entities for me about which I was as certain as I was of the sun and the stars." His postwar revelation exposed his "naive confidence" and left him a realist and relativist struggling not to become a cynic. "It is not impossible for society to overcome conflict and develop into a brotherhood," he allowed, "but there is something divinely foolish about the hope of such a consummation. . . . None of the ideals to which our hopes cling is impossible, but none of them is easy." The war, he said, was no anachronism. "If we thought it so that was only because we were out of touch with reality. The world war was life, lived as it is lived on this little sphere."[46]

As with Croly and White, Niebuhr's journey followed a winding, nomadic route with many stops along the way. In the twenties, although already a philosophical conservative, he remained a political activist, participating gamely in the pacifist Fellowship of Reconciliation and civil rights and labor movements. Henry Ford was a favorite target. In the thirties, he seemed as unrelenting as ever in his quest for social justice, advocating full-scale socialization, exposing the inadequacies of the New Deal, and backing Norman Thomas's candidacy in 1936. George Mowry remarked, "By some mental alchemy Niebuhr remained a political radical and a reformer."[47] But if Niebuhr's energies were not diminished, his convictions steadily were. In 1939 he recalled the circumstances that prompted his leaving his Detroit ministry ten years earlier for the privacy of academic life at Union Theological Seminary. "The simple little moral homilies . . . seemed completely irrelevant to the brutal facts of life in a great industrial center. Whether irrelevant or not, they were certainly futile. They did not change human actions or attitudes in any problem of collective behavior by a hair's breadth, though they may well have helped to preserve private amenities and to assuage individual frustrations." In *Moral Man and Immoral Society,* which appeared in 1932, Niebuhr elaborated for the first time on his maturing belief and lifelong sentiment that human society was inherently, irremediably corrupt and that politics could thus only hope to promote a semblance of "justice"—leaving the higher virtues of love and morality to the province of the individual and his pastor. Individuals, he granted, were capable of love and morality, of "interests other than their own," but these achievements were "more difficult, if not impossible, for human societies and social groups." He went on to a critique of both the Social Gospel and the secular liberalism of progressivism, rejecting the old assumptions one by one: that history was progressive, or at least that society made "moral" progress; that ignorance yielded to education; that appeals to brotherhood were efficacious; that wars were "stupid" and therefore caused by stupid people; that virtue could be engineered into the society. A special whipping boy was Dewey, whom he reproached for overestimating the possibilities of science and the capabilities of man as a social animal.[48]

Curiously, and somewhat paradoxically, Niebuhr carried on a serious affair with communism in the thirties. He came to Marx more out of default than embrace, only as a possible alternative to a sputtering capitalism, and it turned out to be a passing infatuation. Although he believed the communist system might prove more humane and just, he never entertained the illusion that claimed Steffens and other enthusiastic converts of a magical utopia on the other side of the revolution; nor did he suppose the transformation would come without great suffering. "The disintegration of a social system and the birth of a new one," he wrote in 1934, "are certain to be attended by more struggle and conflict, by more tragedy and pathos than our wise men anticipate." Arthur Schlesinger, Jr., has commented that Niebuhr's allegiance to Marxism was always limited, "both the price of indifference to the achievements of piecemeal reform and a symptom of despair." In any case, by the close of the thirties, he was berating Marxist intellectuals for "participating essentially in all the liberal illusions" and, although he had never shared their utopian fancies, repenting his own error. He became critical, too, of the doctrinaire Christian pacifism to which he subscribed in the twenties as a member and national chairman of the Fellowship of Reconciliation. He found the old Bourne argument that "War and not Germany was the enemy" embarrassingly inane in the face of a Nazi regime that threatened to enslave civilization. When isolationist senators on the Senate Foreign Relations Committee baited him with the question of how a man of the cloth could speak so complacently of war, Niebuhr replied that all human beings had a terror of war but that there were perhaps worse terrors. "There is no political question that does not have to face ultimately the problem of possibility of war, if we decide there are some things we want to maintain at all costs." It was vintage *Realpolitik,* reminiscent of Laski telling Bourne in 1920 that one could not stand at Armageddon and philosophize on the abstract injustice of war.[49]

Niebuhr's testimony before the Senate in behalf of Lend-Lease signaled his emergence after World War II as a Cold War liberal. He would go on to assail communism as a sinister, demonic creed, become a supporter of Roosevelt and conventional reform politics, and, improbably, establish himself as a leading figure in Americans for Democratic Action. Christopher Lasch contends that at this point in the twilight of his life, "after passing through various intermediate stages of political disenchantment," Niebuhr relapsed "into a bland and innocuous liberalism almost indistinguishable . . . from the liberalism against which he had initially rebelled." But in books like *The Children of Light and the Children of Darkness* (1944) and countless articles that appeared during the postwar years and up until his death in June 1971, Niebuhr continued to chant the muted message of his neo-orthodox philosophy—preoccupied with sin and evil, more comforting than inspiring, dispensing almost Machiavellian advice on how to manage in an essentially immoral world. If, as Schlesinger sympathetically maintains, he was a man who reconstructed the democratic faith in more realistic terms rather than one who repudiated democracy altogether, Niebuhr had nonetheless strayed far from the Social Gospel of his youth. He had left the pulpit for a roost in the seminary, discredited the notion of perfectibility and seriously challenged the notion of progress in human affairs, and settled into the contemplation of "tentative and tolerable" solutions. Whether after World War II he recovered his "liberalism" or became a "pragmatic realist," as some have called him, or simply played out his conservatism, Niebuhr remained as resigned as ever to what he conceded very early in life was "the inevitable tragedy of human existence and the tortuous character of human history."[50]

For liberals like Niebuhr and Becker who survived into the thirties and forties, it is true that the disillusionment to some extent had run its course. In the challenge posed by the depression and in reaction to the unfolding excesses of fascism and communism abroad, many liberals seemed to reacquire a grudging appreciation or sympathy for American democracy and rediscover the sources of their original faith. The iconoclastic *American Mercury* lost ground to the more conscientious analysis of the *Nation* and *New Republic*, which were winning back old readers and recruiting new ones.[51] Fugitives like Fred Howe made their way back to Washington to contribute where they could to the work of the New Deal. Among the intellectuals, Van Wyck Brooks, who since 1920 had been decrying America's emotional and aesthetic starvation (*Civilization in America, The Ordeal of Mark Twain, The Pilgrimage of Henry James*), published a book in 1936 entitled *The Flowering of New England* in which he recaptured the forgotten heritage of Emerson and Thoreau. Carl Sandburg, a prewar socialist and folk poet who stopped celebrating contemporary America in the twenties and like Whitlock diverted his attention to Lincoln and Washington, sounded a Whitmanesque note of reaffirmation in 1936 with the publication of "The People, Yes." Becker's biographer suggests that his paralyzing relativism evaporated some in the charged atmosphere of the early forties. Becker's colleague Charles Beard reassessed his conspiratorial interpretation of the Founding Fathers in the light of European totalitarianism and acquired a new respect for the Constitution and the American political tradition. All these men had seemingly experienced a renaissance of sorts. Robert Osgood notes, "Slowly, cautiously, shell-shocked reformers ventured out of the spiritual ruins of disillusionment. . . . Resignation gradually gave way to the constructive reassertion of liberal and humanitarian principles."[52]

One wonders, however, if these men were not merely performing a final ritual of conciliation, indistinct from Whitlock's mellowing on the Riviera or Bliss's obliging tour in behalf of pacifism in the twenties. In the recovery of these "shell-shocked reformers" one detects a note more of reconciliation than genuine recommitment or rejuvenation—a matter more of simply making their peace with America and the society that nurtured them than a confident "reassertion." Becker provided an interesting clue to their temper in his observation in 1936 that their behavior was "not unlike that of certain Protestant sects whose habit of going to church has outlived their religious convictions." Warhorses like Howe, Baker, White, Niebuhr, and Becker, to the extent that they became reinvolved in the thirties, were simply going through the motions of instinctive reformers. Becker experienced no sudden resurgence of faith. In 1938, unbent, he told Max Lerner, "You have a romantic faith in the humanity and good sense of the people which I do not share." Brooks's *The Flowering of New England* was less the product of renewed faith than of plain nostalgia; resigned to the failure of the cultural renaissance he had thought possible in his 1915 *America's Coming-of-Age*, Brooks was content to accent the bright spots in America's antiquarian past, forsaking provocative criticism for what a dismayed associate termed "scholarly storytelling . . . completely insulated from the life that used to inspire him to hope or anger." As for Beard, his new-found appreciation for the American system was cultivated only at the price of another disillusion: a persevering internationalist in the twenties, he became America's foremost isolationist in the thirties.[53]

When one scans the "spiritual ruins of disillusionment" one finds salvaged equipment and unfurled banners but really very few signs of vitality in the group that journeyed from conviction. The year 1929 offers a particularly grim vantage point. Donald Richberg wrote an article for the *Survey* in which he counted few of his generation who had "survived the bludgeoning of these years. Death and defeat and discouragement have taken most of them out of the public service." "The world may be rejuvenated in one way or another," Joseph Wood Krutch wrote in *The Modern Temper*, "but we will not. Skepticism has entered too deeply into our souls ever to be replaced by faith." Lippmann's *Preface to Morals* agonized over "The Problem of Unbelief," "False Prophecies," and "Deep Dissolution." John Jay Chapman's "Last Words" tolled a crusader's unrequited death:

> I'll strive no more to be a man:
>   Cold world, bad world, Adieu!
> I've done you all the good I can
>   Or ever mean to do.
> In fact—I say it in your ear—
> It was a grand mistake, I fear,
>   To try to better you.[54]

The thirties and forties offer a slightly different perspective, turning up a contingent of survivors—stragglers and vagabonds wending their way back, weary campaigners looking for a light in the road. But the landscape is still a desolate one, lined more with stumbling blocks than paving stones, and with still more requiems than reveilles. Ray Stannard Baker scrawled in his notebook late in 1936 that he was sure he could not settle "the tremendous problems now plaguing the world. Most often I cannot fully understand. The factors are too complex." Becker cited the gnawing dilemma of liberals who had deserted reform but were unable to take to the path of revolution. Adrift, the liberal "peers cautiously out of doorways, shuffles along the shadow of walls, slinks around corners into side streets." In 1932 Lerner reviewed Becker's existentialist *Heavenly City of the Eighteenth-Century Philosophers* and pronounced it a "product of our entire present generation, one which has not only learned to question existing institutions but, whether out of philosophy or out of despair, has become skeptical of the very questioning itself." Armistice Day 1934 prompted the morbid reflection, "It was not our dead that we mourned on this day [but] our faith that we buried again."[55]

The sense of emptiness with which these liberals picked up their lives in 1919 was never quite relieved. The "travail of the spirit" which eluded Jefferson had seared them all—some more deeply than others but all of them irreparably. Newton Baker visited his friend Whitlock on the Riviera in February 1934, a few weeks before the latter's death. "Our conversation," Baker recalled two years later, "was that of two men who had seen the vast tragedies of life." The river of life had flowed for both "only rarely in calm places. Most of the time there were riffles and shoal places where the going was hard, and sometimes it had fallen over great ledges into chasms and abysses." "These experiences," he said, "had left their mark."[56] Baker, Whitlock, Howe, Lippmann, Croly, White, Becker, Niebuhr—they were part of a company that never did truly return. Their journeys from conviction were no mere excursions. They were emigrations, and they took them steadily and irretrievably from their moorings of 1914 and the once sparkling and manifest promise of American life.

JOURNEYS TOWARD CONVICTION

For a third group of liberals the postwar years had yet another significance. Once they said farewell to progressivism, disillusioned liberals could take to one of two routes. Villard had said that they could move either to the Right or to the Left. John Chamberlain defined the alternatives as cynicism or revolution. Englishman Charles Montague wrote that they could linger to "smash and delete all the old institutions that disappointed in the day of trial" or they could be fired "with a new craving." As early as 1920 William Bullitt noticed prewar liberals gravitating into the two camps: "The more courageous liberals have begun to align themselves with the parties which draw their strength from the labouring class, while the less courageous are lapsing into an impotent faction scarcely distinguishable from the conservatives." Liberals like Croly and White oscillated indecisively between the two through the twenties. By 1930, however, the ranks were fairly well fixed, the issue joined. James Wechsler remembered reading during his sophomore year at Columbia Lippmann's elegiac *Preface to Morals* and John Strachey's exhortative *The Coming Struggle for Power*. "It was," Wechsler said, "the solitary man futilely contemplating the spectacle of the West's decline arrayed against the man of the future. One road was lonely escape; the other was valiant struggle."[57]

The road to the future generally led to communism, or to proletarianism of one form or another, and those prewar liberals who traveled it were mostly younger ones seeking to avert a premature retirement and a few graybeards like Steffens seeking some miraculous transfusion in their old age. Most of them had soured on middle-class progressivism before the war and were charting new directions and what Lewis Mumford called "surrogate heavens" well before the debacle at Paris. Bullitt and John Reed had blazed a trail to Russia; others had won their spurs in the labor movement at home; Steffens was already a "camp follower of revolutions."[58]Although stunned by the wreck of the new order, they could attribute the collapse to what they long suspected to be progressivism's shortcomings and get recharged on their own spare and untested illusions. Where the Crolys and Whites withdrew to nurse old idols, they proceeded on their journeys toward conviction.

At first glance, progressivism's *enfants terribles* would appear to be improbable candidates for conviction after the war. Ever since Hemingway heard Gertrude Stein speak of a "lost generation" and immortalized the phrase by inserting it opposite the title page of *The Sun Also Rises*, the young radical intelligentsia has customarily been portrayed as emerging from the war bitter and alienated, like Fitzgerald's Amory Blaine, "to find all Gods dead, all wars fought, all faiths in man shaken." Malcolm Cowley said, "After the war, they would all suffer from the same emotional collapse: they would be left standing like someone who has just expelled a deep breath and feels no wish to take another."[59]

According to the stereotype, the young radicals were as cynically disposed as disillusioned progressives and became even more sulking and escapist. Certainly there was bitterness. Hemingway in *A Farewell to Arms* would cringe at the "obscenity" of cheap words like "honor" and "justice" placed beside the monuments of leveled villages, khaki-stained rivers, and regimental casualty lists. Dos Passos would say that the "sacrifices" were no nobler or more purposeful than those at the Chicago stockyards. Besides Fitzgerald's *This Side of Paradise*, there was Dos Passos's *Three Soldiers*, Cummings's *The Enormous*

Room, and Eliot's *The Waste Land* as testaments to youthful despair. And there were, of course, the aimless, desultory expatriations.

But the postwar malaise was no more a permanent phenomenon among all of the young than it was among all of the old. There were permanently lost individuals; there was no lost generation. In fact, the Hemingways and Fitzgeralds and the others who burned themselves out on alcohol and jazz in the twenties were in a meager minority. The band of expatriates described by Fitzgerald in *Tender Is the Night* were a special breed of neurotics, alcoholics, and suicides. Matthew Josephson exploded the mythology some years later. "The very idea of a generation is only a convenient mental construct," he suggested. The young exiles were merely following a practice dating to Pound and Eliot before the war and Washington Irving a century earlier of apprentice writers and artists going abroad to obtain perspective on their own culture. "This does not mean we were 'lost,' " he said. Though the impact of the war was immense, "it is nonsense to hold that a generation of American youth were 'lost' or driven to despair." The movement to Europe, Josephson added, "was in no sense an exodus of massive proportions. . . . In numbers they represented only about one per cent of those who listed themselves in the U.S. census as professional writers." Walter Millis agreed. "How far I may be typical of what came to be called the 'Lost Generation' I do not know," he wrote in 1940. "So far as I know, I was never 'lost'; but then, very few of my contemporaries seem to have been either." Dos Passos remarked in an interview that despite his wide travels abroad he was never a party to the expatriation movement and that Cowley, who was, popularized the expatriate and lost-generation phenomena beyond their true dimension. He personally had opposed expatriation and "didn't spend very much time with any of those people." Cowley "always had a genius for getting things wrong—just a little bit wrong, wrong enough to be not quite true."[60]

No doubt most of the young radicals experienced in part the travail of spirit that numbed the Whitlocks and Lippmanns, and no doubt for a spell they engaged in similar bouts of soul-searching. Cowley's "long furlough" and Floyd Dell's "intellectual vagabondage" were not altogether inaccurate characterizations of their postwar course, nor were they metaphors applicable solely to spreeing derelicts like Fitzgerald. Dos Passos wandered from French battlefields and gruesome memories of the ambulance corps to the sheltering quietude of Spain and Portugal. Bullitt, after his Senate testimony, insulated himself on the Riviera in much the same manner as Whitlock; Janet Flanner said he became a "bookworm, rolling stone, and domestic man." But despite these fitful retreats, as Arno Mayer has observed of the radical intelligentsia, they "were neither temperamentally nor morally disposed to forsake the world." When he was almost 70 years old, Cowley himself, detached and philosophical, would admit that the war left the young radicals "not so much disillusioned as disaffiliated"; their capacity for illusion, he said, "was not so much destroyed as displaced."[61] Cowley added that the war had ended too soon for most of them. They had primed themselves for a colossal adventure and when the war ended rather abruptly there were reserves of energy and illusion yet untapped. Like the overheated patriots who channeled their excesses into the postwar Red Scare, they could be expected to release their adrenalin in some new arena of conflict. It was only natural that as they disowned Wilson and abandoned progressivism they should find a new outlet for their residual energies and displaced illusions in the beckoning revolution of communism.

Since the overthrow of the tsar in 1917, liberals searching for an alternative to progressivism had followed the communist experiment with rapt, sometimes mystical attachment. As early as July 1917, James Oppenheim, a cohort of Bourne's on the *Seven Arts*, was deliriously convinced that events in Russia were ushering in a great and wonderful change and a "new Humanity." "We see Russia now as that hopeful chaos, that confusion of the nebula, out of which a new world shapes itself," Oppenheim wrote. They were "riding on the storm." The romance became more serious with disclosure of the secret treaties, the apparent Allied betrayal of the Fourteen Points, and the emergence of Lenin as a rival prophet. By 1919, John Reed's *Ten Days That Shook the World* had sold ten thousand copies, and the contagion among young radicals was such that Dos Passos would later say they caught communism the way other people caught the flu. When the great crusade foundered and resulted in the triumph of reaction, it was easy for them to transfer their frayed allegiance from Wilson to Lenin. As Mayer comments, "Lenin was their surrogate conscience all the time that they rode Wilson's coattails."[62]

The process by which illusions were displaced from a fading Wilsonianism to an ascendant communism unfolded dramatically in the pages of the *Liberator*, "A Journal of Revolutionary Progress" which succeeded the disbanded *Masses* in March 1918 under the familiar editorship of Max Eastman and Floyd Dell. In their introductory issues the editors praised Wilson for his "openness of vision and pliancy of will" and were cautiously optimistic about his chances at the peace table. By September, however, Eastman was heralding Lenin as "a statesman of the new order" and in a barely veiled comparison with Wilson lauding the Bolshevik leader as "a democrat by nature, and not by presbyterian reasoning. . . . He speaks not condescendingly or tolerantly, but with affectionate appreciation, of these disorganized and disorderly assemblies of the masses." Wilson steadily fell into the *Liberator*'s disfavor, as evidenced in a series of barbed editorials and culminating in an article in March 1919 in which Eastman matched the rival prophets in a hypothetical conversation. Wilson came off as neurotic and pretentious; Lenin, sure and direct. Eastman had switched messiahs and decided in the same stroke that the Soviet experiment was "the greatest revolution and creative political act in the history of mankind." After the war, he interpreted Attorney General Palmer's deportation of undesirable aliens aboard the *Buford* as a voyage laden with symbol and significance. "The dreamers and revolters," he reported, "are travelling East instead of West, and the eyes of all the world are turning in the same direction as they go." When Bertrand Russell returned from a factfinding trip and warned the editors that they were merely trading one illusion for another, Eastman and Dell dismissed his caveat as that of a "bourgeois professor."[63]

Dos Passos, yet in France in 1919 attending the Sorbonne, remembered how easy it was to get reillusioned even with the arresting knowledge of the world's "idiocy and corruption." The politicians and diplomats huddled like festering caterpillars, but it was spring, and the "young hotheads," fueled by the new aspirations, would burn them out. Bullitt wrote confidently in March 1920 that the hope of peace had passed from liberalism to labor.[64]

Steffens, too wise and hardened by experience to be swayed by the manifestoes of younger radicals, agreed that something vital and promising was taking place in Russia. Near the conclusion of the peace conference he wrote his brother-in-law that it did not matter that the peacemakers had failed. The problems would be solved. "Other, newer men, with a fresher culture,—the men I have seen lately—they will have their turn now. . . . They know that liberty, democracy, fraternity,—all these lovely old desires can come only after men have made sure that there is food enough to eat, safety for themselves and their children, warmth, shelter, work and full pay." The mission to Moscow with Bullitt and travels throughout Europe convinced Steffens that the future belonged to communism and he became increasingly aroused by the possibilities that excited his younger colleagues. In an expansive tribute to Reed he proclaimed, "The future is coming; it is in sight. And it is good." Reed's death in Moscow "must have been a vision of resurrection." Throughout the ranks of the young intelligentsia and even in the dens of old walruses like Steffens, despite the trauma of disillusionment, the glow of revolution had sparked new enthusiasms and involvements. "I can be gloomy, tired, bitter, sordid, selfish, cynical and disgusted with the world," sighed Michael Gold, "but I can never despair." While others were blowing out the candles and journeying from conviction, the radicals gained a second wind and a new lease on idealism.[65]

The cult of proletarianism gathered momentum in the twenties. "The light of hope now burns elsewhere," John Haynes Holmes wrote in the *Survey.* "Idealism is not dead. It is still with us, only it fixes its attention . . . upon the British Labour Party, upon the League of Nations, upon Soviet Russia, upon Gandhi and India." Eastman left for Europe and a firsthand glimpse of the Promised Land in 1922, when the *Liberator* was expropriated by the American Communist party. Meeting comrades and swapping recipes for revolution, he did not return until 1927. Bullitt, a chronic sulk, cavorted between Vienna and Cannes and talked every so often of lying on the sand and watching the world go to hell; but he married Reed's widow and remained a passionate booster of the Russian cause, and in 1933 would be a felicitous choice to become America's first ambassador to the Soviet Union. Dos Passos went through a dark period of limbo following his stint in the ambulance corps, spinning his surrealist war novels and peregrinating through Spain, the Near East, Italy, Russia, and assorted other way stations before returning to the United States in 1922 and putting his reillusionment to the test. In 1917, as a fresh and recklessly determined alumnus of Harvard, Dos Passos had written a friend that his only hope was in the "wholesale assassination of all statesmen, capitalists, war-mongers, jingoists, inventors, scientists— in the destruction of all the machinery of the industrial world." With time out for reflection and sobering up he continued his journey toward conviction five years later as a discriminating Marxist. In the twenties he championed Sacco and Vanzetti and founded the *New Masses* with Gold and Joseph Freeman.[66]

Perhaps the most interesting, and certainly the most imposing figure in the group was Steffens. In 1920, at the age of 54, in the downswing of an orbit that had taken him from urban muckraking in Philadelphia and St. Louis to revolution in Mexico, Steffens had established himself as one of America's most protean and versatile reformers. It was a fitting climax to an enigmatic career that in 1920 he should want "to spend the evening of my life watching the morning of the new world." He was one of the very few old radicals, excluding the "most unwearied hopers," who were not "tired" after the war, perhaps because he had prepared himself for the failure at Versailles, perhaps because he had gulped a heady whiff of the future on his Moscow visit. After the signing of the treaty, Steffens stayed on in Europe "to watch the consequences," challenging a group of reporters "to name all the wars, big and little, that were going on in the world." His muffled correspondence through 1919 and his idle tramping through Copenhagen, Berlin, Rome, Vienna, and Prague before sailing back to New York in the fall of 1920 suggest he was not totally immune to the inertia that claimed other weathered reformers after the war. But the brush with communism had made a lasting impression, and "thinking it all out again in the new light" crystallized his vision of a communist future and restored him to the road of conviction. By the summer of 1923 he was back in Europe and brimming with enthusiasm about life and politics. From San Remo in December 1924, he wrote Whitlock that he had become "an utter optimist." His marriage to Ella Winter, a woman thirty years younger, and bright and vigorous, provided an additional tonic. Life was fun and very rich. He told Whitlock of his discovery that "whenever I lose an illusion I can find in the facts that destroyed it a better or at any rate another illusion."[67]

By the late twenties many of the radicals could detect middle-class America itself succumbing to the new *Zeitgeist*. Willy-nilly, by some infectious process, America seemed to be redeeming its old promise. Matthew Josephson remembered a marked break in the oppressive monotony of industrial society, "at some point in time such as 1925 or 1926." He wrote an "open letter" to Ezra Pound and the other exiles urging them to return and chided Pound for "still weeping into his wine glass and railing at his fatherland." The business culture seemed suddenly more dynamic, less selfish, more humane. Mass-production capitalism, some sensed, for all its materialism and technocracy, might in the end prove as benevolent as Soviet communism. Steffens, working on his autobiography in 1928, took a curious liking to "the new United States." The American way was not the Russian way, yet in a peculiar manner they were more alike than any other two countries he had seen. "Wasn't it this," he asked, "that these two young peoples, the Russians and the Americans, are driving, the one consciously, the other unwittingly, toward the same end?"[68]

Steffens returned to America in 1927. Although Pound remained ensconced in Italy, the exile colony gradually drifted back, some seeking employment and respectability, others another field for revolution, all of them attracted by what appeared to be the more civilized aspects of the new capitalism. Cowley became literary editor of the *New Republic* in 1929. Waldo Frank, another veteran of Bourne's *Seven Arts*, wrote a transcendental piece in 1928 proposing "the rediscovery of America." Josephson perhaps best explained the psychology of recommitment: "The enigma of America's future civilization continued to haunt me. . . . So far as my country was concerned

I wanted to be *engagé*, for better or worse, in the 'progress' or the 'evolution' of its society, rather than take flight to some island of Majorca or Capri where one practiced a pleasurable sort of delayed suicide."[69]

But these were men moved by something more compelling than the simple longing for roots and reconciliation that lured Fred Howe back from Nantucket, and when America disappointed them once again with the depression in 1929 they were on the road anew—this time for a longer and stormier engagement. It was really only after the depression that most of them became full-fledged fellow travelers.

Steffens plunged headlong into the proletarian cause after 1931, paying his last respects to "bankrupt liberalism" and making up his mind once and for all that "all roads lead to Moscow." Josephson agreed that "the scene of optimism" in America had reverted to the "abysmal state" of 1921 and that Russia was "the only large-scale experiment of a collective state now going forward." His "road of indignation" produced two epic Marxist critiques of American history—*The Robber Barons* (1934) and *The Politicos* (1938). Edmund Wilson appealed to progressives to stop "betting on capitalism," scrap finally the "old shibboleths" for "new ones as shocking as possible," and take their bearing from the Soviets. Waldo Frank shelved the "useable American past," one of the key ingredients of his recent rediscovery, and scouted the future during a depression vacation to Moscow. In *Dawn in Russia: The Record of a Journey,* Frank concluded, "What is taking place to-day in Russia is the most precious social event . . . of our crucial epoch. Russia is our time's most conspicuous stronghold . . . of the human spirit. We must defend the Soviet Union with our spirit; if need be, we must defend it with our bodies." Although few of them actually became card-carrying members of the party, they worked for the election of Communist candidate William Z. Foster in 1932, proselytized among their friends and braved the harassment of their enemies, and were possessed with the same consuming sense of urgency and purpose that stoked the progressive fires in 1917.[70]

Despite Eugene Lyons's facile contention that the radical intelligentsia "migrated from the Left Bank of Paris to the political Left of Moscow," there had been considerable foot dragging and more than one detour on the journey toward conviction. Daniel Aaron indicates that Malcolm Cowley's interest in the Soviet Union was whetted in the twenties but that he "did not take revolutionary ideas very seriously" until after the depression. In a radical symposium in September 1932, Waldo Frank stated that his movement to the left was "a steady, logical evolution . . . a clarifying and solidifying and organizing of convictions present in my work from its beginning." Granville Hicks, who quit the *New Republic* for the *New Masses* in 1934 and became a party member a year later, testified that in his youth he had fallen "under the influence of Wilsonian liberalism" and been "a fairly typical liberal, with a mild interest in socialism"; events in the twenties, especially the Sacco-Vanzetti affair, "crushed" the remnants of his conventional liberalism, and with the cathartic effect of the depression he was finally able "to get the virus . . . out of my system . . . to break through the fog of self-deception and confusion." Most of the radicals threw themselves into the communist cause in the thirties as both a logical and desperate last step in their postwar search for a habitable future. All their other prospects—such as a grassroots farmer-labor movement and even a regenerate capitalism in the United States— had gone up in smoke by 1931. Whittaker Chambers, who became an early convert in 1925, said that communism offered "what nothing else in the dying world had power to offer at the same intensity— faith and a vision."[71]

And so it was the apocalypse, Armageddon, the moment of truth all over again. Surrogate illusions would finally have to undergo their own acid test. What happened, of course, was another betrayal. "The future" turned out to be as dehumanizing as the capitalist past, in many ways more oppressive—and every bit as deceiving. American radicals had casually overlooked the misadventures that riddled the Marxist movement through the twenties—the feuds, the factionalism, the cults of personality; aberrations and imperfections could be excused, indeed expected, in a period of transition. But experiment gave way to rigid conformity, revolutionary dialogue to unquestioning discipline. The Stalinist excesses of the thirties produced a pattern of repression and betrayal more odious than anything experienced under progressivism. The famine of 1932–1933, the purges of 1937– 1938, capped with the Nazi-Soviet Non-Aggression Pact of August 1939, were gross Marxist versions of the capitalist depression, Wilsonian censorship, and the Allied secret treaties. Progressivism's fault had been that it was too timid and complacent; Marxism had become vicious. Dos Passos, always attracted more to the emancipating than the collectivist possibilities of communism, had hoped that "the soviets might develop into something like the New England town meeting, but of course they developed into something entirely different, something more like the boss-controlled conventions which we disliked at home." Eastman, a Trotskyite who resented Stalin from the start, remembered "the crude instinctive nationalistic bossism of the Russian leaders," even in the twenties "so sharply in conflict with their creed and profession of internationalism."[72]

Disillusionment struck erratically and unevenly—there was no lightning rod as that provided by the Paris conference in 1919. Dos Passos soured after the Communist party invaded a Socialist rally in Madison Square Garden in February 1934 and bullied the Socialists into a united front. Cowley, a late devotee and a late defector, insisted into April 1937 that "Stalin, with all his faults and virtues, represents the Communist revolution" and that "with its strength and weaknesses, its present shortcomings and its promise for the future," Russia was "still the most progressive force in the world"; not until the pact with Hitler did he demand "a complete reexamination not only of Russian practice but of Marxian theory from the beginning." Bullitt left his post in Moscow in 1936 for a more congenial one in Paris, appalled by Stalin's police state and the perversion of Lenin's faithful principles. Hicks resigned from the party in 1939. Eastman traced his disaffection to a falling out in the spring of 1921, then only "fractional" and "half-hearted . . . destined only after many years to be complete"; by 1938, his "ideological journey was approaching its inevitable end in the abandonment of the socialist hypothesis as disproven by two decades of experimentation." The *Liberator* editor who in 1918 had hailed the Bolshevik ascendancy as "the greatest revolution and creative political act in the history of mankind" finished out the thirties with a trilogy of debunking themes—*The End of Socialism in Russia* (1937), *Stalin's Russia and the Crisis in Socialism* (1939), and *Marxism: Is It Science?* (1940).[73]

When the break came, it came as cleanly and swiftly as the break with progressivism. The involvement with communism had always been more emotional than cerebral; there were none of the ideological fixations that beget diehards or martyrs. Whittaker Chambers wrote, "The ultimate choice I made was not for a theory or a party. It was— and I submit that this is true for almost every man and woman who has made it—a choice against death and for life."[74] The radical intelligentsia who wandered from the ruins of Versailles were carpetbaggers carrying and trading their illusions from one outpost to another. The effect of the Russian fiasco was merely to send them packing again—in the case of some, for the third or fourth time in a quarter-century. This time, however, the future offered few pathways. Both progressivism and communism were behind them; no new prophets or cathedrals beaconed ahead. In the absence of alternatives, the only routes really left open to them were the journeys *from* conviction mapped by the Whitlocks and Beckers twenty years earlier. And, like a ghost caravan, they followed those same trails.

Scott Nearing, fifty years old and a veteran of three decades in the socialist struggle, retired in 1932 to lead a "decent, kindly and orderly" life in the woods of Vermont; in the 1950s, about the same time that Walter Lippmann was recapitulating "the decline of the West" in *The Public Philosophy*, Nearing would collaborate with his wife Helen on a survival handbook entitled *Living the Good Life: How to Live Sanely and Simply in a Troubled World*. Harold Stearns, an exile in France, took Howe's reconciliation route in the thirties and returned to the United States and the "real world," an American "for better or worse." Characteristically, the disillusionment with Marxism provoked a shift to the right more pronounced than even Lippmann's postwar course. Cowley wrote in 1940 that a blind enthusiasm led to an equally blind revulsion. "Some have turned their values upside down, believing that they will thereby rid themselves of all their illusions." Eastman's "convalescing from socialism" led to a ringing endorsement of the American war effort, fraternization with Commonwealth and Southern boss Wendell Willkie, and such hard-hitting attacks on communism that a left-wing paper highlighted his defection with a notice "In Memoriam—Max Eastman." In the fifties and sixties, Eastman donned the mantle of the "bourgeois professor" whom he formerly ridiculed, writing crotchety memoirs, serving innocuously as "roving editor" for the *Reader's Digest*, and letting his name appear for a time on the masthead of William F. Buckley's *National Review*. Bullitt became an intense nationalist during the war, assailed the concessions made to the Russians at Yalta, and in the fifties pressed for the recapture of the Chinese mainland and eradication of the Chinese communists. In the sixties the onetime liberal prodigy finally made good his promise to watch the world go to hell and spent his remaining days in disinterested retirement on the Riviera.[75]

Dos Passos was a classic example of the "far-left-to-far-right" syndrome. His decompression in the thirties produced an affectionate work, *The Ground We Stand On*, in the manner of Van Wyck Brooks's "rediscovery" of the New England literary heritage, but by the late forties he had become a petulant critic of democracy and mass culture. Granville Hicks gauged the degree of his reversal in 1950: "Twenty years ago, he was as romantic a rebel as American letters had seen since the death of John Reed, passionate in his attack on capitalism, quick to support a radical cause. Today this pioneer fellow-traveler defends the profit motive, quarrels not merely with communism but also with the New Deal . . . and finds in Senator Taft the qualities of leadership he thinks America needs."[76]

Dos Passos voted the Republican ticket in every election between the end of the Second World War and his death in 1970. Barry Goldwater was a favorite candidate and the American intervention in Vietnam a favorite cause. He always maintained that he had not really changed through the turbulence of two major wars and a depression, that throughout his life he remained at bottom an individualist: in the twenties, it meant being a radical resisting the conformity and standardization of the business culture; in the forties and fifties, it meant being a conservative resisting the totalitarianism of the collectivist state that threatened to transplant itself from Russia to America. "The theme," he said in 1956, had always been "freedom."[77]

Semantics aside, however, Dos Passos's transformation was more substantial than he would admit. He had become more concerned with preservation than change, and had revised fundamentally his estimate of the "individuals" he was trying to save. As a tired radical—or conservative—he had come to distrust the "plain men" and to admire such former villains as McKinley, Bryan, Pershing, and even Wilson. During a television broadcast in 1962 he explained that he "got to understand Pershing much better. As a buck private in the rear rank I very much disliked him but looking at it from a rather dispassionate distance of many years, you see the man's charm, his virtues, and you become involved in problems, the day to day problems that had to be solved."[78]

Others who underwent "the great reversal," as Hicks termed it, included Whittaker Chambers, after 1940 a mystic and fatalist painfully collecting his thoughts in a moving correspondence with William Buckley; John Chamberlain, the author of *Farewell to Reform*, giving up on revolution as well, defending Joseph McCarthy in the fifties and, like Eastman and Dos Passos, graduating from the *New Masses* to the *National Review*; William Henry Chamberlin, like Dos Passos a gut individualist, making the quantum leap from Bolshevism to the *Wall Street Journal*; and Edmund Wilson, another individualist, fleeing the masses after "travels in two democracies" and toying with the concept of selective breeding. Chamberlain became a frequent contributor to *Fortune*, condensing several of his pieces into *The Enterprising Americans* (1963), a reverential history of American business written by a former Marxist.[79]

The gyrations of Eastman and the group that swung violently right were breathtaking and spectacular, and a remarkable number took the spin, but the majority of the disillusioned reached a level of equilibrium still within the compass of liberalism. Hicks emphasized that although the trails of the ex-fellow travelers crisscrossed the map of American politics, most ended up "closer to Norman Thomas or Harry S. Truman than to Senator Taft." Cowley and Josephson gingerly made their way back into farmer-labor politics. Early in 1940, Hicks and Max Lerner organized a series of meetings among those ex-communists who still considered themselves radicals to decide what they "ought to be doing in the United States." Cowley offered his "sixteen propositions" for reconstruction. "In view of what has happened in the world," said Cowley, "neither the liberalism of Woodrow Wilson's day nor the optimistic radicalism of the 1930's seems any longer a valid position." Russia had still "to be studied," but this time "not as a portent and working model of the future, but rather for the lessons to be drawn from Russian mistakes and Russian achievements." Hicks continued writing and editing, serving as literary consultant to the *New Leader* and teaching his course in proletarian literature at the New School, New York University, and Syracuse University.[80]

Lerner remained a dedicated "democrat," though he admonished flustered colleagues that liberalism would have to make smaller claims and be satisfied with smaller gains. He was pleased that the hard core of liberals still active was "working realistically with the trade unions and middle-class groups, . . . willing to acknowledge that it has made serious miscalculations [and] anxious to recast its theory and its tactic." In an introduction to a Modern Library edition of *The Prince*, Lerner stated that Machiavelli had underestimated the possibilities for creative human behavior and social commitment, but generally applauded the work for its unsentimental realism and hard-boiled principles, which seemed to him as axiomatic in 1940 as four centuries earlier:

> . . . that men, whether in politics, in business or in private life, do not act according to their professions of virtue; that leaders in every field seek power ruthlessly and hold on to it tenaciously; that the masses who are coerced in a dictatorship have to be wooed and duped in a democracy; that deceit and ruthlessness invariably crop up in every state; and that while the art of being ruled has always been a relatively easy one, the art of ruling ourselves is monstrously difficult.[81]

Even among those whose blind enthusiasm did not lead to a blind revulsion there was considerable rethinking and retrenchment—evidence that the iron had entered their souls and that the journey toward conviction had finally been derailed.

Only the education of Lincoln Steffens remained unfinished. Steffens died in 1936, spared the last ugly chapter in Russia's totalitarian slide. To the end he tolerated the Stalinist excesses. Christopher Lasch attributes his perseverance to being more thick-skinned and "scientifically" inclined than most of the fellow travelers—more willing to put up with moral injustices and accept the revolution on its own terms. "Secure in his faith," adds Daniel Aaron, "Steffens could look unmoved at the boils and carbuncles on the Soviet body politic that sickened the squeamish liberals." No doubt, too, the old muck-raker had finally tired of a career of exposés and skepticism. Hicks said in a 1952 article that Steffens "urged his mind" in a "quest for certainty." He had managed to lose and renurture illusions all his life until he was desperate for a future that offered some assurance; even Mussolini appealed to him briefly in the existentialist void of the twenties. At the time of his death Steffens had planned to emigrate to Russia to be closer to Reed and the resurrection. Carl Sandburg eulogized that "he had enough doubts and faiths to make a classic." A suitable epitaph for them all.[82]

POSTSCRIPT, 1940

By 1940, at the end of a generation in the crucible, liberalism's ranks were as variant, splintered, and uncategorical as ever, but they were also uniformly wiser, more restrained, and toughened with calluses. Even the optimists were keeping their eyes open. Cowley referred to himself as a "progressive," with a lower profile and paler corollaries than the term implied in 1914. Niebuhr was called by others a "pragmatic realist." Opening his mail one summer morning in 1940, he found a letter from a person asking him to set "moral force against Hitler's battalions." "It fails to explain," he thought, "how this moral force is to be effective against tanks, flame-throwers, and bombing planes." Niebuhr directed such irreconcilables "to retire to the monastery, where medieval perfectionists found their asylum."[83]

Max Lerner insisted on a "liberalism without tears." "We may as well understand," he said, "that there has been no age in modern history . . . so desperately a victim of its own accepted ideas. . . . Because of our errors of commission and omission in the past, we stand—even under the best outcome we can envisage—on the threshold of an ice age, in which we shall have to fight and endure, steel our will, nourish our patience." Dos Passos penned a "Preface Twenty-Five Years Later," trusting that "perhaps the disillusionments of the last quarter of a century have taught us that there are no short cuts to a decent ordering of human affairs, that the climb back out of the pit of savagery to a society of even approximate justice and freedom must necessarily be hard and slow. We can only manage one small step at a time." Felix Frankfurter, whose optimism in the twenties had amazed Carl Becker, told a gathering of the *Survey* Associates in December 1937, "We are in a much more chastened mood. We do not speak so glibly of progress." Frankfurter was now prepared to face "the grim realities of an intractable world."[84]

When they talked about reform, it was piecemeal and gradualist reform, not root-and-branch stuff. When they talked about American intervention and the impending war with Hitler, they studiously eschewed the crusading idiom. Lerner implored the intellectuals to accept war as a fact of modern life without having to justify or celebrate it. "We can no longer go on believing in the liberal notion of the unaided final triumph of the idea," he wrote in the *Nation* in August 1940. In an essay entitled "Randolph Bourne and Two Generations," Lerner urged them to view war as a necessary resort for the purpose of survival even if there were no social benefits to be accrued.[85]

Walter Millis, a lifelong pacifist and best-selling author in 1935 of *The Road to War*, a cynical interpretation of American intervention in World War I, became an outspoken supporter of intervention in 1940. In a semiautobiographical essay he admitted that his generation had regarded war too abstractly and dogmatically, that wars were inevitable and in fact "the deepest expression of our social life," and that their indignant reaction to Woodrow Wilson's failure was naive and immature. "Greed and littleness and unwisdom," Millis said, "are the commonplaces of all existence; no triumph of peace has ever been achieved without their presence, and while the effort to reduce them should be unrelenting, their existence should neither cause surprise nor be an excuse for defeatism."[86]

In 1943, looking ahead to another peace conference, Carl Becker cautioned against the "war to end imperialism" blather. He was confident that most liberals had outgrown such sentiments: "We have probably learned something since 1919. We have rightly set our hopes on making a better world, but most of us are less sure that a military victory alone will provide us with a great opportunity to do so overnight, and we are more aware that, in any case, the difficulties will be formidable."[87]

Van Wyck Brooks and Lewis Mumford, in the course of a correspondence that would last over forty years, had reduced their ambition from "What can we conquer?" to "What can we save?" In an address at Hunter College, Brooks lamented the tendency of contemporary writers to be sodden and withdrawn, but he could understand what had happened and was still picking up the pieces himself. His friend Mumford, in several articles and books through the early forties, skillfully diagnosed the pathology of liberalism and prescribed a more stringent regimen for the future. In *Faith for Living* Mumford cited their childish belief "in being permanently able to dispose of evil," "their immodest expectations of human goodness," their "too-virtuous idealism" and "too exacting purity." "Faith for living," he said,

> means being able to go on stoutly in a world where even the closest lovers quarrel and true friends misunderstand one another. We must recognize that it is fantastic to think that we can establish a perfect justice, which will call for no further remedies, or discover a perfect truth, which will call for no corrections. It is even more puerile, if that were possible, to believe that once we get the mechanism properly adjusted, creating full employment in the factory or balancing the endocrines in the human personality, the community will remain in that utterly blissful state.[88]

In "The Aftermath of Utopianism," written at the request of Niebuhr for *Christianity and Crisis*, Mumford painfully recounted their errors. They "never faced with candor the issues and results of the great World War." They read *All Quiet on the Western Front*, brooded over the horrors of fighting, became acutely conscious of the blunders of statesmen, recognized the implacable selfishness of the ruling classes. "But they lost sight of what the war itself was about. . . . They had hoped for a new heaven and earth to descend from the skies; and when they found that they had only cleared the ground for the City of Man, they were unprepared to survey the site or to set the cornerstone." "My generation, old and young, smug and cynical," Mumford said, "was wrong; it expected too high a reward for its virtue and sacrifice." In the face of the present war he called for a fresh maturity. They should prepare "for a century of resolute struggle." There would be delays, mistakes, mismanagements. "When the war is over we will not enter utopia; we will pass into the next phase of life. . . . There are no final solutions to human problems . . . only the courage to take the next step." Twenty years after Versailles, Mumford beseeched them finally to abandon their "juvenile conception of human nature . . . false hopes, lazy wishful attitudes, and perfectionist illusions."[89]

It is easy to criticize the generation of reformers who cut their teeth on progressivism and went on to "chase rainbows" or "grouch between their knees" and then grow long of tooth on adolescent fancies or senile anecdotage. It is easy to criticize their naïveté, their stubborn persistence in the wrong methods and wrong assumptions, their offended sensibilities. Perhaps this study has been too critical of their efforts, just as Mumford and the other self-accusers may have been too disparaging of themselves.

Perhaps the important lesson is that they aspired, not that they blundered or failed. Because they grew up and practiced their liberal profession in a pivotal, what often seemed to be an apocalyptic juncture in American history ànd Western civilization, they were especially vulnerable to the foolish illusions and hasty disillusions that snare reformers of every generation, and as a result they often appear peculiarly comic or tragic. But certainly their experience was not unique. The Lippmanns and Beckers and Eastmans had no monopoly on idealism or resignation. The prophylactic cycle of hope and disappointment is a recurring phenomenon in human history. The titles of John Gardner's works in the sixties, from his expectant *Excellence* (1961) to groping *Self-Renewal* (1964) and *No Easy Victories* (1968) to *The Recovery of Confidence* (1970), reflect the gamut of every reformer's ordeal. The *engagés* of 1970 and Kent State were already the dropouts of 1972. In an echo of Stuart Chase's *Survey* report a half century earlier, a young veteran of Woodstock and Harvard Square testified that he

> knew a whole mess of people who were out there on the streets together but look what's happened to them. One went to Africa with a Quaker program. One guy bought a farm in Nova Scotia. Another guy has a ranch in Wyoming. Another is studying communism in the London School of Economics. Another went to British Honduras to learn how to be a medicine man.[90]

In his last letter to William Buckley, Whittaker Chambers wrote, "History hit us with a freight train." Ultimately, it is the fate of all earnest people to begin as innocents and to make their way through billowing doubts and initiations toward an appointment with reality. The rendezvous with the freight train is inescapable. What distinguishes the stout hearts from the weak knees, the survivors from the victims, is one's course after the collision: whether, in Mumford's terms, the jilted idealist becomes a useful man or a resentful neurotic.[91] It is that crucial test which must be the final measure of the progressives' failure, and a beckoning challenge for those of us who uncertainly approach the crossroads in the seventies.

NOTES

Because of the mass of published material consulted, and because, at long stretches, I have let the liberals tell their own story, there are necessarily many references. For reasons of both economy and clarity I have attempted to consolidate notes where possible.

Periodicals consulted include *American Magazine*, the *American Review of Reviews*, the *Atlantic Monthly*, *Collier's*, the *Dial*, *Harper's*, the *Liberator*, the *Literary Digest*, the *Masses*, *McClure's*, the *Nation*, the *New Republic*, the *Saturday Evening Post*, *Scribner's*, and the *Seven Arts*; only the *New Republic*, frequently cited, is abbreviated (*NR*).

The Carl Becker Papers are at Cornell University in the Collection of Regional History and University Archives, and are cited as Becker Papers. The John Dos Passos Manuscript Collection, cited as Dos Passos MS., is in the Alderman Library of the University of Virginia. Although I usually found it more convenient to cite from their published letters or journals, I also examined the Lincoln Steffens Papers and Randolph Bourne Papers in Columbia University Library; the William Bullitt Papers in Yale University Library (now held privately by the family); and the Brand Whitlock, William Allen White, and Ray Stannard Baker collections in the Library of Congress.

To list a complete bibliography would require several dozen pages, since I have canvassed virtually all of the extant published materials, primary and secondary, for some thirty individuals. The notes should furnish an ample bibliographical network. Those wanting something more comprehensive or formalized may refer to my Ph.D. dissertation, "The Dynamics of Disillusionment in the American Liberal Community, 1914-1920," pp. 397-424, in the University of Virginia's Alderman Library.

Chapter 1

1. Walter Weyl, *Tired Radicals and Other Papers* (New York, 1921), 12.
2. Lewis Mumford, *Faith for Living* (New York, 1940), 4; Charles Edward Russell, *After the Whirlwind* (New York, 1919), 190-91.
3. Henry F. May, *The End of American Innocence* (New York, 1959); May, "The Rebellion of the Intellectuals, 1912-1917," *American Quarterly* 8 (Summer 1956): 114-26; Christopher Lasch, *The New Radicalism in America, 1889-1963* (New York, 1965).

4. Max Lerner, *It Is Later Than You Think* (New York, 1938), 3; C. H. Cramer, *Newton D. Baker: A Biography* (Cleveland, 1961), 63; Carl Becker, "The Dilemma of Liberals in Our Time," in *Detachment and the Writing of History: Essays and Letters of Carl L. Becker,* ed. Phil L. Snyder (Ithaca, N.Y., 1958), 188.

5. Wolfgang J. Helbich, "American Liberals in the League of Nations Controversy," *Public Opinion Quarterly* 31 (Winter 1967-68): 570.

6. Arno J. Mayer, *Political Origins of the New Diplomacy, 1917-1918* (New Haven, 1959), 393.

Chapter 2

1. Matthew Josephson, *Life Among the Surrealists* (New York, 1962), 15-16; carbon typescript in Dos Passos MS., n.d.; Elmer Davis, "Good Old 1913, Reminiscences of a Golden Age," *Forum* 85 (May 1931): 266; Mumford, *Faith for Living*, 4.

2. Jane Addams, *Newer Ideals of Peace* (New York, 1907), 209-38; Scott Nearing, *The Making of a Radical: A Political Autobiography* (New York, 1972), 177; Newton D. Baker, *Frontiers of Freedom* (New York, 1918), 116-17; Norman Angell, *The Great Illusion: A Study of the Relation of Military Power in Nations to Their Economic and Social Advantage* (London, 1911).

3. Upton Sinclair, *The Industrial Republic: A Study of America Ten Years Hence* (London, 1907); William English Walling, *Progressivism—and After* (New York, 1914), xvi; Brand Whitlock, *Forty Years Of It* (New York, 1914), 371; Donald Richberg, "We Thought It Was Armageddon," *Survey* 61 (1 Mar. 1929): 723; Carl Becker, "The New History," review of James Harvey Robinson's *The New History*, in *Dial* 53 (1 July 1912): 20.

4. John Dewey et al., *Creative Intelligence: Essays in the Pragmatic Attitude* (New York, 1917), 69; Holmes to Harold Laski, 31 Dec. 1916, *Holmes-Laski Letters: The Correspondence of Mr. Justice Holmes and Harold J. Laski, 1916-1935*, ed. Mark DeWolfe Howe (Cambridge, 1953), 1: 49; Horace Meyer Kallen, *The Structure of Lasting Peace* (Boston, 1918), 187 (italics mine).

5. William Allen White, *The Old Order Changeth: A View of American Democracy* (New York, 1910); Randolph Bourne, *The Gary Schools* (Boston, 1916) and *Education and Living* (New York, 1917); John Dewey, *Democracy and Education* (New York, 1916); Jane Addams, *A New Conscience and an Ancient Evil* (New York, 1912); Addams, *The Spirit of Youth and the City Streets* (New York, 1911).

6. Speeches of 23 Oct. 1917 and 31 Jan. 1918, in Baker, *Frontiers of Freedom*, 91, 225-36.

7. Walter Lippmann, *A Preface to Politics* (New York, 1913) and *Drift and Mastery* (New York, 1914).

8. Mumford, *Faith for Living*, 220.

9. Malcolm Cowley, *Exile's Return* (New York, 1934), 19-20. For Cowley's version of "the revolt against gentility" in literature, see his foreword in *After the Genteel Tradition* (New York, 1937), 9-25.

10. Josephson, *Life Among the Surrealists*, 13-14; Pound to Harriet Monroe, 24 Sept. 1914, *The Letters of Ezra Pound, 1907-1941*, ed. D. D. Paige (New York, 1950), 10; Van Wyck Brooks, *America's Coming-of-Age* (New York, 1915); May, "Rebellion of the Intellectuals," 125.

11. Henry Dan Piper, "Fitzgerald's Cult of Disillusion," *American Quarterly* 3 (Spring 1951): 79; Bourne to Alyse Gregory, 8 Sept. 1913, cited in "Randolph Bourne and Two Generations," in Max Lerner, *Ideas for the Ice Age* (New York, 1941), 129.

12. Heinz Eulau, "Mover and Shaker: Walter Lippmann as a Young Man," *Antioch Review* 11 (Sept. 1951): 302; Cowley, *After the Genteel Tradition*, 229-30.

13. Holmes to Laski, 7 Sept. 1916, *Holmes-Laski Letters*, 1:17; Laski to Holmes, 9 Sept. 1916, *Letters*, 1:17.

14. Steffens to Brand Whitlock, 25 Apr. 1910, *The Letters of Lincoln Steffens*, ed. Ella Winter and Granville Hicks (New York, 1938), 1:245; *The Autobiography of Lincoln Steffens* (New York, 1931), 2:575; George Santayana, *The Life of Reason* (New York, 1905), 2:136.

15. Recounted in John Haynes Holmes, "What Is Worth Fighting For in American Life?" *Survey* 57 (1 Feb. 1927): 550.

16. Walter Lord, *The Good Years: From 1900 to the First World War* (New York, 1960), ix; William Allen White, "A Theory of Spiritual Progress," Phi Beta Kappa address delivered at Columbia, 1908 (published Emporia, Kansas, 1910); Whitlock, *Forty Years Of It*, 373; John Chamberlain, *Farewell to Reform* (New York, 1932), 275.

Chapter 3

1. *Literary Digest* 48 (20 June 1914): 1469-70; *Atlantic Monthly* 113 (June 1914): 721-32; *Munsey's* 52 (June 1914): 72-82; *American Review of Reviews* 49 (June 1914): 641-65; *Scribner's* 55 (June 1914): 762-73.

2. Edith Wharton, *A Backward Glance* (New York, 1934), 336-38; Brand Whitlock, *Belgium: A Personal Narrative* (New York, 1919), 1:7; Harold Stearns, *The Street I Know* (New York, 1935), 98-99.

3. Walter Lippmann, *U.S. Foreign Policy: Shield of the Republic* (Boston, 1943), xi; Nearing, *Making of a Radical*, 105-6; Russell, *After the Whirlwind*, 26.

4. *The Autobiography of William Allen White* (New York, 1946), 549, 558; Davis, "Good Old 1913," 267.

5. Herbert Croly, *The Promise of American Life* (New York, 1909), 312; Russell, *After the Whirlwind*, 72.

6. Max Eastman, *Love and Revolution: My Journey Through an Epoch* (New York, 1964), 22; Wharton, *A Backward Glance*, 338; David Starr Jordan and Harvey Ernest Jordan, *War's Aftermath: A Preliminary Study of the Eugenics of War* (Boston, 1914), xviii.

7. Santayana to Mrs. Frederick Winslow, 16 Aug. 1914, *The Letters of George Santayana*, ed. Daniel Cory (New York, 1955), 139-40; John Haynes Holmes, "War and the Social Movement," *Survey* 32 (26 Sept. 1914): 629; Charles William Eliot, address to Business Women's Club of Boston, 15 Oct. 1914, in Eliot, *The Road Toward Peace* (Boston, 1915), 101.

8. May, "Rebellion of the Intellectuals," 115; John Dos Passos, *The Best Times: An Informal Memoir* (New York, 1966), 23; Harold Stearns, *Liberalism in America* (New York, 1919), 80 (italics are Stearns's); Bourne letter of 25 Aug. 1914, cited in "Bourne and Two Generations," 126.

9. "The Conquest of America!" *McClure's* 45 (May 1915): 9 ff.; Richard Harding Davis, *With the Allies* (New York, 1914); *Sixty Opinions on the War* (London, 1915); Hugo Münsterberg, *The War and America* (New York, 1914) and *The Peace and America* (New York, 1915).

10. Holmes, "War and the Social Movement," 630; "Mental Unpreparedness," NR 4 (11 Sept. 1915): 143-44.

11. William Howard Taft, "A Message to the People of the United States," *Independent* 79 (10 Aug. 1914): 199; "Mental Unpreparedness," 144.

12. *Towards An Enduring Peace: A Symposium of Peace Proposals and Programs, 1914-1916*, compiled by Randolph S. Bourne (New York, 1916), 13, 143, 189-99, 36, 135, 203-4. (Italics in the Walling excerpt are mine.)

13. A useful compilation of the various peace programs is David Starr Jordan, *Ways to Lasting Peace* (Indianapolis, 1916).

14. Eliot, *The Road Toward Peace*, 16, 236-46; Eliot to *New York Times*, 4 Sept., 17 Nov., and 11 Dec. 1914, and 1 July 1919.

15. *Towards An Enduring Peace*, 59-60. Another response conspicuous for its insight was that of A. Lawrence Lowell, Eliot's successor as president of Harvard, who perceived that the proposed settlement could not "meet all possible contingencies" or "prevent all future wars" (p. 158).

16. Walter Lippmann, *The Stakes of Diplomacy* (New York, 1915), 9-10, 6, 204, 224.

17. David Starr Jordan, *War and the Breed: The Relation of War to the Downfall of Nations* (Boston, 1915), 216; Laski to Holmes, 13 Dec. and 28 Dec. 1916, *Holmes-Laski Letters*, 42, 48; Laski to Holmes, 9 Sept. 1916, *Letters*, 17; John Dos Passos, "A Humble Protest," *Harvard Monthly* 62 (June 1916): 120.

18. Edith Wharton, ed., *The Book of the Homeless* (New York, 1916), 45.

19. *Enforced Peace: Proceedings of the First Annual National Assemblage of the League to Enforce Peace*, Washington, D.C. (26-27 May 1916), 5, 6.

20. Newton D. Baker, "National Ideals," *Survey* 37 (25 Nov. 1916): 189.

21. Herron to Sinclair, 20 Sept. 1915, in Upton Sinclair, *My Lifetime in Letters* (Columbia, Mo., 1960), 192-93.

22. Whitlock to House, 17 May 1916, *The Letters and Journal of Brand Whitlock*, ed. Allan Nevins (New York, 1936), 1:193-94.

Chapter 4

1. See, for instance, *Sixty Opinions on the War*, 8, 69-71, 118-20.

2. Chapman to his mother, 12 Aug. 1914, *John Jay Chapman and His Letters*, ed. M. A. DeWolfe Howe (Boston, 1937), 282; "A Memorandum on Compulsory Disarmament," 12 Aug. 1914, *Letters*, 283; diary, 28 Aug. 1914, *Letters*, 286.

3. Diary, 1 Sept. 1914, *Letters*, 287.

4. Eliot to *New York Times*, 12 Mar. 1916; see also Eliot to *Times*, 27 July 1916; John E. Semonche, *Ray Stannard Baker* (Chapel Hill, N.C., 1969), 306.

5. Lippmann, "Notes for a Biography," *NR* 63 (16 July 1930): 250-52.

6. "Notes for a Biography," 251; "Timid Neutrality," *NR* 1 (14 Nov. 1914): 7-8; "Pacifism vs. Passivism," *NR* 1 (12 Dec. 1914): 6-7; "The Goose and the Gander," *NR* 2 (20 Feb. 1915): 59-60. See also untitled editorial, 2 (27 Feb.): 83; "Getting It Both Ways," 2 (27 Feb.): 86-87; and "The Difficult Peace," 2 (May 1): 315-16.

7. "The Temper of Two Nations," *NR* 3 (5 June 1915): 107-8; "Not Our War," *NR* 3 (5 June 1915): 108-9.

8. *NR* 9 (2 Dec. 1916): 106; "Moving Toward Peace," *NR* 9 (25 Nov. 1916): 81-82. Among the several scholars who have examined the *New Republic* editorials during this period, the most thorough investigations of this dilemma have been by Charles Forcey, *The Crossroads of Liberalism: Croly, Weyl, Lippmann, and the Progressive Era, 1900-1925* (New York, 1961), chap. 7; David W. Noble, *The Paradox of Progressive Thought* (Minneapolis, 1958), chap. 2; and Robert Endicott Osgood, *Ideals and Self-Interest in America's Foreign Relations* (Chicago, 1953), 121-25.

9. "The Note as Americanism," *NR* 9 (30 Dec. 1916): 228-29; "Beneath the Outcry," *NR* 9 (30 Dec. 1916): 232.

10. "The Note as Americanism," 228-29; "Beneath the Outcry," 232.

11. Stearns, *Liberalism in America*, 146.

12. Pinchot to New York *Evening Post*, 27 Mar. 1917, cited in Lasch, *New Radicalism in America*, 205.

13. Josephson, *Life Among the Surrealists*, 54; Randolph Bourne, *Untimely Papers*, ed. James Oppenheim (New York, 1919). *Seven Arts* was intended to be exclusively an

"arts" magazine, but it assumed a steadily increasing interest in politics and the war. "We felt," said one of the editors, "the war also was a cultural crisis." See John Adam Moreau, *Randolph Bourne—Legend and Reality* (Washington, D.C., 1966), 145. For a distillation of Bourne's views on the war, see Moreau, chaps. 8 and 9.

14. *Masses*, Nov. 1916; Eastman, *Love and Revolution*, 25-26; Nearing, *Making of a Radical*, 110. The *Masses* was founded in 1911 by a group of socialist artists and writers and was, in its infancy, according to Eastman, "more interested in consumers' cooperatives than in the class struggle." When Eastman became editor, the magazine embarked on a career of radicalism. The best summary of its stormy evolution is in Daniel Aaron, *Writers on the Left: Episodes in American Literary Communism* (New York, 1964), 18-23.

15. Norman A. Graebner, ed., *Ideas and Diplomacy* (New York, 1964), 411.

16. "Notes for a Biography," 251; "Beneath the Outcry," 232.

17. *New York Times*, 23 and 24 Jan. 1917; Semonche, *Ray Stannard Baker*, 306; Stephen Wise, *Challenging Years: The Autobiography of Stephen Wise* (New York, 1949), 175-77.

18. Untitled editorial, NR 9 (6 Jan. 1917): 253; "The Will to Believe," NR 9 (13 Jan. 1917): 283-84.

19. "America Speaks," NR 9 (27 Jan. 1917): 342; NR 10 (3 Feb. 1917), cover; Arthur S. Link, *Woodrow Wilson and the Progressive Era, 1910-1917* (New York, 1954), 267-69; "New Russia and the War," *Nation* 104 (22 Mar. 1917): 330.

20. Frederick Lewis Allen, "The American Tradition and the War," *Nation* 104 (26 Apr. 1917): 484; Henry van Dyke, "Liberty Enlightening the World," London *Times*, 10 Apr. 1917, in *A Treasury of War Poetry*, ed. George Herbert Clarke (Boston, 1917), 4-5; Wise to Wilson, 11 Apr. 1917, *Challenging Years*, 177; Russell, *After the Whirlwind*, 271-72; Stearns, *Liberalism in America*, 90; Cowley, *Exile's Return*, 45.

21. Kennan develops his theme in several works, notably *American Diplomacy, 1900-1950* (Chicago, 1951), 58-59 and *Russia and the West* (Boston, 1960), 5-6; White to George Brett, 29 June 1917, *Selected Letters of William Allen White*, ed. Walter Johnson (New York, 1947), 181; Gustavus Myers, "Why Idealists Quit the Socialist Party," *Nation* 104 (15 Feb. 1917): 181-82. Stearns found it bitterly amusing that erstwhile socialists, once they had joined the cause, were given daily space in the conservative press to air their displeasure with pacifists and later the Bolsheviks. Stearns, *Liberalism in America*, 111-12.

22. *The Autobiography of Upton Sinclair* (New York, 1962), 218-19. Sinclair commented in 1927: "It was my task, self-assumed, to hold the radical movement in line for Woodrow Wilson's policies. Needless to say, I never asked or received a cent from anyone, and the little magazine which I edited and published cost me a deficit of six or eight thousand dollars for the ten months of its history." Sinclair, *Money Writes!* (New York, 1927), 52-53.

23. David Starr Jordan, *The Days of a Man: Being Memoirs of a Naturalist, Teacher and Minor Prophet of Democracy* (New York, 1922), 2: 735; "In the War with a Free Hand," *Nation* 104 (3 May 1917): 518; untitled editorial, *Nation* 104 (17 May 1917): 589.

24. Louis Filler, *Crusaders for American Liberalism* (New York, 1939), 375; Max Lerner, "The Attitude of the Intellectuals," *Nation* 151 (3 Aug. 1940): 89; Forcey, *Crossroads of Liberalism*, 210; Jane Addams, *Peace and Bread in Time of War* (New York, 1945 [New York, 1922]), 142; Stearns, *Liberalism in America*, 102-6.

25. Untitled editorial, NR 9 (25 Nov. 1916): 79. On this general theme, see Allen F. Davis, "Welfare, Reform and World War I," *American Quarterly* 19 (Fall 1967): 516-33; Charles Hirschfeld, "Nationalist Progressivism and World War I," *Mid-America* 45 (July 1963): 139-56; and William E. Leuchtenburg, "The New Deal and the Analogue of War," in John Braeman et al., eds., *Change and Continuity in Twentieth Century America* (Columbus, O., 1964), 81-143.

26. Albert J. Beveridge, *What Is Back of the War* (Indianapolis, 1915), 426.

27. Addams, *Peace and Bread*, 132-33. Veblen reverted to form and bowed out of his post after five months. See Joseph Dorfman, *Thorstein Veblen and His America* (New York, 1934), 383. Darrow wrote his piece for *Santa Fe Magazine*; it was reprinted in the *War Information Series*, no. 14 (Mar. 1918), 26-27.

28. Eric F. Goldman, *Rendezvous With Destiny* (New York, 1952), 250-51; *Letters and Journal of Brand Whitlock*, 1: xix; Russell, *After the Whirlwind*, 185-86, 267-68; Donald B. Meyer, *The Protestant Search for Political Realism, 1919-1941* (Berkeley, 1961), 11.

29. Dewey, "What America Will Fight For," *NR* 12 (18 Aug. 1917): 69.

30. Lippmann, "Angels to the Rescue," *NR* 5 (1 Jan. 1916): 221; "The White Passion," *NR* 8 (21 Oct. 1916): 293-95.

31. "The World Conflict In Its Relation to American Democracy," address before the American Academy of Political and Social Science, Philadelphia, Apr. 1917, printed in full in Lippmann, *The Political Scene: An Essay on the Victory of 1918* (New York, 1919), 83-103.

32. *Stakes of Diplomacy*, 7; Heinz Eulau, "Wilsonian Idealist: Walter Lippmann Goes to War," *Antioch Review* 14 (Mar. 1954): 87-93; Eulau, "Man Against Himself: Walter Lippmann's Years of Doubt," *American Quarterly* 4 (Winter 1952): 303; Osgood, *Ideals and Self-Interest*, 121.

33. Eulau, "Wilsonian Idealist," 104.

34. Charles Chatfield, "World War I and the Liberal Pacifist in the United States," *American Historical Review* 75 (Dec. 1970): 1920-37; Nearing, *Making of a Radical*, 112; James Weinstein, "Anti-War Sentiment and the Socialist Party, 1917-1918," *Political Science Quarterly* 74 (June 1959): 219.

35. Bourne, "The War and the Intellectuals," *Seven Arts* 2 (June 1917): 133-46.

36. "War and the Intellectuals," 144; Laski, "The Liberalism of Randolph Bourne," *Freeman* 1 (19 May 1920): 237.

37. *New York Times*, 23 Jan. 1917; Laski to Holmes, 18 Apr. 1917, *Holmes-Laski Letters*, 1: 79.

38. "International Security," *NR* 9 (11 Nov. 1916): 35; *War Information Series*, no. 4 (Aug. 1917), 15; Lippmann, *Political Scene*, 102.

39. "Mental Unpreparedness," 144; Croly, "American Withdrawal From Europe," *NR* 36 (12 Sept. 1923): 66.

Chapter 5

1. Helbich, "American Liberals in the League of Nations Controversy," 573; Baker, *American Chronicle* (New York, 1945), 303; *War Information Series*, no. 14 (Mar. 1918), 42.

2. Speeches of 4 July and 12 Dec. 1917, in Baker, *Frontiers of Freedom*, 52, 203.

3. Edward T. Devine, "Social Organization for War Needs," *Survey* 38 (7 July 1917): 316-17.

4. Kallen, *Structure of Lasting Peace*, 56-57; Weyl, *The End of the War* (New York, 1918), 303-4; Angell, *The British Revolution and the American Democracy* (New York, 1919); Dewey, "What Are We Fighting For?" *Independent* 94 (22 June 1918): 474.

5. Addams, *Peace and Bread*, 135.

6. Fitzgerald to his mother, 14 Nov. 1917, *The Letters of F. Scott Fitzgerald*, ed. Andrew Turnbull (New York, 1963), 451-52; Cowley, *Exile's Return*, 47-52; May, *The End of American Innocence*, 381.

7. Cowley lecture at University of Virginia, 1 Nov. 1967; Dos Passos interview with David Sanders for the *Paris Review*, 1962, carbon typescript in Dos Passos MS. (also, Dos Passos, *Best Times*, 24); Josephson, *Life Among the Surrealists*, 55-56 (he borrowed the phrase from Dos Passos).

8. American Historical Association meeting, Washington, D C , 30 Dec. 1969. See Roland N. Stromberg, "European Intellectuals and the Coming of the War," *Journal of European Studies* 3 (1973): 109-22.

9. Walter Millis, "The Faith of an American," in Stephen Vincent Benét et al., *Zero Hour* (New York, 1940), 218-19.

10. Eastman, "Wilson and the World's Future," *Liberator* 1 (May 1918): 24; undated note, cited in Beatrice Farnsworth, *William C. Bullitt and the Soviet Union* (Bloomington, Ind., 1967), 13.

11. Cowley mentioned the "Seegerette" anecdote in his Virginia lecture; Seeger to his mother, 28 Sept. 1914, *Letters and Diary of Alan Seeger* (New York, 1917), 2-3; Seeger to his mother, 18 June 1915, *Letters and Diary*, 119-20; Charles V. Genthe, *American War Narratives, 1917-1918: A Study and Bibliography* (New York, 1969).

12. Chapman, *Deutschland Über Alles, or Germany Speaks* (New York, 1914), 92; Eliot to *New York Times*, 4 Sept. and 2 Oct. 1914; untitled editorial, *NR* 10 (10 Feb. 1917): 31.

13. Steffens to Allen H. Suggett, 30 Sept. 1917, *Letters*, 1: 405-6; Baker, *American Chronicle*, 303.

14. Ida Tarbell, *All In The Day's Work* (New York, 1939), 330; Allen, "The American Tradition and the War," 484; Angell, *After All: The Autobiography of Norman Angell* (New York, 1952), 200.

15. Baker, *Frontiers of Freedom*, 29-30.

16. Allen, "The American Tradition and the War," 485; Frederic C. Howe, *The Confessions of a Reformer* (New York, 1925), 267; "Bourne and Two Generations," 130; Villard, *Fighting Years: Memoirs of a Liberal Editor* (New York, 1939), chap. 18; Eastman gives an amusing recollection of the lynching episode in *Love and Revolution*, chap. 7.

17. Stearns, *The Street I Know*, 165-66; Edward A. Steiner, "What the War Did to My Mind," *Christian Century* 45 (15 Feb. 1928): 203-4; C. Hartley Gratton, "The Historians Cut Loose," *American Mercury* 11 (Aug. 1927): 421. Gratton's account of the irrationality that gripped the historical profession is brutally humorous if sensationalized; more serious is James R. Mock and Cedric Larson, *Words That Won the War: The Story of the Committee on Public Information, 1917-1919* (Princeton, 1939), chap. 7.

18. Granville Hicks, "The Parsons and the War," *American Mercury* 10 (Feb. 1927): 129-42. Hicks later admitted some "flippancy" but insisted that his charges were thoroughly documented and that he was serious about them. See Hicks, *Part of the Truth* (New York, 1965), 62-64. Harry Emerson Fosdick defended the preachers against the Hicks indictment in "What the War Did to My Mind," *Christian Century* 45 (5 Jan. 1928): 10.

19. Addams, *Peace and Bread*, 140; Holmes to Laski, 9 June 1917, *Holmes-Laski Letters*, 1: 89-90; "The Case of the Columbia Professors," *Nation* 105 (11 Oct. 1917): 388-89; Whitlock to Meredith Nicholson, 17 Sept. 1918, *Letters and Journal*, 1: 265. See also Whitlock's diary entries, *Letters and Journal*, 2: 466-528.

20. Becker to Professor W. A. Hammond, 17 Apr. 1918, cited in Burleigh Taylor Wilkins, *Carl Becker* (Cambridge, 1961), 143; Kallen, *Structure of Lasting Peace*, xiii-xiv; Dewey, "In Explanation of Our Lapse," *NR* 13 (3 Nov. 1917): 17-18; Beard to Butler, 8 Oct. 1917, printed in *New York Times*, 9 Oct. 1917.

21. Kallen, *Structure of Lasting Peace*, xiv-xv; Baker, *Frontiers of Freedom*, 148.

22. "Seeing the War Through," *NR* 14 (30 Mar. 1918): 248-51; "Mob Violence and War Psychology," *NR* 16 (3 Aug. 1918), 5-7.

23. *Win the War for Permanent Peace: Addresses Made at the National Convention of the League to Enforce Peace*, Philadelphia (16-17 May 1918), 27, 41, 51, 34.

24. H. L. Mencken to Sinclair, 19 Aug. 1918, in Sinclair, *My Lifetime in Letters*, 230; Albert Jay Nock to Baker, 9 June 1918, cited in Cramer, *Newton D. Baker*, 158.

25. A classic instance is Villard's untitled editorial, *Nation* 111 (3 Nov. 1920): 489.

26. Osgood, *Ideals and Self-Interest*, 287.

27. Baker notebook entry, cited in Semonche, *Ray Stannard Baker*, 311; Straight to his wife, 23 Dec. 1917, cited in Herbert Croly, *Willard Straight* (New York, 1924), 481; Santayana to Mrs. Frederick Winslow, 6 Apr. 1918, *Letters*, 164-65.

28. John Reed, "Almost Thirty," written in 1917, published in *NR* 86 (15 and 29 Apr. 1936): 267-70, 332-36; Bourne to Everette Benjamin, 26 Nov. 1917, cited in Moreau, *Bourne*, 166; Fitzgerald to "Ceci" (his cousin), 10 June 1917, and to Edmund Wilson (his classmate at Princeton), 10 Jan. 1918, *Letters*, 76, 324; Steffens to Mrs. J. James Hollister, 5 Jan. 1918, *Letters*, 1: 416.

29. Croly, *Willard Straight*, 481; Croly to Hand, 31 Oct. 1918, cited in Forcey, *Crossroads of Liberalism*, 285.

30. *Letters and Journal*, 1: 257, 260-61, 263; 2: 420, 471, 473.

31. Goldman, *Rendezvous With Destiny*, 253.

32. *The End of the War*, 2-4, 31; *Tired Radicals*, 12.

33. *John Jay Chapman and His Letters*, 341; *Letters and Journal*, 2: 509; Santayana to B. A. G. Fuller, 10 Sept. 1919, *Letters*, 171.

34. Meyer, *Protestant Search for Political Realism*, 15-16.

Chapter 6

1. Baker to Whitlock, 2 Nov. 1918, cited in Frederick Palmer, *Newton D. Baker: America at War* (New York, 1931), 2: 379.

2. Wolfgang J. Helbich, granted access to the Foreign Policy Association files, has examined extensive minutes and memoranda of the LFNA and written a lengthy article on its activities. See Helbich, "American Liberals in the League of Nations Controversy," *Public Opinion Quarterly* 31 (Winter 1967-68): 568-96.

3. "The Pivot of History," *NR* 17 (16 Nov. 1918): 59; "The Progress Towards Peace," *Nation* 107 (19 Oct. 1918): 436; "The German Collapse," *Nation* 107 (2 Nov. 1918): 502; untitled editorials in *Dial* 65 (5 and 19 Oct. 1918): 265, 311.

4. Steffens to Laura Suggett, 1 Nov. 1918, *Letters*, 1: 439; Steffens, *Letters*, 1: 402-52 passim; Straight to his wife, 20 Aug., 14 Oct., 25 Oct. 1918, cited in Croly, *Willard Straight*, 516, 526, 528; diary, 7 Nov. 1918, *Letters and Journal*, 2: 514.

5. Eulau, "Wilsonian Idealist," 99; *Political Scene*, 9-10, xii, 80.

6. Steffens to Laura and Allen Suggett, 27 Oct. 1918, *Letters*, 1: 436.

7. Frank H. Simonds, *When Europe Made Peace Without America* (Garden City, N.Y., 1927), 65; White, *Autobiography*, 549; Harold Nicolson, *Peacemaking 1919* (London, 1933), 31-32; Herron to Sinclair, 4 Dec. 1918, in Sinclair, *My Lifetime in Letters*, 194.

8. Ray Stannard Baker, *Woodrow Wilson and World Settlement* (Garden City, N.Y., 1922), 1: 9-11.

9. Charles T. Thompson, *The Peace Conference Day By Day* (New York, 1920), 3-5; Edward M. House, "The Versailles Peace in Retrospect," in *What Really Happened at Paris: The Story of the Peace Conference, 1918-1919, by American Delegates* (New York, 1921), 431; Whitlock to House, 28 Nov. 1918, *Letters and Journal*, 1: 271-72.

10. John Dos Passos, *Mr. Wilson's War* (Garden City, N.Y., 1962), 459; James T. Shotwell, *At the Paris Peace Conference* (New York, 1937), 69 (curiously, on Wilson's second voyage to Europe his ship landed on March 13).

11. Westermann diary, 4 Dec. 1918, cited in Lawrence E. Gelfand, *The Inquiry: American Preparations for Peace, 1917-1919* (New Haven, 1963), 169; Bullitt diary, 4 Dec. 1918, cited in Gelfand, *Inquiry*, 170.

12. George Creel, *The War, the World and Wilson* (New York, 1920), 163. Creel's precise function at Paris was unclear. Dos Passos remarked cynically that Creel hoped "to go on transmitting to the world the Wilsonian slogans as they fell from his master's lips" (*Mr. Wilson's War*, 444).

13. Herbert Hoover, *Memoirs* (New York, 1952), 1: 452; diary, 2 Jan. 1919, in Stephen Bonsal, *Unfinished Business* (Garden City, N.Y., 1944), 15; Vernon Bartlett, *Behind the Scenes at the Paris Peace Conference* (London, 1919), 13.

14. Villard, *Memoirs*, 362-63. Villard noted that he finally won over the British visa officer by telling him that during the Venezuela episode in 1895 his *Evening Post* sided with the British and broke with President Cleveland.

15. *The Intimate Papers of Colonel House*, ed. Charles Seymour (Boston, 1928), 4: 255.

16. *Manchester Guardian*, 19 Dec. 1918, cited in Baker, *Woodrow Wilson and World Settlement*, 1: 84; *L'Oeuvre*, 10 Jan. 1919, cited in Baker, 1: 86; *Nation* 107 (21 Dec. 1918): 759; *Dial* 65 (14 Dec. 1918): 561; *NR* 17 (21 Dec. 1918): 206.

17. Lippmann, *Political Scene*, ix-x; "The Meaning of Reconstruction," *NR* 17 (14 Dec. 1918): 182-83; *Liberator* 1 (Dec. 1918): 8; Eastman, *Love and Revolution*, 135; Granville Hicks, *John Reed: The Making of a Revolutionary* (New York, 1936), 327.

18. Shotwell diary, 22 Jan. 1919, *At the Peace Conference*, 136; Steffens to Laura Suggett, 24 Dec. 1918, *Letters*, 1: 451 (italics are Steffens's); Villard to his wife, 1 Jan. 1919, cited in Wreszin, *Villard*, 109; White to his wife, 8 Jan. 1919, *Selected Letters*, 195; Walter Johnson, *William Allen White's America* (New York, 1947), 296.

19. Bartlett, *Behind the Scenes*, 71.

20. The text of the statement is printed in Baker, *Woodrow Wilson and World Settlement*, 3: 47-49. As numerous scholars have pointed out, Wilson never actually intended open "diplomacy" but rather open "results"—i.e., disclosure of the final treaties.

21. "Secrecy at Versailles," *Nation* 108 (25 Jan. 1919): 122-23; *NR* 17 (25 Jan. 1919): 353-54; Sisley Huddleston, *Peace-Making at Paris* (London, 1919), 28; Bartlett, *Behind the Scenes*, 16.

22. For a detailed record, see Baker, *Woodrow Wilson and World Settlement*, v. 1, pt. 3.

23. Baker, *Woodrow Wilson and World Settlement*, 1: 291; letter dated 15 Feb. 1919, in Charles Seymour, *Letters From the Paris Peace Conference*, ed. Harold B. Whiteman, Jr. (New Haven, 1965), 163; "The Net Result," *Nation* 108 (22 Feb. 1919): 268. The *New Republic* was delighted with Wilson's progress up to this point: "No one who will read without bias the provisions of the proposed constitution can doubt for a moment that if such an organization had been in existence in 1914 there would have been no war." "The Constitution of 1919," *NR* 18 (22 Feb. 1919): 101.

24. Bartlett, *Behind the Scenes*, 18-19; Villard, *Memoirs*, 386-87.

25. Shotwell, and particularly Gelfand in his study of the Inquiry, may be overstating the case somewhat. Sidney Mezes, CCNY professor and director of the Inquiry, wrote a brief account of their activities with no trace of bitterness. He said that the decisions which they had a part in negotiating "were only in the rarest instances modified by the supreme council." See Mezes, "Preparations for Peace," in *What Really Happened at Paris*, 1-14.

26. Straight to his wife, 14 Nov. 1918, cited in Croly, *Willard Straight*, 535; Forcey, *Crossroads of Liberalism*, 289.

27. White to his wife, 9 Feb. 1919, *Letters*, 197.

28. Nicolson to his father, 9 Mar. 1919, *Peacemaking 1919*, 281.

29. Bliss to his wife, 18 Dec. 1918, and 21 Jan. and 26 Feb. 1919, in Frederick Palmer, *Bliss, Peacemaker: The Life and Letters of General Tasker Howard Bliss* (New York, 1934), 359, 370, 375.

30. Bliss to Major Enoch H. Crowder, 3 Mar. 1919, in Palmer, *Life and Letters*, 376.

Chapter 7

1. Baker, *Woodrow Wilson and World Settlement*, 1: 296; Thompson, *The Peace Conference Day By Day*, 231.

2. George Bernard Noble, *Policies and Opinions at Paris, 1919* (New York, 1935), 420.

3. Whitlock diary, 12 Oct. 1920, *Letters and Journal*, 2: 635; Steffens, *Autobiography*, 2: 781-82.

4. Noble, *Policies and Opinions at Paris*, 419; Nicolson to Valentine Wilson, 14 May 1919, *Peacemaking 1919*, 337; Douglas Wilson Johnson, "Fiume and the Adriatic Problem," in *What Really Happened at Paris*, 123; Robert Lansing, *The Peace Negotiations: A Personal Narrative* (Boston, 1921), 100-101.

5. Seymour letters dated 30 Jan. and 7 Apr. 1919, *Letters From the Paris Peace Conference*, 137, 194.

6. Steffens to Whitlock, 28 Jan. 1925, *Letters and Journal of Brand Whitlock*, 1: 366.

7. Lewis Mumford, "The Aftermath of Utopianism," *Christianity and Crisis*, 1 (24 Mar. 1941): 3.

8. Nicolson to his father, 23 Mar. 1919, and to Valentine Wilson, 24 Mar. 1919, *Peacemaking 1919*, 288, 289; "Peace by Ultimatum," *NR* 18 (22 Mar. 1919): 231; untitled editorial, *NR* 18 (29 Mar. 1919): 257; House diary, 4 Apr. 1919, *Intimate Papers*, 4: 391.

9. *Dial* 66 (22 Mar. 1919): 309; Bliss memorandum, 25 Mar. 1919, in Baker, *Woodrow Wilson and World Settlement*, 3: 449-57.

10. Bliss to his wife, 25 Mar. 1919, in Palmer, *Life and Letters*, 379; Bonsal, *Unfinished Business*, 179; Reinhold Niebuhr, *Leaves From the Notebook of a Tamed Cynic* (New York, 1929), 22.

11. Wilson's actual intentions here have been discussed at length by those present at Paris and by later historians. Many of the British and French felt that Wilson was bluffing; most Americans at Paris felt that he was so physically drained and mentally depressed that he really did intend to leave. See, for instance, Hoover, *Memoirs*, 1: 460; Thompson, *The Peace Conference Day By Day*, chap. 26; and Ray Stannard Baker, *What Wilson Did At Paris* (Garden City, N.Y., 1920), chap. 7. Historian Noble examined the evidence relating to the episode and concluded it seemed "planned as a dramatic gesture to indicate to the world in general, and the French government . . . in particular, that the American President had reached the limit of his patience" (*Policies and Opinions at Paris*, 323).

12. Bonsal diary, 1 Apr. 1919, *Unfinished Business*, 181-82.

13. Baker, *Woodrow Wilson and World Settlement*, 2: 66.

14. A lively if not entirely accurate account of the Fiume intrigue appears in Bartlett, *Behind the Scenes*, chap. 7; Baker presents a documented record of the episode in *Woodrow Wilson and World Settlement*, v. 3, pt. 4, and a summary in his small monograph *What Wilson Did At Paris*, chap. 9; an incisive analysis of the entire "Italian Question" was written by Douglas Wilson Johnson, Chief of Division on Boundaries in the American delegation at Paris ("Fiume and the Adriatic Problem," in *What Really Happened at Paris*, 112-39). The best accounts of the Shantung settlement, though overly apologetic, are in Baker, *Woodrow Wilson and World Settlement*, v. 2, pt. 7, and *What Wilson Did At Paris*, chap. 11; for a more critical, somewhat cynical view, see Lansing, *The Peace Negotiations*, chap. 18.

The *Dial* devoted its lead editorials to the Siberian intervention and was so exercised by it that it passed over the actual negotiations in Paris.

15. "The Truth About the Peace Conference," *Nation* 108 (26 Apr. 1919): 646-47 (italics are Villard's).

16. Whitlock diary, 2 May 1919, *Letters and Journal* 2: 559; Herron to Sinclair, 22 Apr. 1919, in Sinclair, *My Lifetime in Letters*, 195; Seymour letter dated 28 Apr. 1919, *Letters From the Paris Peace Conference*, 215-16; Shotwell diary, 1 May 1919, *At the Peace Conference*, 305.

17. Baker, *Woodrow Wilson and World Settlement*, 2: 108; Nicolson diary, 8 May 1919, *Peacemaking 1919*, 329; Keynes to his mother, 14 May 1919, cited in R. F. Harrod, *The Life of John Maynard Keynes* (New York, 1963), 249; Lansing, *The Peace Negotiations*, 274-75.

18. William C. Bullitt, *The Bullitt Mission to Russia* (New York, 1919); Steffens, *Autobiography*, 2: 792; Huddleston, *Peace-Making at Paris*, 204. The text of Bullitt's letter is printed in full in *Mission to Russia*, 96-97.

19. *NR* 19 (17 May 1919), cover; *Dial* 66 (17 May 1919): 511-13; "The Madness at Versailles," *Nation* 108 (17 May 1919): 778-80.

20. Smuts to Wilson, 30 May 1919, in Baker, *Woodrow Wilson and World Settlement*, 3: 466-68; Keynes to Lloyd George, 5 June 1919, cited in Harrod, *Life of John Maynard Keynes*, 253; Bliss to his wife, 16 June 1919, in Palmer, *Life and Letters*, 399.

21. Joseph C. Grew, *Turbulent Era: A Diplomatic Record of Forty Years, 1904-1945*, ed. Walter Johnson (Boston, 1952), 1: 392; Steffens, *Autobiography*, 2: 788; Hoover, *Memoirs*, 1: 468, 482; House diary, 28 June 1919, *Intimate Papers*, 4: 487.

22. *Humanité*, 28 June 1919, cited in Noble, *Policies and Opinions at Paris*, 382; Nicolson diary, 28 June 1919, *Peacemaking 1919*, 371.

Chapter 8

1. C. E. Montague, *Disenchantment* (New York, 1922), 172, 250; Bliss to his wife, 16 June 1919, in Palmer, *Life and Letters*, 399.

2. Baker, *What Wilson Did At Paris*, 75; Bullitt, "The Tragedy of Paris," *Freeman* 1 (17 Mar. 1920): 20; White to Hays, 6 Aug. 1919, *Letters*, 199-200; White to Herbert Croly, 11 Sept. 1920, *Letters*, 207-8.

3. Robert Herrick, "In General," *Nation* 113 (7 Dec. 1921): 658; Davis, "Welfare, Reform and World War I," 516-33.

4. Theodore Peterson, *Magazines in the Twentieth Century* (Urbana, Ill., 1956), 373; Wreszin, *Villard*, 149; James Westfall Thompson, "The Aftermath of the Black Death and the Aftermath of the Great War," *American Journal of Sociology* 26 (Mar. 1920): 565-72.

5. Weyl, *Tired Radicals*, 13; Cowley, *After the Genteel Tradition*, 232; White to Theodore Roosevelt, Jr., 5 July 1926, *Letters*, 261; Whitlock to White, 8 Oct. 1926, *Letters and Journal of Brand Whitlock*, 1: 389.

6. Steffens to Whitlock, 3 July 1925, *Letters and Journal of Brand Whitlock*, 1: 370; Tarbell, *All In The Day's Work*, 345; Mumford, *Faith for Living*, 222; Dos Passos, "A Preface Twenty-Five Years Later," in *First Encounter* (New York, 1945), 9.

7. Lippmann, *Stakes of Diplomacy*, 9.

8. Niebuhr, *Leaves From the Notebook*, 42; Sinclair, *Money Writes!*, 53; Herron to Sinclair, 5 Mar. 1924, in Sinclair, *My Lifetime in Letters*, 202.

9. Bourne, "A War Diary," *Seven Arts* 2 (Sept. 1917): 540; Howe, *Confessions of a Reformer*, 279; Stearns, *Liberalism in America*, 24; Lippmann, "Notes for a Biography," 252; Harry Elmer Barnes, *The Genesis of the World War* (New York, 1927), 685. On the subject of historical revisionism, see also Osgood, *Ideals and Self-Interest*, 318, and Selig Adler, "The War-Guilt Question and American Disillusionment, 1918-1928," *Journal of Modern History* 23 (Mar. 1951): 1-28.

10. "The Madness at Versailles," 779; Weyl, "Prophet and Politician," *NR* 19 (7 June 1919): 178; John Maynard Keynes, *The Economic Consequences of the Peace* (New York, 1920), 39; Eastman, "Wilson and the World's Future," *Liberator* 1 (May 1918): 19; Eastman, "Wilson's Failure," *Liberator* 2 (May 1919): 6; "The Paradox of Woodrow Wilson," *NR* 37 (13 Feb. 1924): 299.

11. Weyl, *The End of the War*, 2-4; Stearns, *Liberalism in America*, 146-47; Jordan, *The Days of a Man*, 2: 759; untitled editorial, *Nation* 111 (3 Nov. 1920): 489.

12. *The American Liberals and the Russian Revolution* (New York, 1962), xv, 212-14.

13. Dewey, "The Discrediting of Idealism," *NR* 20 (8 Oct. 1919), 285-86; Becker to Dodd, 17 June 1920, Becker Papers; Becker to Dodd, 26 Feb. 1923, Becker Papers; Bliss to Sullivan, 26 Nov. 1922, in Palmer, *Life and Letters*, 431.

14. Croly, "Liberalism vs. War," *NR* 25 (8 Dec. 1920): 35-39; Lippmann, "Liberalism in America," *NR* 21 (31 Dec. 1919): 151; Santayana, "Marginal Notes," *Dial* 72 (June 1922): 553-68.

15. "Where Are the Pre-War Radicals?" *Survey* 55 (1 Feb. 1926): 563-64, 557, 558.

16. "Mental Unpreparedness," 143-44; White, *Autobiography*, 576.

17. *War Information Series*, no. 14 (Mar. 1918), 41; Whitlock, *Forty Years Of It*, 374; *Win the War for Permanent Peace*, 122; Mencken to Sinclair, 23 Feb. 1920, in Sinclair, *My Lifetime in Letters*, 231-32.

18. Bonsal, *Unfinished Business*, 291; Addams, *Peace and Bread*, 68; Millis, "The Faith of an American," 224-25.

19. Nicolson, *Peacemaking 1919*, 187.

20. Niebuhr, "What the War Did to My Mind," *Christian Century* 45 (27 Sept. 1928): 1161; Cowley, *After the Genteel Tradition*, 232-33; Cowley lecture at University of Virginia, 1 Nov. 1967.

21. See, for example, Paul W. Glad, "Progressives and the Business Culture of the 1920's," *Journal of American History* 53 (June 1966): 75-89; William E. Leuchtenburg, *The Perils of Prosperity, 1914-1932* (Chicago, 1958), chap. 7; Arthur S. Link, "What Happened to the Progressive Movement in the 1920's?," *American Historical Review* 64 (July 1959): 833-51; Clarke Chambers, *Seedtime of Reform: American Social Service and Social Action, 1918-1933* (Minneapolis, 1963); and a historiographical essay by Herbert Margulies, "Recent Opinion on the Decline of the Progressive Movement," *Mid-America* 45 (Oct. 1963): 250-68.

22. Lloyd Morris, *Postscript to Yesterday* (New York, 1947); Max Lerner, in rebuttal to George Mowry's article "The First World War and American Democracy," in *War as a Social Institution*, ed. J. D. Clarkson and T. C. Cochran (New York, 1941), 184-88.

23. Lasch, *New Radicalism in America*, 251-56; Piper, "Fitzgerald's Cult of Disillusion," 69-80; Larzer Ziff, *The American 1890's: Life and Times of a Lost Generation* (New York, 1966).

24. May, "Rebellion of the Intellectuals," 115; *The End of American Innocence*, passim; J. C. Furnas, *The Americans: A Social History of the United States, 1587-1914* (New York, 1969), 927; Thomas Beer, "Toward Sunrise, 1920-1930," *Scribner's* 87 (May 1930): 542.

25. See Phil L. Snyder, "Carl L. Becker and the Great War: A Crisis for a Humane Intelligence," *Western Political Quarterly* 9 (Mar. 1956): 8-10.

26. Davis, "Welfare, Reform and World War I," 532-33; May, "Rebellion of the Intellectuals," 125-26.

27. Steffens to Roosevelt, 9 June 1908, *Letters*, 1: 195; to Johnson, 1 Sept. 1909, *Letters*, 1: 223; to Reed, 6 June 1914, *Letters*, 1: 342; to Marie Howe, 3 Apr. 1919, *Letters*, 1: 463. For wider insight into Steffens's thinking, see *Letters*, 1: 402-40 and *Autobiography*, 2: 712-13.

28. "The Pivot of History," *NR* 17 (16 Nov. 1918): 59; Baker, *Frontiers of Freedom*, 217.

29. Whitlock to Steffens, 7 Feb. 1919, *Letters and Journal of Brand Whitlock*, 1: 278; Steffens to Laura and Allen Suggett, 26 July 1919, *Letters*, 1: 477.

Chapter 9

1. "Where Are the Pre-War Radicals?," 566.
2. "Where Are the Pre-War Radicals?," 564, 563, 560, 565, 558, 564, 566.
3. Arthur M. Schlesinger, Jr., *The Crisis of the Old Order, 1919-1933* (Boston, 1957), 150.
4. Osgood, *Ideals and Self-Interest*, 309; Addams, *Peace and Bread*, 62, 246; Butler, *Looking Forward: Essays and Addresses on Matters National and International* (New York, 1932), 316.
5. Paul Jones, "What the War Did to My Mind," *Christian Century* 45 (8 Mar. 1928): 310-12; Sherwood Eddy, "What the War Did to My Mind," *Christian Century* 45 (26 July 1928): 925-27; "Where Are the Pre-War Radicals?," 565. The best treatment of Protestant thought after the war is Meyer, *The Protestant Search for Political Realism, 1919-1941*.
6. Chambers, *Seedtime of Reform*, 26.
7. Sidney Kaplan, "Social Engineers As Saviors: Effects of World War I on Some American Liberals," *Journal of the History of Ideas* 17 (June 1956): 363; Dewey, "A Sick World," *NR* 33 (24 Jan. 1923): 217-18; "Practical Democracy," review of Walter Lippmann's *The Phantom Public, NR* 45 (2 Dec. 1925): 52-54; "Education As a Religion," "Education As Engineering," and "Education As Politics," *NR* 32 (13 Sept., 20 Sept., and 4 Oct. 1922): 63-65, 89-91, 139-41; Lippmann, *A Preface to Morals* (New York, 1929); Dewey, *The Public and Its Problems* (New York, 1927), 110, 146.
8. Dewey, *The Quest for Certainty* (New York, 1929); "Why I Am Not a Communist," *Modern Monthly* (Apr. 1934); Otis L. Graham, Jr., *An Encore For Reform: The Old Progressives and the New Deal* (New York, 1967), 134; Lerner, "The Attitude of the Intellectuals," 89; Kaplan, "Social Engineers As Saviors," 362.
9. Sinclair, *Autobiography*, 329.
10. Russell, *After the Whirlwind*, 190-97, 251-54, 317; *Bare Hands and Stone Walls: Some Recollections of a Side-Line Reformer* (New York, 1933), 298.
11. Graham, *Encore For Reform*, 138; *Bare Hands and Stone Walls*, 421-23; "An Old Reporter Looks at the Mad-House World," *Scribner's* 94 (Oct. 1933): 225-30.
12. Villard, "Issues and Men," *Nation* 150 (13 Jan. 1940): 47; "Valedictory," *Nation* 150 (29 June 1940): 782; *Fighting Years: Memoirs of a Liberal Editor* (New York, 1939), 518.
13. Graham, *Encore For Reform*, 116.
14. Osgood, *Ideals and Self-Interest*, 313-14.
15. Villard to his wife, 30 Mar. 1919, cited in Wreszin, *Villard*, 121; Fitzgerald to Shane Leslie, 17 Sept. 1920, *Letters*, 377; Weyl, *The End of the War*, 27-30.
16. Osgood, *Ideals and Self-Interest*, 333.
17. Bourne, "Twilight of Idols," *Seven Arts* 2 (Oct. 1917): 689; Dewey, "The Discrediting of Idealism," *NR* 20 (8 Oct. 1919): 285; "Our National Dilemma," *NR* 22 (24 Mar. 1920): 117, 118; "Shall We Join the League?," *NR* 34 (7 Mar. 1923): 36-37; "What Outlawry of War Is Not," *NR* 36 (3 Oct. 1923): 149-52; "Shall We Join the League?," 37. Dewey retained an avid interest in foreign affairs, writing frequently on events in Russia, China, Turkey, and Mexico, but it was the interest of a traveler and commentator.
18. "Murray Butler Makes Moan," *NR* 29 (21 Dec. 1921): 89-90; James A. Wechsler, *The Age of Suspicion* (New York, 1953), 16; Villard, *Memoirs*, 517; Villard to White, 28 Jan. 1939, cited in Graham, *Encore For Reform*, 184.
19. Villard, *Memoirs*, 461.
20. "Where Are the Pre-War Radicals?," 564.
21. Howe, *Confessions of a Reformer*, 317, 320, 340, 337.
22. "Where Are the Pre-War Radicals?," 560-61, 557-58, 563.
23. Whitlock, *Belgium: A Personal Narrative*, 1: 274.

24. Whitlock diary, 23 May 1920, *Letters and Journal*, 2: 602; Whitlock to John Van Schaick, 20 Dec. 1921, *Letters and Journal*, 1: 337.

25. Whitlock to Marshall Sheppey, 4 Apr. 1922, and Rutger Jewett, 7 Apr. 1922, *Letters and Journal*, 1: 339-40; to Trumbull White, 10 Oct. 1920, *Letters and Journal*, 1: 319-20; to Jewett, 30 Nov. 1921, *Letters and Journal*, 1: 334; to Van Schaick, 20 Dec. 1921, *Letters and Journal*, 1: 337; to Sheppey, 4 Apr. 1922, *Letters and Journal*, 1: 339 (italics are Whitlock's); diary, 13 June 1920, *Letters and Journal*, 2: 611.

26. Whitlock to Colonel House, 24 Nov. 1916, *Letters and Journal*, 1: 206; diary, 24 July 1920, *Letters and Journal*, 2: 620; diary, 23 Dec. 1921, *Letters and Journal*, 2: 720-21; to Jewett, 7 Apr. and 17 May 1922, and 30 Aug. 1924, *Letters and Journal*, 1: 341-43, 353.

27. *Letters and Journal*, 1: lxv (Nevins does not identify his source).

28. David W. Noble, "The New Republic and the Idea of Progress, 1914-1920," *Mississippi Valley Historical Review* 38 (Dec. 1951): 388.

29. Lippmann to House, 19 July 1919, cited in Lasch, *New Radicalism in America*, 219; Francine Curro Cary, *The Influence of War on Walter Lippmann, 1914-1944* (Madison, Wis., 1967), 55; Eulau, "Wilsonian Idealist," 108; Laski to Holmes, 4 Jan. 1920, *Holmes-Laski Letters*, 1: 231.

30. Lippmann, "Unrest," *NR* 20 (12 Nov. 1919): 315; *Stakes of Diplomacy*, 20; "Why I Shall Vote For Davis," *NR* 40 (29 Oct. 1924): 218-19; "Mr. Kahn Would Like to Know," *NR* 35 (4 July 1923): 144-46.

31. Forcey, *Crossroads of Liberalism*, 299.

32. Lippmann, *Interpretations, 1931-1932*, ed. Allan Nevins (New York, 1932), 261-62; "The Scholar in a Troubled World," Phi Beta Kappa address at Columbia, 31 May 1932; Broun column in *New York World Telegram*, 21 Nov. 1933, cited in Goldberg, *American Radicals*, 72. Lippmann's "journey" attracted the interest of many of his contemporaries. Articles appearing in the transition years of the thirties include: Amos Pinchot, "Walter Lippmann: 'The Great Elucidator,' " *Nation* 137 (5 July 1933): 7-10; "What Has Happened to Walter Lippmann?," *Christian Century* 53 (23 Sept. 1936): 1245-46; Louis J. A. Mercier, "Walter Lippmann's Evolution," *Commonweal* 30 (4 Aug. 1939): 348-50; and J. C. Aldrich, "Lippmann Retreats to Yesterday," *Scholastic* 38 (17 Mar. 1941): 1-T.

33. Lippmann sharpened his *Realpolitik* in "The Atlantic and America: The Why and When of Intervention," *Life* 10 (7 Apr. 1941): 84 ff., and *U.S. Foreign Policy: Shield of the Republic* (Boston, 1943). A good summary of the maturation of his foreign policy views is in David Elliott Weingast, *Walter Lippmann: A Study in Personal Journalism* (New Brunswick, N.J., 1949), 86-92.

34. Lippmann, *The Good Society* (Boston, 1937); Eulau, "Mover and Shaker," 291; Washington *Evening Star* cartoon, 22 May 1967; "Walter Lippmann at 80," *Washington Post*, 31 May 1970; interview in Baltimore *Sun*, 21 Sept. 1969.

35. George H. Soule, "Herbert Croly's Liberalism, 1920-1928," *NR* 63 (16 July 1930): 253; Croly, "The Eclipse of Progressivism," *NR* 24 (27 Oct. 1920): 210-16; "Why I Shall Vote For La Follette," *NR* 40 (29 Oct. 1924): 221-24; "Hope, History and H. G. Wells," *NR* 29 (30 Nov. 1921): 12; "American Withdrawal From Europe," *NR* 36 (12 Sept. 1923): 68; "Liberalism vs. War," 38; "The Meaning of the Conference," *NR* 28 (16 Nov. 1921, suppl.): 14.

36. Croly, "Surely Good Americanism," *NR* 32 (15 Nov. 1922): 294-96; Edmund Wilson, "H. C.," *NR* 63 (16 July 1930): 268; Forcey, *Crossroads of Liberalism*, 305; Croly, "Christianity as a Way of Life," *NR* 39 (23 July 1924): 230-37; "Consciousness and the Religious Life," *NR* 45 (27 Jan. 1926): 262-65; "Religion as a Method," *NR* 47 (30 June 1926): 174-77; Goldman, *Rendezvous With Destiny*, 288.

37. Kaplan, "Social Engineers As Saviors," 363. Croly died on 17 May 1930. The editors of the *New Republic* and others who had worked with him prepared a memorial

issue that appeared on 16 July and remains the best collection of articles on Croly. Besides the Soule and Wilson articles, two other very revealing ones are Waldo Frank, "The Promise of Herbert Croly," 260-63, and Walter Lippmann, "Notes for a Biography," 250-52.

38. White, *Autobiography*, 578; *The Editor and His People: Editorials by William Allen White*, ed. Helen Ogden Mahin (New York, 1924), 236; "We Who Are About to Die," *NR* 26 (9 Mar. 1921): 36-38; Emporia *Gazette*, 24 Dec. 1921 and 24 July 1922.

39. White to Nevins, 24 May 1934, *Selected Letters*, 346; *Selected Letters*, 366; *Autobiography*, 640, 642.

40. "America's War Aims and Peace Program," *War Information Series*, no. 21 (Nov. 1918); Becker to Dodd, 17 June 1920, Becker Papers; Noble, *Paradox of Progressive Thought*, 31.

41. Becker to Dodd, 25 Oct. 1920, Becker Papers; Burleigh Taylor Wilkins, *Carl Becker* (Cambridge, 1961), chap. 8; *The Declaration of Independence* (New York, 1922), 218-19; undated letter to Frankfurter (1927), Becker Papers.

42. "The New History," 21; *Progress and Power* (Stanford, 1936), 8, 6, 13; "Everyman His Own Historian," *American Historical Review* 37 (Jan. 1932): 236. Wilkins contends that Becker lost his certitude but never his compassion; he softens Noble's portrait by emphasizing Becker's partiality to liberalism even in his despair and the eventual recovery of his democratic faith in the forties in the wake of fascism abroad. Becker died in 1945.

43. Baker to Whitlock, 19 Dec. 1930, *Letters and Journal of Brand Whitlock*, 1: 479; to Shotwell, 1 Apr. 1936, cited in Cramer, *Newton D. Baker*, 234; "The Decay of Self-Reliance," *Atlantic Monthly* 154 (Dec. 1934): 726-33; Cramer, *Newton D. Baker*, 193.

44. "Where Are the Pre-War Radicals?," 566; *Letters and Journal of Brand Whitlock*, 1: lxiv.

45. Bliss address at Carnegie Institute of Technology, 14 June 1924, in Palmer, *Life and Letters*, 439; Bliss to Bok, 2 Oct. 1923, *Life and Letters*, 435; undated letters from 1923, *Life and Letters*, 436-37.

46. Niebuhr, *Leaves From the Notebook*, 14-15, 42; "What the War Did to My Mind," 1161-63.

47. "How Philanthropic Is Henry Ford?," *Christian Century* 43 (9 Dec. 1926): 1516-17; "Ford's Five-Day Week Shrinks," *Christian Century* 44 (9 June 1927): 713-14; George E. Mowry, *The Urban Nation, 1920-1960* (New York, 1965), 217.

48. "Ten Years That Shook My World," *Christian Century* 56 (26 Apr. 1939): 545; *Moral Man and Immoral Society* (New York, 1932), xi; "The Blindness of Liberalism," *Radical Religion* 1 (Autumn 1936): 4.

49. "After Capitalism—What?," *World Tomorrow* 16 (1 Mar. 1933), 203-5; "Marx, Barth and Israel's Prophets," *Christian Century* 52 (30 Jan. 1935): 138-40; "Russia and Karl Marx," *Nation* 146 (7 May 1938), 530-31; *Reflections On The End of An Era* (New York, 1934), 35; Arthur Schlesinger, Jr., "Reinhold Niebuhr's Role in American Political Thought and Life," in *Reinhold Niebuhr: His Religious, Social, and Political Thought*, ed. Charles W. Kegley and Robert W. Bretall, (New York, 1956), 139-41; "Ten Years That Shook My World," 543; "An End to Illusions," *Nation* 150 (29 June 1940): 778-79; *Christianity and Power Politics* (New York, 1940); Gordon Harland, *The Thought of Reinhold Niebuhr* (New York, 1960), 215-24; Kegley and Bretall, *Reinhold Niebuhr*, 7-8; Osgood, *Ideals and Self-Interest*, 381-83; U.S. Congress, Senate, Committee on Foreign Relations, *Hearings*, 77th Cong., 1st sess., Jan.-Feb. 1941.

50. "Why Is Communism So Evil?," in *Christian Realism and Political Problems* (New York, 1953), 33-42; Lasch, *New Radicalism in America*, 299-306; *The Children of Light and the Children of Darkness* (New York, 1944); Schlesinger, "Reinhold Niebuhr's Role," 143-50; "The Blindness of Liberalism," 4. For a detractor's view of Niebuhr as cynic, see

Holton P. Odegard, *Sin and Science: Reinhold Niebuhr as Political Theologian* (Yellow Springs, O., 1956).

51. The *Mercury's* circulation dropped from 77,000 readers in 1927 to 33,000 when Mencken resigned in 1933. The *New Republic*, which had been dying a slow death, picked up from a low of 12,000 in 1929 to a level of about 25,000 in the thirties. Peterson, *Magazines in the Twentieth Century*, 373, 379.

52. Beard, "What About the Constitution?," *Nation* 143 (1 Apr. 1936): 406; Richard Hofstadter, "Charles Beard and the Constitution," in *Charles A. Beard: An Appraisal*, ed. Howard K. Beale (Lexington, 1954), 91; Osgood, *Ideals and Self-Interest*, 320-21.

53. Becker, *Progress and Power*, 10; Becker to Lerner, 25 Mar. 1938, Becker Papers; Cowley, *After the Genteel Tradition*, 77, 232. Eric Goldman, a close friend of Beard's from his graduate school days at Johns Hopkins, recounts the circumstances of Beard's isolationist conversion in *Rendezvous With Destiny*, 283.

54. Richberg, "We Thought It Was Armageddon," *Survey* 61 (1 Mar. 1929): 763; Krutch, *The Modern Temper* (New York, 1929), 247; Lippmann, *Preface to Morals*, chapter headings; Chapman, "Last Words," *Scribner's* 86 (July 1929): 78.

55. Graham, *Encore For Reform*, 179; Becker, "The Dilemma of Liberals in Our Time," 188; Becker, "Liberalism—A Way Station," in *Everyman His Own Historian: Essays on History and Politics* (New York, 1935), 91-100; Lerner, *Ideas Are Weapons* (New York, 1939), 236; H. N. Brailsford, "Machinery Turns Nationalist," *NR* 81 (5 Dec. 1934): 92. Brailsford, English socialist and veteran *New Republic* correspondent, spent most of World War I on assignment in America.

56. *Letters and Journal of Brand Whitlock*, 1: viii.

57. Montague, *Disenchantment*, 250-51; Chamberlain, *Farewell to Reform*, 323; Bullitt, "The Tragedy at Paris," 20; Wechsler, *Age of Suspicion*, 37.

58. Schlesinger, *Crisis of the Old Order*, 208.

59. Fitzgerald, *This Side of Paradise* (New York, 1920), 304; Cowley, *Exile's Return*, 9.

60. Josephson, *Life Among the Surrealists*, 6-7, 12; Millis, "The Faith of an American," 217; "An Interview With John Dos Passos," *Idol* (literary quarterly of Union College), 45 (1969): 16. See also Warren I. Susman, "A Second Country: The Expatriate Image," University of Texas *Studies in Literature and Language* 3 (Summer 1961): 171-83.

61. Janet Flanner, *An American In Paris* (New York, 1940), 68; Arno J. Mayer, *Politics and Diplomacy of Peacemaking: Containment and Counterrevolution at Versailles, 1918-1919* (New Haven, 1967), 892; Cowley lecture at University of Virginia, 1 Nov. 1967.

62. James Oppenheim, editorial, *Seven Arts* 2 (July 1917): 342-43; Mayer, *Politics and Diplomacy of Peacemaking*, 893.

63. Eastman, "Wilson and the World's Future," 19-24; "A Statesman of the New Order," *Liberator* 1 (Sept. and Oct. 1918): 10-13, 28-33; "Lenin and Wilson," *Liberator* 2 (Mar. 1919): 8-11; "November Seventh, 1918," *Liberator* 1 (Dec. 1918): 23; editorial, *Liberator* 3 (Feb. 1920): 5; Bertrand Russell, "Soviet Russia—1920," *Nation* 111 (31 July and 7 Aug. 1920): 121-26, 152-54; Floyd Dell, "Communist But," *Liberator* 3 (Sept. 1920): 7. Eastman was sensitive to Russell's charge and repeatedly insisted that the Russian venture was no pious and sentimental crusade but a sophisticated experiment, firmly grounded in history and science. For example, "John Reed," *Liberator* 3 (Dec. 1920): 5.

64. Dos Passos, *Occasions and Protests* (New York, 1964), 26-27; Dos Passos, introduction to 1969 edition of *One Man's Initiation: 1917* (Ithaca, N.Y., 1969), 2-4; Bullitt, "The Tragedy at Paris," 20-21.

65. Steffens to Allen H. Suggett, 13 Apr. 1919, *Letters*, 1: 466; Steffens, "John Reed," *Freeman* 2 (3 Nov. 1920): 181; Michael Gold, "Hope for America," *Liberator* 4 (Dec. 1921): 14-17.

66. Holmes, "What Is Worth Fighting For in American Life?," 605; "Where Are the

Pre-War Radicals?," 565; Dos Passos to Arthur McComb, 28 June 1917, cited in Aaron, *Writers on the Left*, 346.

67. Steffens to Mrs. J. James Hollister (his sister), 19 Sept. 1920, *Letters*, 2: 554; *Autobiography*, 2: 803; Steffens to Whitlock, 20 Dec. 1924, *Letters and Journal of Brand Whitlock*, 1: 357; to Whitlock, 28 Jan. 1925, *Letters and Journal of Brand Whitlock*, 1: 367.

68. Josephson, *Life Among the Surrealists*, 354; Josephson, "Open Letters to Mr. Ezra Pound, and the Other 'Exiles,' " *Transition* (Summer 1928): 98-102; Steffens, *Autobiography*, 2: 851.

69. Cowley, *Exile's Return*, 215; Nancy Evans, "Goodbye Bohemia," *Scribner's* 89 (June 1931): 643-46; Waldo Frank, *The Re-discovery of America* (New York, 1929); Josephson, *Life Among the Surrealists*, 364.

70. Steffens, "Bankrupt Liberalism," *NR* 70 (17 Feb. 1932): 15-16; Josephson, "The Road of Indignation," *NR* 66 (18 Feb. 1931): 13-14; Wilson, "An Appeal to Progressives," *NR* 65 (14 Jan. 1931): 234-38; Frank, *Dawn in Russia: The Record of a Journey* (New York, 1932), 272.

71. Eugene Lyons, *The Red Decade* (Indianapolis, 1941), 129; Aaron, *Writers on the Left*, 232; "How I Came to Communism: Symposium," *New Masses* 8 (Sept. 1932): 6-10; Whittaker Chambers, *Witness* (New York, 1952), 196. See also Frank A. Warren, *Liberals and Communism: The "Red Decade" Revisited* (Bloomington, Ind., 1966).

72. Dos Passos interview with David Sanders, 1962, Dos Passos MS.; Eastman, *Love and Revolution*, 242.

73. Granville Hicks, "The Politics of John Dos Passos," *Antioch Review* 10 (Mar. 1950): 93; Cowley, "The Record of a Trial," *NR* 90 (7 Apr. 1937): 267-70; Cowley, "Sixteen Propositions," *NR* 102 (26 Feb. 1940): 264-65; Eastman, *Love and Revolution*, 242, 631.

74. Chambers, *Witness*, 196.

75. Stearns, *Rediscovering America* (New York, 1934), 23-24, 43; Cowley, "Sixteen Propositions," 264-65; Bullitt, *Report to the American People* (Boston, 1940); *The Great Globe Itself* (New York, 1946); "Should We Support An Attack on Red China?," *Look* 18 (24 Aug. 1954): 32-33. Eastman died in 1969 at the age of 86. A crop of Bullitt articles appeared in *Reader's Digest, Life,* and the *New Republic* in the late forties. Dying from leukemia in February 1967, Bullitt attempted to return to America and his native Philadelphia, but was tragically unsuccessful because of snowstorms on the Eastern seaboard. The best treatment of his disillusionment with Russia is Farnsworth, *Bullitt and the Soviet Union*, chap. 7.

76. Dos Passos, *The Ground We Stand On* (New York, 1941); *The Grand Design* (Boston, 1949); Hicks, "The Politics of John Dos Passos," 85.

77. Interview with David Sanders, Dos Passos MS.; *The Theme Is Freedom* (New York, 1956).

78. Martin Kallich, "John Dos Passos: Liberty and the Father-Image," *Antioch Review* 10 (Mar. 1950): 99-106; Dos Passos to "Mr. Teague," 12 Feb. 1963, Dos Passos MS.; "World War I: New Interest In An Old War," NBC *Open Mind* series, 9 Dec. 1962, typescript in Dos Passos MS.

79. Hicks, "The Great Reversal," *New Leader* 37 (29 Mar. 1954): 15-19; William F. Buckley, *Odyssey of a Friend* (New York, 1969); Louis Filler, "John Chamberlain and American Liberalism," *Colorado Quarterly* 6 (Autumn 1957): 200-11; William Henry Chamberlin, *The Confessions of an Individualist* (New York, 1940); Malcolm Cowley, "Flight From the Masses," a review of Wilson's *Travels in Two Democracies*, *NR* 87 (3 and 10 June 1936): 106-8, 134-35. Chamberlin is probably most famous for *America's Second Crusade* (New York, 1950), a crude indictment of Roosevelt's war policy and diplomacy at Yalta.

80. Hicks, "The Politics of John Dos Passos," 85-86; Hicks, *Part of the Truth*, 187-88; Cowley, "Sixteen Propositions," 265.

81. Lerner, *It Is Later Than You Think*, 66-67; "The Left: End and Beginning," *Nation* 150 (10 Feb. 1940): 164-66; introduction to Machiavelli's *The Prince and the Discourses* (New York, 1940), xxv-xlvi.

82. Lasch, *New Radicalism in America*, 273-85; Aaron, *Writers on the Left*, 128; Hicks, "Lincoln Steffens: He Covered the Future," *Commentary* 13 (Feb. 1952): 155; Carl Sandburg, introduction to *Letters of Lincoln Steffens* 1: ix. See also Alfred B. Rollins, Jr., "The Heart of Lincoln Steffens," *South Atlantic Quarterly* 59 (Spring 1960): 239-50.

83. Niebuhr, "An End to Illusions," 778-79.

84. Lerner, *Ideas for the Ice Age*, viii; Dos Passos, "A Preface Twenty-Five Years Later," 9-10; Frankfurter address to *Survey* Associates, Dec. 1937, in *Law and Politics: Occasional Papers of Felix Frankfurter, 1913-1938*, ed. Archibald MacLeish and E. F. Prichard, Jr. (New York, 1939), 345-47.

85. Lerner, "The Attitude of the Intellectuals," 92; *Ideas for the Ice Age*, 140.

86. Millis, "The Faith of an American," 234-41; Millis, "1939 Is Not 1914," *Life* 7 (6 Nov. 1939): 69 ff. Robert Sherwood offers an uncanny parallel to Millis. The author of *Idiot's Delight*, a tart 1935 antiwar play that won a Pulitzer prize, Sherwood four years later wrote an embattled sequel, *There Shall Be No Night*, and drafted the widely publicized "Stop Hitler Now" advertisement for the Committee to Aid the Allies.

87. Becker, "How New Will the Better World Be?," *Yale Review* 32 (Mar. 1943): 417-39.

88. Brooks, *On Literature Today* (New York, 1941); Mumford, *Faith for Living*, 221-23.

89. "The Aftermath of Utopianism," 2-7; "The Corruption of Liberalism," *NR* 102 (29 Apr. 1940): 568-73.

90. "Uncommon Conversations," Baltimore *Evening Sun*, 12 June 1972.

91. Chambers to Buckley, 9 Apr. 1961, in *American Conservative Thought in the Twentieth Century*, ed. William F. Buckley, Jr. (Indianapolis, 1970), 531; Mumford, *Faith for Living*, 222.

INDEX